W9-ABI-188

TECHNICAL COLLEGE OF THE LOWCOUNTRY
LEARNING RESOURCES CENTER
POST OFFICE BOX 1288
BEAUFORT, SOUTH CAROLINA 29901-1288

Percy Bysshe Shelley

Updated Edition

Twayne's English Authors Series

Herbert Sussman, Editor

Northeastern University

TEAS 81

PERCY BYSSHE SHELLEY
By Edward Ellerker Williams
Courtesy of the Pierpont Morgan Library, New York (#1949.3)

Percy Bysshe Shelley

Updated Edition

By Donald H. Reiman

The Carl H. Pforzheimer Shelley and His Circle Collection,
The New York Public Library

TECHNICAL COLLEGE OF THE LOWCOUNTRY
LEARNING RESOURCES CENTER
POST OFFICE BOX 1288
BEAUFORT, SOUTH CAROLINA 29901-1288

Twayne Publishers
A Division of G. K. Hall & Co. • *Boston*

TECHNICAL COLLEGE OF THE LOWCOUNTRY
LEARNING RESOURCES CENTER
POST OFFICE BOX 1288
BEAUFORT, SOUTH CAROLINA 29901-1288

Percy Bysshe Shelley, Updated Edition
Donald H. Reiman

Copyright 1990 by G. K. Hall & Co.
All rights reserved.
Published by Twayne Publishers
A division of G. K. Hall & Co.
70 Lincoln Street, Boston, Massachusetts

First Edition copyright 1969 by Twayne Publishers, Inc.

Printed on permanent/durable acid-free paper
and bound in the United States of America

Library of Congress Cataloging-in-Publication Data

Reiman, Donald H.
    Percy Bysshe Shelley / by Donald H. Reiman.—Updated ed.
       p.   cm.—(Twayne's English authors series ; TEAS 81)
    Bibliography: p.
    Includes index.
    ISBN 0-8057-6981-1 (alk. paper)
    1. Shelley, Percy Bysshe, 1792–1822—Criticism and interpretation.
I. Title. II. Series.
PR5431.R4   1989
821'.7—dc20
                                                        89-15458
                                                          CIP

For My Parents,
Mildred A. Reiman and †Henry W. Reiman

Contents

About the Author

Born at Erie, Pennsylvania, in 1934, Donald H. Reiman graduated from Strong Vincent High School there, earned his B.A. at the College of Wooster, and his M.A. and Ph.D. degrees in English at the University of Illinois. He taught English at the University of Illinois, Duke University, and the University of Wisconsin–Milwaukee, before coming to New York in 1965 as editor of *Shelley and his Circle* (a multivolume catalogue and edition of the manuscripts of Shelley, Byron, their families and their associates), first at The Carl H. Pforzheimer Library and since 1987 at The Carl H. Pforzheimer Shelley and His Circle Collection, New York Public Library. During those years, he has taught courses at the City University of New York, Columbia University, St. John's University, and the University of Washington and has lectured frequently in the United States, Canada, England, and Italy. In 1988–89 he was the James P. R. Lyell Reader in Bibliography at Oxford University.

Besides editing four volumes of *Shelley and his Circle*, Dr. Reiman has written, edited, or compiled over one hundred and forty other volumes on Shelley, the English Romantic poets, and their times, including the Norton Critical Edition of *Shelley's Poetry and Prose*, *The Romantics Reviewed* (9 volumes), *The Romantic Context: Poetry* (128 volumes), and most recently *Romantic Texts and Contexts*, a selection of Dr. Reiman's major essays and reviews (1987), and *Intervals of Inspiration: The Skeptical Tradition and the Psychology of Romanticism* (1988). He serves as editor-in-chief of *The Bodleian Shelley Manuscripts* and general editor of *The Manuscripts of the Younger Romantics*, two multivolume series of facsimile editions of the literary manuscripts of Shelley, Byron, and Keats.

A life member of both the Modern Language Association of America and the Modern Humanities Research Association, Dr. Reiman founded the Wordsworth-Coleridge Association. He presently serves as treasurer and executive director of the Keats-Shelley Association of America, as a director of the Society for Textual Scholarship and the American Byron Society, and as a member of the editorial or advisory board of *Studies in Romanticism*, *Nineteenth-Century Contexts*, *Nineteenth-Century Literature*, and *TEXT*. A member of Phi Beta Kappa, he has been awarded research fellowships and grants-in-aid from universities and foundations, the American Council of Learned Societies, and the National Endowment for the Humanities. His other honors include an Litt.D. from the College of Wooster in 1981 and, in 1987, a Distinguished Scholar Award for career achievement from the Keats-Shelley Association of America.

Preface to the Updated Edition

Percy Bysshe Shelley was first published in mid-year 1969, after I had spent over ten years in intensive research and writing on Shelley's life, thought, and art. A product of my thinking during the years when I first learned about the poet and his age, the book also reflected my teaching of literature to introductory and advanced undergraduates and to graduate students who were seriously engaging Shelley's poetry for the first time. Though twenty years of further research and writing on Shelley and his contemporaries have added to my factual knowledge about Shelley's life, thought, and art, as well as about those of his contemporaries, I doubt that I could write as fresh and useful an introductory book, were I to begin again today.

Not only are the basic outlines and conceptions of the original study uncluttered in a way that would be difficult to replicate out of my more complicated understanding of the issues, but most of the facts and a substantial proportion of the judgments and opinions expressed here have stood the test of time. I still hold most of the views expressed here, and even those that I would no longer express in quite the same form have been adopted by other scholar-critics of the English Romantic period. The readings deserve a hearing as possible ways of approaching Shelley and his writings, though they are not now—any more than they were when they were written—total or comprehensive studies; they do not pretend to exhaust the complexity and richness of Shelley's thought and art. Rather than attempt a new, but still partial account, I have chosen to reissue the volume essentially intact, with some factual corrections; updated Chronology, Notes, and Bibliography; and this new Preface, in the confidence that readers will recognize the merits of a sane and accurate introduction to the main events of Percy Bysshe Shelley's life and to his most enduring writings in poetry and prose.

I have taken advantage of this opportunity, however, to correct a few statements that no longer seem accurate in the light of current knowledge. I have rechecked and totally revised the Chronology, Notes, and Selected Bibliography to guide readers to the best current evidence in support of the text and the most reliable authorities for further study. Finally, I have added this new Preface to survey briefly some issues in which Shelley studies of the past twenty years—my own and others'—

have advanced in both the information available and in depth of understanding, as Shelley's writings moved from the periphery to the
center of scholarship and criticism on English literature.

After Shelley was recognized as a man of superior intellect and out-
standing poetic talent and large numbers of scholars and critics studied
his writings with respect instead of condescension, many of the difficulties that hostile critics—Matthew Arnold, the New Humanists, and
the New Critics—had attributed to his poetry began to evaporate.[1] But
as the tone of criticism on Shelley and his writings changed from the
hostile and the defensive to the celebratory, shallow and lazy critics,
who parade behind whatever author's bandwagon is rolling through
the academic world at the moment, began to praise Shelley with almost
as limited understanding of him as his detractors had formerly evi-
denced. In the late-Victorian and Edwardian periods (1870 through
the beginning of World War I), Shelley's poetry was praised by many
who attributed to Shelley their own superficial ideas, making him a
symbol of the eccentric behavior and sentimental ideas that they favored.[2] Since the late 1960s, Shelley's name and quotations, wrenched
from their contexts in his works, have been used to further the life-
styles of hippies and druggies, the ideologies of Marxists and nihilists,
and the fads of various pop subcultures, as well as the careers of academic trend-followers.[3]

Behind the trends, however, a renewed recognition of Shelley's genius was achieved, not primarily by critical counter-assertions, but by
destroying the mythic caricatures of Shelley as an angelic (or demonic)
spirit, devoted to unearthly beauty (or fiendish selfishness)—caricatures meant as compliments (or dismissals) by his late-Victorian and
Edwardian admirers (and their enemies). Younger generations, disillusioned by the trauma of two world wars and the Great Depression,
reacted to the praise of Shelley as a disembodied angel by declaring
him both immature and irrelevant to the twentieth century. Shelley
regained his place in the canon when both caricatures were replaced by
a more nearly authentic portrait of him as a hard-headed idealist, who
used Academic Skepticism to protect his own hopes from the disillusionment he faced through both his personal misfortunes and the
suppression of the progressive reforms he favored. Such political repression had occurred first in the 1790s, during Shelley's babyhood, after
the French Revolution had turned into the Reign of Terror; a renewal
of French imperialism had persisted throughout the Napoleonic Wars,

while Shelley was coming to maturity; then, when a revived reform movement arose again after the downfall of Napoleon and the restoration of reactionary regimes in continental Europe, the British ruling classes renewed their repression of both popular agitation and reasoned proposals for the peaceful redistribution of political power.

The new understanding of Shelley's intelligent awareness of the political and social realities of his time was achieved primarily through patient biographical, bibliographical, textual, and contextual scholarship, matching that of the period from 1870 through 1911 that saw—alongside the popular misconceptions of Shelley—the best work of William Michael Rossetti, Harry Buxton Forman, Richard Garnett, Edward Dowden, and George Edward Woodberry. The chief names associated with the early stages of the twentieth-century renewal of scholarship were Newman Ivey White, Edmund Blunden, Kenneth Neill Cameron, Frederick L. Jones, Carlos Baker, James A. Notopoulos, and C. E. Pulos. Later, it was spearheaded by Earl R. Wasserman, G(eoffrey) M. Matthews, Donald H. Reiman, Stuart Curran, Timothy Webb, and William Keach, aided by parallel editions and studies of Shelley's friends and contemporaries, notably the editions of *The Journals of Claire Clairmont* by Marion Kingston Stocking and *The Letters of Mary Wollstonecraft Shelley* by Betty T. Bennett.[4] These and a host of other responsible scholar-critics in the United States, Great Britain, the Commonwealth, and Japan have, through textual studies and new editions of Shelley's poetry, clarified what Shelley wrote; through studies of the historical, intellectual, and literary contexts of his writings, they have determined which public events and intellectual patterns help shape his themes and ideas; through careful biographical analysis, they have identified his private emotional experiences and have come nearer to understanding what his intentions were—what particular audience he hoped to reach with each work and what he wished that group of readers to understand by it; finally, through structural and verbal analysis of his works, they have clarified how the interactions of the various parts—structure, diction, symbols, and allusions—contribute to each poem's overall intended meaning.

The study of Percy Bysshe Shelley and his writings since the 1960s has advanced in four areas. First, the basic documents underlying the texts of his writings have been reexamined and are now well on their way to being published in full, so that all can examine for themselves the primary evidence on particular cruxes, rather than relying on other people's interpretation of the evidence. Second, the reexamination of Shelley's manuscripts and the concomitant awareness of his care and artistry in diction, imagery, and rhetoric have initiated extended analyses of his concept of language and his ideas on the relationship of language to human thought and action. Third, with this detailed study of Shelley's language and intentions has come a growing awareness of the complexity of his personality and how powerfully he repressed his first feelings and reactions in an attempt to conform to his *beau idéal* of moral human behavior. Finally, there has emerged a deepened understanding of Shelley's social and political philosophy vis-à-vis the thinking of both his contemporaries and ours.

I shall take up each of these four areas briefly, supplementing the original book with a brief overview that sketches the developments and problems in recent writings on Shelley. The chapters of the text itself provide an introduction to matters of primary concern to the reader or teacher approaching Shelley for the first (or second) time—namely, the aesthetic structures of individual poems or essays and the development of Shelley's ideas both within particular works and from one chronological period to another. This Preface delineates some of the issues to be explored by advanced students who have read Shelley's publications and are already familiar with the outlines of his life and times.

I

The primary documents relating to Shelley's life and writings have been assiduously collected and religiously preserved over the years in three major collections: the archives of Lord Abinger, the Bodleian Library, Oxford, and The Carl H. Pforzheimer Shelley and His Circle Collection (now an endowed special collection of The New York Public Library). In 1952, Carl H. Pforzheimer engaged Kenneth Neill Cameron to publish his collection of manuscripts relating to Shelley and his associates in the edition *Shelley and his Circle, 1773–1822*. In 1965, Donald H. Reiman succeeded Cameron as editor and continues the work today.[5] After thirty-five years of further purchases that more than doubled the size of the collection and intensive scholarship by a team of resident researchers and contributing editors, the edition has produced eight volumes, totaling almost five thousand pages, with four volumes yet to come. *Shelley and his Circle* presents the documents themselves in diplomatic transcription and with extensive scholarly aids (including translations of most letters and documents in other languages) and with full commentaries on the implications of the texts and evidence presented. Analyses of both sides of Shelley's correspondence with his friends lead not only to correction of factual errors in previous scholarship, but to examination of nuances and speculations about motives that others have lacked the time to notice, or at least to explore.

In 1983, as an outgrowth of this research, Donald H. Reiman undertook a project designed to make available Shelley's literary manuscripts in other collections, as well as major literary documents of Byron, Keats, Mary W. Shelley, and other contemporary writers. After some refinements suggested by David G. Vaisey and Bruce Barker-Benfield at the Bodleian, the program evolved as *The Bodleian Shelley Manuscripts* and *The Manuscripts of the Younger Romantics*.[6] These two series are reproducing in photofacsimile—accompanied always by scholarly helps and annotation and, where necessary or appropriate, by complete transcriptions of the text—the major literary manuscripts of Shelley, as well as notebooks and letters preserving literary drafts or texts. With Lord Abinger's Shelleyana now on deposit at the Bodleian Library, as well as available on microfilm in several research centers in the United States and Canada, the major archives are being systematically studied and made more widely available.

As Stuart Curran has emphasized, "neither Shelley's poetry nor his prose is completely available in a reliable version,"[7] but the best texts now available are these: 1) the Norton Critical Edition, *Shelley's Poetry and Prose*, edited by Donald H. Reiman and Sharon B. Powers, for the major poetry and the three essays it contains; 2) for most of the other poetry, the Oxford Standard Authors edition, edited by Thomas Hutchinson and corrected by G. M. Matthews; 3) for the text of "A Philosophical View of Reform," the scholar will use the literal transcription of the manuscript in *Shelley and his Circle*, volume VI; and 4) until the Oxford English Text edition of Shelley's prose appears, volumes V, VI, and VII of the Julian Edition of *The Complete Works of Percy Bysshe Shelley* for the remainder of the prose. Curran's further comment, "it is sardonically amusing that so much critical writing fleets over such thin textual ice," might well be taken to heart and turned into an advantage, if teachers and students would learn to check the soundness of their interpretations by comparing the crucial points in them with the original documents—manuscripts and early editions—that underlie the texts.

II

During the past twenty years, contemporary literary studies have followed the trend of modern philosophy by moving from the discussion of referents and the signified to analysis of the signs and signifiers—the words, tropes, and silences in both the personal and the literary writings of Shelley. My study *Shelley's "The Triumph of Life"* (1965) had anticipated this trend by devoting a chapter to the close analysis of Shelley's prosody, his use of simile, metaphor, and synaesthetic imagery, and his simpler rhetorical structures. Some more recent rhetorical analyses (here I mean especially those by disciples of Paul de Man) have vitiated the greater sophistication that they drew from recent linguistic and rhetorical theories by their naïveté in forgetting that Shelley had a better education in Classical rhetoric than they do and was probably as aware of the effects of his poetic tropes, at both their superficial and subliminal levels, as they have become through their belated labors. Those scholar-critics who have given Shelley credit for knowing what he was doing—among them, Richard Cronin, Tilottama Rajan, Jerrold E. Hogle, and especially William Keach—have made the real advances in analyzing Shelley's theory of language, his stylistic techniques, and the implications of these for other areas of his thought and practice.

We must remember that Shelley was trained from his youth in Classical rhetoric from textbooks that graduate professors must now seek out in rare-book libraries to read as scholarly exercises. He used the techniques that worked to his purposes as a matter of course, without sweating and straining. "A Defence of Poetry," for example, follows the structure of a Classical oration just as clearly as does Milton's *Areopagitica,* and with just as little need to advertise its formal divisions. Shelley, a genius who became a poetic master, deployed figures of speech and rhetorical devices in his mature works as naturally as a basketball star eludes the defense and arcs the ball into the net. For the critic to say that Shelley achieved his successful poetic effects fortuitously—that he was trying to repress something unsaid, rather than say what he did say—is like a sportscaster claiming to know that Larry Bird did not intend to bank the ball off the backboard and that it went into the basket by accident. As an athlete's trained eyes and muscles respond automatically to a game situation, the hand and ear of a skilled poet such as Byron form his poems almost effortlessly according to his underlying, preconsidered purpose. Shelley, more like Wordsworth, added to his trained poetic responses a regimen of careful revision and restructuring of most of his major works, demonstrating a superior critical faculty as well as imaginative genius.

This much understood, the analyst of Shelley's language (and his silences) must first confront the author's articulated (and otherwise apparent) values and his stated purpose in writing a particular work and, only after analyzing both the verbal textures and the larger, generic and rhetorical structures, measure the extent to which these reinforce that declared intention. Where there are discrepancies between the two, we may say that the artist failed to fulfill his intention (e.g., wrote a military march in waltz-time), or that he had another intention, in addition to the stated one, that 1) he was ignorant of, or 2) he chose to hide from his readers. A third possibility—and the most likely to be the case, taking all critics as a group—is that the particular critical analysis is faulty and that the work being judged as an imperfect duck is actually a swan.

In my experience, Shelley's poetry—and recent critiques of it—provide examples of all three situations. Certainly Shelley could be devious, as his manipulative letters to businessmen, his father, and even his closest friends demonstrate. He was also at times, we believe, partially blinded by his desires or the difficulty of his personal situations into acting in ways that he could not consciously approve and that, like other mortals, he rationalized such actions. When he attacked the *Quarterly Review*ers, ostensibly, for their treatment of Keats, he really meant to hit back at them for their attacks on himself. But how much of this displacement came about because of Shelley's conscious decision that it was rhetorically more effective for him to appear as the defender of a dead youth whose last months had been poisoned by callous reviewers, rather than simply to brand as unfair their reviews of him? That question is in the sphere of competence of the biographical scholar who studies the history of Shelley's relations with Robert Southey, or for the textual scholar who analyzes Shelley's drafts for *Adonais* and unravels the shifts and revisions that show Shelley implementing his purpose (conscious or subliminal), rather than in that of the rhetorical critic, tripping on tropes. From an analyst of language, one may learn about language; from a scholar-critic who studies the whole life, thought, works, and age of an artist, one can sometimes learn— through the scholar-critic's mastery of the native idiom—about the more vital questions of the author's doubt and belief, hate and love, or blindness and insight.

III

As an individual, Shelley had personal problems that seemed to follow him throughout life, no matter how well he managed to hide them from strangers, from most of his friends, and (perhaps) even himself. Though the roots of his psychological predispositions and insecurities must lie in his childhood relationships with his parents, siblings, and servants, too little is known of these interactions to afford us more than guesses as to these origins. Clearly, however, by the time that Shelley started writing his poetry that survives in *The Esdaile Notebook,* he felt lonely, isolated, and unloved. His inability to get on well with the majority of his school contemporaries at Syon House Academy and at Eton is well documented. Having begun as the heir to a large fortune, raised in a house that—though not exceptionally large or grand—dominated the surrounding landscape (as no human habitation could in the mountainous Lake Country where Wordsworth grew up), Shelley, an intellectual prodigy with adoring younger sisters who were not only his followers but his disciples, clearly began with an inflated impression of his importance in the world.

Many of Shelley's problems may have arisen from his later efforts to re-create the feelings of personal superiority and power that were his during childhood. He refused to surrender his exalted vision of the self to the bullying he encountered at Syon House Academy, at Eton, and (at an intellectual level) at Oxford. Throughout his adult life, Shelley tended to seek friends among those whom he could patronize, and he sought lovers and wives among impressionable, intellectual, adolescent girls (sixteen seems to have been the favored age) who admired him and with whom he could enjoy the master / disciple relationship that had been his as a boy on his family's estates and among his younger sisters. At the same time, he also formed relationships with such paternal or maternal figures as Dr. Lind, Robert Southey, William Godwin, Madame de Boinville, Maria Gisborne, and Lady Mount Cashell ("Mrs. Mason"), from whom he sought sympathy and counsel such as he may have lacked in his relations with his own parents, or may have been trying to recapture from his reminiscences of his childhood.[8]

Shelley's quest for sympathy, portrayed in *Alastor* and "Athanase: A Fragment" (later named by Mary W. Shelley "Prince Athanase"[9]), as well as in many poems in *The Esdaile Notebook,* led him as an author to seek the understanding of the reading public and to employ every psychological and rhetorical means of ingratiating himself with his potential readers in his prose Prefaces. The extension of his quest for sympathy from his family and friends to the British reading public contributed to Shelley's sense of identification of his personal goals and his social goals, and as recent studies of his literary manuscripts are beginning to show, he often begins a poem with such an intermixture of personal feeling and social idealism that the two subjects are hard to disentangle until the poet commits himself to a particular genre and structure. For Shelley, the best social order was the one with the most love and sympathy among its members. His ideal here, as so often, reflects both his gift for friendship and his feeling that the response of others to him was inadequate—a sense that may have arisen from the insatiable demands of idealized emotional recollections.

In his later works—as I argue in my reading of *Epipsychidion* (pp. 125–33)—Shelley modified his ideal of love by attempting to fix the goal of its quest for perfection, not in living human beings, but in the realm of art. If he could not capture the sense of perfect understanding and mutual love in actual human relationships, he could at least embody aspects of the ideal itself in works of art that would endure to transmit his feelings in a purified form to generations yet to come. Thus he would transform the failure of his mortal quest into a hope for victory in the future, just as Laon and Cythna die in the assurance that their ideal of a regenerated social order will be fulfilled in some dimly foreseen future rebirth of their ideals. Shelley expressed his hopes for social and political regeneration—paralleling the personal hopes he expressed in the envoy to *Epipsychidion*—in the final chorus of *Hellas,* his last completed work:

> Another Athens shall arise,
>   And to remoter time
> Bequeath, like sunset to the skies,
>   The splendour of its prime,
> And leave, if nought so bright may live,
> All earth can take or Heaven can give.

Shelley, as Earl R. Wasserman pointed out in his analysis of *The Cenci* in *Shelley: A Critical Reading,* did not believe that introspection was morally useful, since to discover and articulate the dark desires normally trapped beneath consciousness often results in releasing them into overt action.[10] We are not warranted, however, in assuming that, just because Shelley (unlike Coleridge in his revelatory Notebooks) did not dwell on his own mixed motives, he was unaware of them. His very portrayal of the various introspective characters in *The Cenci* itself—most of whose motives, as he analyzes them, embody aspects of his own thinking—reveals the subtlety of his psychological understanding. From the drafts of *Adonais,* for example, we learn how much effort Shelley devoted to eliminating from his finished writings most traces of his personal animus against Robert Southey, whom Shelley believed to have been the author of a scurrilous anonymous review of *Laon and Cythna (The Revolt of Islam)* in the *Quarterly Review.*[11] With great effort and artistry, Shelley sublimated his hostility toward anonymous reviewers into an immortal tribute to the genius of Keats to produce what, in the Preface to *Prometheus Unbound,* he refers to as an "idealism of moral excellence." Thus, when all the evidence is in, it is clear that not only was Shelley's "grasp on the actual" very strong indeed, but that his moral sense was stronger still and demanded that he fulfill the role that he set for himself in one of the notes to *Hellas*: "it is the province of the poet to attach himself to those ideas which exalt and ennoble humanity."

IV

When we look at all of Shelley's words and recorded actions, not in the light of our times but in the context of his own age, we find that his political ideas and programs also evolved from his experience as the son of a landed aristocrat whose family had been political allies of the Duke of Norfolk and the old Whig agricultural magnates—the so-called Whig Connexion.[12] These landed aristocrats, the so-called radical Whigs who followed Charles James Fox in his fight against William Pitt's wars on France, had since the mid-eighteenth century opposed the imperialist economic and political policies of the Tory administrations that, ruling in the name of King George III, had promoted the industrial revolution and were rapidly turning England from a traditional agricultural society into a "nation of shopkeepers"—the first modern urban, industrialized state. The dukes of Norfolk and Bedford and their friends' circles could rationally support the French Revolution, which marked the overthrow of the French feudal-agrarian political elite, because by supporting these developments in France, they heralded the creation of a new France that would compete with and, therefore, weaken their domestic rivals—the industrialists, bankers, merchants, and colonial planters who had gained new wealth and power from colonial exploitation (including slavery), foreign trade, and industrial expansion.

Though Shelley was an idealist influenced by the Enlightenment's optimistic ideas of human progress, especially by William Godwin's *Enquiry concerning Political Justice* and other reformist writings,[13] he was even more profoundly affected by his status as the heir to large agricultural estates. Combining these influences, he hoped to use his wealth and prestige to do good for—to patronize—those less fortunate than himself. During the time of his political awareness, events in France did not augur much good from the Revolution there, which had led to the military dictatorship of Napoleon Buonaparte, a new French imperialism on the Continent, and a partial reaction against the earlier ideals of "Liberty, Equality, and Fraternity." In England, he saw that the British reaction had derailed the progressive program of his father's Whig party and that the extended wars against the French enriched and enhanced the power of the industrial and commercial interests. As a philanthropist, Shelley rejected in principle the combination of force and corruption that gave privileges to the older ruling classes—including his family. But he believed that the real power in England since the Glorious Revolution of 1688—especially since the confirmatory transition in 1714 from the Stuart monarchs (who represented the agrarian and feudal orders) to the house of Hanover (tool of the Protestant urban, commercial and middle-class elements in British society)—had been held by bourgeois forces that were dehumanizing British society in the name of progress.

Shelley was thus not a "liberal" of the same kind as Jeremy Bentham and other middle-class precursors of modern democratic liberalism; he was, rather, a reactionary. He sought to turn back the ideological and social clock to a time when individuals of different social classes knew, respected, and supported one another, before money and the "cash nexus" had dehumanized workers into mere factory "hands."[14] In "A Philosophical View of Reform" (1819–20), for example, Shelley cites the Long Parliament, elected in 1640, as the last Parliament to be elected freely by a representative group of the various classes in English society.

Shelley knew, however, that England would not revert to the old order of Church, Court, and Country interests, but would either remain under the power of a few magnate nobles who sent their sons and nephews to Parliament from "rotten" boroughs that they controlled by limiting the vote to their tenants and dependents, or else would fall under the growing power of big-city bankers, merchants, and indus-

trialists; planters from the West Indies; and military adventurers or
rapacious exploiters who had made fortunes in the East Indies—and
many of whom later bought themselves seats in the unreformed Parliament. Having felt the religious establishment as a repressive force in
his own life whenever he dared to inquire into the truth of the doctrines
that they espoused, Shelley advocated complete religious toleration.
He also supported an expansion of voting rights and transition to the
rule of the majority when the education of the people in their moral
and political responsibilities would enable them to exercise their choice
in a rational way—at least enable them to understand their own long-
term self-interest, so that they would not succumb to unscrupulous
demagogues like Robespierre or Caesarian generals like Napoleon who
were simply more efficient tyrants. Thus, though Shelley held as an
ideal goal universal suffrage, he advocated as an intermediate step
broadening the franchise to include all who paid a small sum in direct
(i.e., real estate or income) taxes—then a limited portion of the
population.[15]

The French Revolution affected Shelley chiefly by making him aware
of the weight of injustice that had burdened the lower classes under
the old regime. But he hoped that by awakening young aristocrats to
the evil of such abuses, he could help initiate a society in which the
upper class would carry out its responsibility to protect, guide, and
educate the lower classes until, at some unspecified future date, all
human beings could live as free and responsible equals, none exploiting
another either in the name of ancient privileges or because of greater
wealth. This stance made him "radical" in the eyes of his contemporaries, but his ideals were contrary to those of the urban, middle-class
"philosophical radicals" (later, Utilitarians) and their allies who were
to become the dominant political force in England during the second
half of the nineteenth century. They looked forward to a new industrialized society in which newly acquired wealth or office would replace
birth, breeding, and moral character as the ultimate criterion of success
and respect.

Shelley himself (like his contemporaries Coleridge and Austen)
looked back to the unfulfilled ideals of earlier ages, hoping to inspirit
limited human beings to live up to the ideals of Western humanism to
which the upper classes still paid lip-service. But unlike many others
who drew their ideals from the past, Shelley—whose early enthusiasm
was for science rather than history—shared the hopes for progress that
had arisen during the Enlightenment and persisted throughout the

nineteenth century. For this reason, he admired not the Middle Ages, with its feudal ideal of stasis, but the Hellenic civilization of the sixth and fifth centuries B.C. and the years of the Italian and the English Renaissance, when the ideal of intellectual progress was reborn during periods of disruptive change like that accompanying the French Revolution. Thus Shelley's reactionary search through the past for a viable ideal also helped him to imagine a future in which the continuing improvement of human society and its members, as depicted in Godwin's *Enquiry concerning Political Justice,* might become a reality.

V

The hope for personal and social amelioration that burns so brightly in the cosmic idealisms of *Queen Mab, Epipsychidion, Adonais,* and *Prometheus Unbound* tends, however, to turn to disillusionment and despair whenever Shelley focuses on the "sad reality" of actual human history, as in "Marenghi," *The Cenci,* or "The Triumph of Life," or when he examines actual human relations, as in *Rosalind and Helen* and "Julian and Maddalo." As I have noted elsewhere, the very strength of Shelley's poetic vision depends upon the unresolved tension between the desired Ideal of his dreams and the imperfect world around him. That is why a recurrent phrase in his poetry speaks of "this world in which I wake to weep."[16] Whereas Shakespeare's characters all find sleep and the dreams that may come to them a fearful thing, Shelley seeks out the world of sleep and dreams. Whereas Prospero in *The Tempest,* in a brief moment of weakness and despair, indicts the worthlessness of human life by saying, "We are such stuff / As dreams are made on; and our little life / Is rounded with a sleep," Shelley can turn to the insubstantiality of the dream as a fitting analogue to the possible insubstantiality of the rival experience of our waking experience:

> in this life
> Of error, ignorance, and strife—
> Where nothing is—but all things seem,
> And we the shadows of the dream,
>
> It is a modest creed, and yet
> Pleasant when one considers it,
> To own that death itself must be,
> Like all the rest,—a mockery.

"For Shelley, . . . dreams of Utopia, the Elysian Fields, the Golden Age, Eden, the New Atlantis, or Plato's Republic were all preferable to the quietistic acceptance of the myriad imperfections of the social, political, and religious establishments that he had encountered."[17]

The virtues of Shelley's unwillingness to accept reality and of his extreme moral idealism form the subject of an important book by Stuart M. Sperry.[18] It takes up a strain previously articulated by a strong tradition of scholars, from Bennett Weaver and Ellsworth Barnard to Ross Woodman and D. J. Hughes. Those of us who have emphasized Shelley's hardheadedness and his keen awareness of the realities of the world around him may have done him a partial disservice by causing students to lose sight of his special contribution of an extreme idealism, almost unique in English literature. By refusing to bow his neck to the yoke of sublunar "reality," he helped set an example for selfless human service and sacrifice to promote radical social reform that has left its mark for good on every aspect of Western society.[19]

Students of the poet must now look once again at his inexhaustible writings with their eyes open to the basic fact that his skeptical epistemology is worked out in complex linguistic patterns that first undercut the easy assertions of the surface meaning, only to undercut the skeptical undercutting itself. By negating the force of the negation— by showing that we can no more know the worst to be true than we can know the best to be so—Shelley keeps alive his hopes for the ultimate triumph of good over evil and life over death. By saying that John Keats "wakes or sleeps with the enduring dead," he both denies any dogmatic knowledge of human destiny and links the fate of Keats's spirit with those of Shakespeare, Milton, and others that the human consciousness would not willingly let die. Shelley remains, after all else is said, the English language's supreme poet of hope—both hope for preserving the good of past ages and hope for perfecting the future course of human life and culture.

Donald H. Reiman

The Bronx, New York

Preface (1969)

In this book I have tried to give a brief, clear, and accurate account of Shelley's life, freshly examining existing accounts in the light of the primary evidence upon which they are based. I have studied Shelley's writings anew and have given inclusive readings of as many of them as space permits—especially those poems and essays that are, in my opinion, most important for a comprehension of his thought and art. One wishing to understand Shelley should read at least these works: *Alastor*, "Mont Blanc," "Hymn to Intellectual Beauty," "Lines written among the Euganean Hills," "Julian and Maddalo," *Prometheus Unbound, The Cenci*, "A Defence of Poetry," *Epipsychidion, Adonais*, and "The Triumph of Life." I have outlined the structure of each of them in detail, hoping to guide the reader's understanding of the whole work (and the relation of individual parts to the whole) by charting its thematic development. In treating such less-read works as *The Revolt of Islam*, "Peter Bell the Third," "The Witch of Atlas," and *Hellas*, I have condensed the thematic analysis but have quoted key passages to give the reader the flavor of poems for which he may not find time during his initial study of Shelley.

The chronological plan of the book is not only the most convenient for the reader wishing to review a phase of Shelley's career; it is, I believe, truest to the essential growth of Shelley as an artist. Some have denied that his thought developed, but an examination of his changing conception of the roles of love and poetry in human life shows how fallacious this denial is. Shelley's goals remained essentially unaltered, but his views on how and to what extent men might achieve these ideals were tempered through an eventful lifetime of testing ideas in the fires of experience. Thus, although Shelley is not essentially an autobiographical poet, an understanding of his life aids one in accounting for certain shifts of emphasis in his poetry.

I accept, of course, full responsibility for the interpretations presented here (a number of which depart from previous readings), but I am greatly indebted to numerous scholars and critics who have written on Shelley. Allusions in the text, as well as in the notes and bibliography, both acknowledge my specific debts and, hopefully, will guide the interested reader from this necessarily brief introduction to more detailed secondary studies and to the primary materials on which they are based. I have usually quoted (and cited locations) of Shelley's published writings from the following editions: poetry from the Oxford Standard Authors edition, ed. Thomas Hutchinson (cited as "OSA"); prose from *The Complete Works of Percy Bysshe Shelley,* ed. Roger Ingpen and Walter E. Peck (Julian Edition; cited as "Julian"); letters from *The Letters of Percy Bysshe Shelley,* ed. Frederick L. Jones (cited as *"Letters"*).

I am grateful to Indiana University Press for permission to quote from Dante, *La Vita Nuova, A New Translation* by Mark Musa (Bloomington, 1962). I wish to thank Duke University and the University of Wisconsin-Milwaukee for generously supporting my research; Miss Evelyn Johnson for faithful work as my student assistant at the University of Wisconsin-Milwaukee; my students at Duke, University of Illinois, and University of Wisconsin-Milwaukee for giving their best and demanding mine; The Carl and Lily Pforzheimer Foundation, Inc., and its president, Mr. Carl H. Pforzheimer, Jr., for a three-month fellowship in the summer of 1965; Miss Doucet Devin for typing early drafts of several chapters; Professor Kenneth Neill Cameron for sharing with me his unsurpassed knowledge of the materials of research in Shelley's life and times; Professor Jack Stillinger for giving the manuscript the benefit of his exceptional critical intelligence; and Mary Warner Reiman for her partnership in every stage of this work.

Donald H. Reiman

New York

Chronology

1789   Storming of the Bastille in Paris, July 14.

1792   Percy Bysshe Shelley (PBS) born August 4 at Field Place, Warnham, near Horsham, West Sussex, the eldest child of Timothy Shelley, M.P., and Elizabeth Pilfold Shelley, and eldest grandchild of (Percy) Bysshe Shelley, a wealthy landowner.

1793   Execution of King Louis XVI (January) and Marie-Antoinette (October); France declares war on England and Holland (February); Reign of Terror, May 1793–July 1794.

1794   Habeas Corpus suspended in England in May (also in August 1799, April 1801, and 1803); London treason trials of Horne Tooke, Hardy, and others, with their acquittals (October–December).

1796   Napoleon Bonaparte leads French army into Italy and defeats Austrians.

1797   On March 29, William Godwin marries Mary Wollstonecraft, who gives birth to their daughter Mary Wollstonecraft Godwin (later Shelley—MWS) on August 30 and dies September 10. Bonaparte imposes Treaty of Campo Formio on Austria, October 17.

1798   PBS studies with local clergyman, the Reverend Evan ("Taffy") Edwards. Irish Rebellion, February–October; Nelson destroys French fleet at Battle of the Nile on August 1.

1799   Napoleon returns to France in October and becomes First Consul in November; title extended for life, August 1802.

1800   Act of Union of Great Britain and Ireland; Napoleon defeats Austrians at Marengo on June 14.

1801   William Pitt ousted; Addington administration (March); in April, Nelson bombards Copenhagen and destroys neutral Danish fleet to prevent it from falling into French hands.

1802   PBS begins boarding school at Syon House Academy, Isleworth, on the Great Western Road in Thames Valley. Peace of Amiens between England and France in March; in October, French invade Switzerland.

1803   Renewal of war between France and England (May).

1804   Napoleon declared Emperor of France in May; second Pitt administration begins in May. PBS begins studies at Eton in September, which continue through spring of 1810.

1805   Napoleon crowned King of Italy in May; in October, Nelson's victory (and death) at Trafalgar balances Napoleon's defeat of the Austrians at Ulm the same month and of both the Austrians and Russians at Austerlitz in December.

1806   Pitt's death in January followed by national unity "Ministry of All the Talents" (February) and abolition of slave trade (June); Bysshe Shelley created Sir Bysshe Shelley, baronet; Charles James Fox dies (September). Earliest possible year for any of PBS's poems in *The Esdaile Notebook* (latest written 1813). In October, Napoleon crushes Prussians at Jena-Auerstädt.

1807   Duke of Portland's coalition administration begins in March. After Napoleon defeats Russians at Friedland (June), he and Czar Alexander sign Treaty of Tilsit in July.

1808   PBS begins corresponding with his Wiltshire cousin Harriet Grove (their "engagement" ends in 1810). British under Wellesley (later Duke of Wellington) open Peninsular Campaign in August with victory at Vimiera, but sign away advantages to French in Convention of Cintra (August 30).

1809   PBS writes five or six poems in *The Esdaile Notebook*. Spencer Perceval, a Tory, becomes Prime Minister in October.

1810   PBS's Gothic novel *Zastrozzi* published (spring); his and his sister Elizabeth's *Original Poetry* by "Victor" and "Cazire" published and withdrawn (autumn). PBS enters University College, Oxford, and meets Thomas Jefferson Hogg in October. PBS's *Posthumous Fragments of Margaret Nicholson* published in November and *St. Irvyne,* his second Gothic novel, in December.

1811   PBS meets Harriet Westbrook (January). Prince of Wales becomes Prince Regent in February. PBS and Hogg write *The Necessity of Atheism* and are expelled from University College on March 25. PBS and Harriet Westbrook elope and are married in Edinburgh on August 29. At York, Hogg tries to seduce Harriet; Shelleys move to Keswick and are befriended by Southey.

1812 Shelleys travel to Dublin, where two pamphlets are published by PBS in February—*Address to the Irish People* and *Proposals for an Association of . . . Philanthropists. Declaration of Rights* printed. Shelleys return to Wales (April 6) and move to Lynmouth, Devon, where PBS writes *Letter to Lord Ellenborough*. Spencer Perceval, assassinated by an insane bankrupt in May, is succeeded as Tory Prime Minister by Robert Banks Jenkinson, 2nd Earl of Liverpool (who serves till his death in 1827). In June, Napoleon invades Russia. Shelleys, joined by Elizabeth Hitchener in July, go to Tremadoc, North Wales, in September, then to London, where PBS meets William Godwin (October); in mid-November, they return to Tremadoc without Hitchener. Napoleon wins Battle of Borodino and captures Moscow in September; in October, Moscow is burned and French begin disastrous retreat, which continues during one of the coldest winters in European history.

1813 Shelleys flee Tremadoc on February 27; go to Ireland to recover manuscript of *The Esdaile Notebook* from printer there, and return to London on April 5. *Queen Mab* issued in May. On June 23, Ianthe Shelley born; Shelleys at Bracknell, with Newton-Boinville circle. Napoleon tries unsuccessfully to defeat the Allies in Germany, with major battles at Dresden in August and Leipzig in October.

1814 In January or February, PBS publishes *A Refutation of Deism*. Allies invade France and capture Paris on March 31; Napoleon is first deposed and then abdicates; Louis XVIII proclaimed king on April 6. On July 27 PBS and Mary Wollstonecraft Godwin (MWS) elope to war-ravaged France, accompanied by MWS's step-sister, Mary Jane (later "Claire") Clairmont (born ?April 27, 1798); from Switzerland they return to England on September 13, after journey down Rhine. Congress of Vienna convenes in September (continues, with interruptions, till June 1815). PBS's first son, Charles, born to Harriet on November 30.

1815 Sir Bysshe Shelley dies on January 5. PBS involved with George Cannon and *Theological Inquirer* (January); PBS, MWS, Claire Clairmont, and Hogg engage in free-love experiment; MWS's first child (a daughter) born prematurely, probably on February 22, but dies on March 6. Napoleon returns to rule France for the Hundred Days in March through June (Waterloo, June 18). In settling legal claims to Sir Bysshe's estate, PBS receives from his father money to pay his debts (some cash he diverts to Godwin), as well as an annual income of £1,000 (£200 earmarked for Harriet; later £120 for her children); PBS and MWS settle near Bishopsgate in August and travel by boat up the Thames with Peacock and Charles Clairmont in September; PBS writes *Alastor.*

1816   William Shelley born January 24; *Alastor . . . and Other Poems* published in February. Byron leaves England April 25. Princess Charlotte, only legitimate child of the Prince Regent (later George IV), marries Leopold of Saxe-Coburg in May. PBS, MWS, and Claire Clairmont leave England for Geneva (arrive mid-May) and remain near Byron till August 29; in June, PBS tours Lake Leman with Byron and writes "Hymn to Intellectual Beauty"; in July, the Shelleys visit Mont Blanc and PBS writes "Mont Blanc." The Shelleys, after reaching Portsmouth September 8, settle at Bath; Fanny Imlay (MWS's half-sister) commits suicide in Wales on October 9; Harriet Shelley drowns herself (her body found December 10); PBS and MWS marry December 30. A year of social unrest caused by unemployment, bad harvests, and food shortages culminates in Spa Fields Riot, December 2.

1817   Allegra Byron, Claire's daughter, born at Bath. Chancery Court denies PBS custody of his children Ianthe and Charles. After Habeas Corpus is suspended March 4 (till February 1818), opposition journalists flee or are imprisoned. Shelleys settle at Marlow in March; PBS's *Proposal for Putting Reform to the Vote* published same month. PBS writes *Laon and Cythna* from ?March to September; it is printed about October–November, then revised and published as *The Revolt of Islam,* December 1817 (but dated 1818). Clara Shelley born September 2. PBS drafts "Essay on Christianity" (?September–December); *History of a Six Weeks' Tour* by MWS and PBS published in November. Also in November, Princess Charlotte dies in childbirth; PBS writes (and perhaps publishes) *An Address to the People on the Death of the Princess Charlotte.* MWS's *Frankenstein* published in December (dated 1818). David Booth and W. T. Baxter break with the Shelleys during December.

1818 Probably in January, PBS begins *Rosalind and Helen*; he and MWS spend time in London before they leave for the Continent on March 12, accompanied by Claire Clairmont, three children, and two female servants—Amelia (Milly) Shields and Louise (Elise) Duvillard; they reach Milan April 4, visit the Italian lakes, send Allegra, with Elise, to Byron April 28, visit Pisa and Livorno (Leghorn), and meet the Gisbornes in May. In June they move to Bagni di (Baths of) Lucca, where PBS translates Plato's *Symposium*, writes "On Love," and completes *Rosalind and Helen*. PBS and Claire go to Venice to see Allegra, beginning August 17; PBS summons MWS and the children (with Milly and new servant, Paolo Foggi); he visits Byron, settles at Este, and begins *Prometheus Unbound*. Little Clara Shelley dies September 24. PBS's depression reflected in "Euganean Hills" and beginning of "Julian and Maddalo," ?September 29–October 11. After visiting Venice, October 12–31, the Shelleys travel to Rome and Naples (November–December 1), remaining in Naples till February 28, 1819, with excursions to Vesuvius, Paestum, etc.

1819 Shelleys reach Rome on March 5; from March through May, PBS drafts Acts II–III of *Prometheus*. William Shelley dies June 7. Shelleys flee to Livorno, where MWS remains in depression, while PBS writes *The Cenci* in summer (printed in Italy, it is sent to England for publication in 1820). News of "Peterloo Massacre" (August 16) provokes PBS to write *Mask of Anarchy* in September. On October 2, Shelleys move to Firenze (Florence), where son Percy Florence Shelley is born November 12 and where PBS finishes *Prometheus* (published August 1820), writes "West Wind" and "Peter Bell the Third" (October–November), and drafts "A Philosophical View of Reform" (?December–January 1820). In December 1819 and January 1820, parliament fears revolution and passes the "Six Acts" to repress dissent.

1820 George III dies and George IV succeeds in January; Cato Street Conspiracy to kill the English ministry foiled in February and leaders executed. Spanish army revolts in January and establishes constitutional monarchy in March. Shelleys move to Pisa January 26; PBS writes "Sensitive Plant" in March, "Ode to Liberty," and "Sky-lark." Shelleys live in Gisbornes' house at

Livorno while they are in England from June to August; PBS
writes "Letter to Maria Gisborne," June 16 ff. Constitutional
revolution in Naples in July. Caroline of Brunswick, estranged
wife of George IV, returns from Italy to England (July) to claim
her rights as queen; she is "tried" by House of Lords (August–
November), but becomes a rallying point for the opposition.
At Bagni di San Giuliano (Bagni di Pisa) from August to October, PBS writes "Witch of Atlas," "Ode to Naples," and
Swellfoot the Tyrant (the last published and suppressed in November or December). Claire Clairmont moves to Firenze;
flood forces Shelleys (with Medwin) to return to Pisa at end of
October. There Shelleys meet Teresa ("Emilia") Viviani in November and Prince Alexander Mavrocordato on December 2.

1821   In January–February, PBS visits Teresa Viviani and writes *Epi-
        psychidion* (published anonymously in May). Edward and Jane
        Williams arrive and meet Shelleys on January 13. PBS writes
        "A Defence of Poetry," February–March. Austrians crush Nea-
        politan liberals and restore hegemony throughout Italy
        (March). Greeks in Morea rise against Turkish rule in March;
        expatriate Greeks from Russia invade Turkish provinces in
        April. On April 11 a letter from London informs PBS of Keats's
        death (Rome, February 23); PBS writes *Adonais* in May and
        June (printed July). Early in May, Williamses move to Pug-
        nano, Shelleys to Bagni di San Giuliano, both on the River
        Serchio. In August PBS visits Byron at Ravenna and urges him
        and the Gambas to move to Pisa; the Gambas arrive in August;
        Byron on November 1. During October and November, PBS
        writes *Hellas* (published February 1822).

1822   PBS works on "Charles the First" (?January). Edward John Tre-
        lawny arrives January 14. "Pisan Circle," centered on Byron
        and PBS, plans theatricals. Allegra Byron dies April 20. Shel-
        leys and Williamses move to San Terenzo, on Bay of Lerici,
        April 30; PBS's boat, the *Don Juan,* arrives May 12. PBS writes
        "The Triumph of Life" after May 20. MWS miscarries on June
        16. PBS and Williams sail to Leghorn July 1 to meet Hunts
        but drown during return voyage on July 8; their bodies are
        found and after temporary burial (mid-July) cremated on Au-
        gust 13 and 14. MWS and Hunts live together and near Byron

at Albaro, outside Genoa, from September 1822 till July 1823; there MWS begins to study and transcribe PBS's manuscripts.

1823 MWS returns to England in July.

1824 MWS's edition of PBS's *Posthumous Poems* published in June but suppressed in September at insistence of Sir Timothy Shelley.

Chapter One
A World to Reform

Percy Bysshe Shelley, born August 4, 1792, near Horsham, Sussex, was the eldest child of Timothy Shelley, Member of Parliament, and the grandson of Bysshe Shelley, who in 1806 was to be made Sir Bysshe Shelley, Baronet. Grandfather Bysshe (pronounced "Bish") had been born at Newark, New Jersey; but *his* father, another Timothy—apparently a merchant—had returned to England, inheriting the family estate of Fen Place, Sussex, when one of his elder brothers died and the other was declared insane in 1743. On the death of an uncle in 1748, Timothy inherited Field Place. Bysshe Shelley came into very little of his father's modest property until 1790, when his elder brother John died without issue; and by that time Bysshe had established his own fortune with two successful marriages (both elopements) that made him one of the wealthiest men in Sussex.

Timothy Shelley, the poet's father, was the eldest of Bysshe's ten legitimate children (three by the first marriage; seven by the second); after attending University College, Oxford, and taking the "grand tour" of the Continent, he entered Parliament. In October, 1791, he married Elizabeth Pilfold; they established residence at Field Place, his father's newly inherited estate. There followed a succession of children: Percy Bysshe; Elizabeth (May 10, 1794); Hellen (January 29, 1796; died four months later); Mary (June 9, 1797); a second Hellen (September 26, 1799); Margaret (January 20, 1801); and John (March 15, 1806). The young poet thus grew up the eldest in a family of girls, seeing his baby brother only on school holidays. "Bysshe," as he was called at home, seems to have been the apple of his parents' eye, the beloved guide and protector of his sisters, and a favorite among the servants.[1]

The most important influences that shaped the character of Percy Bysshe Shelley lie hidden in his early relationships with his family, servants, neighbors, teachers, and schoolmates. Compared with Wordsworth and Byron, Shelley was relatively unautobiographical in his poetry and characteristically so in his letters. Discussions of ideas,

1

descriptions of scenes viewed or books read, directions concerning financial or household affairs—these objective topics provide the staple of Shelley's correspondence. In the period of intellectual and psychological ferment during his short stay in Oxford and following his expulsion, Shelley wrote some revealing letters to Thomas Jefferson Hogg, Elizabeth Hitchener, and William Godwin; but these contain few references to his earlier years at Field Place, Syon House Academy, and Eton. From these scattered comments and from later reminiscences of his sister Hellen, his cousins Charles Grove and Thomas Medwin, and such confidants as Hogg, Leigh Hunt, Thomas Love Peacock, and Mary Shelley, there emerges a picture of a boy increasingly uneasy in the position of privilege to which he had been born and increasingly unwilling to submit to the system which fostered that privilege.

Four ironic juxtapositions seem to have contributed to Shelley's revolt against the conventions of his era. The first was the contrast between his grandfather, the vulgar founder of the family fortunes, and the poet's father Timothy, who attempted to live down the stigma of old Bysshe's peculiarities by conforming rigorously to the stereotyped patterns of behavior expected of a country gentleman and member of parliament. Second, the contrast between the indulgence Shelley enjoyed as the willful favorite at the family estate and his later experience of the petty tyranny of English school life at Syon House Academy (1802–4) and, more seriously, at Eton affected him. Third, he observed the contrast between the social realities of England during the Napoleonic wars and the ideals of human virtue and social justice in the Bible, the Classical school texts, and eighteenth-century humanitarian writers. Finally, he noted a sharp discrepancy between England's traditional role as the defender of individual liberty and constitutional government (a role historically championed by the Whig party of his father and grandfather) and England's hostility toward those same ideals following the French Revolution. Shelley—too young to have been disillusioned by the Reign of Terror, the subjugation of Switzerland, and the earliest and gravest threats of French invasion—saw only that England was allied with reactionary Austria, Prussia, and Russia in an effort to restore the hated Bourbons to the throne and to do so against the will of the French people. To one who had been nurtured on admiration of Milton and the Glorious Revolution of 1688, no course could have seemed more incongruous.

About those individuals who were probably strong influences on Shelley's character during his formative years, we know only the scantiest details. His grandfather, Bysshe, was, according to Shelley, in religion "a complete Atheist" and in politics a Whig supporter of the Duke of Norfolk, a peer who continually sought parliamentary reform and the abolition of the slave trade and who in 1798 lost his military appointments for toasting "our Sovereign's health—the Majesty of the People." Shelley's father, Timothy, less outspoken than Sir Bysshe (who used to argue politics with farmers in a local pub), served the Duke of Norfolk's interests in parliament, though he is on record as having made only a single speech in his long career.[2]

Of Shelley's mother we know that she was an excellent letter writer, that she was no bigot in religion, and that she and Shelley had a genuine affection for each other. Peacock records that Shelley retained great respect for "the Reverend Mr. Edwards of Horsham" from whom "he received his first instructions."[3] Dr. Greenlaw, the Scottish master of Syon House Academy, was a stern disciplinarian but a "man of rather liberal opinions."[4] Adam Walker, a popularizer of the sciences, came to lecture at Syon House and at Eton during Shelley's time in those schools, and his demonstrations in chemistry and astronomy may have first stimulated Shelley's life-long interest in the sciences.

In the patrician confines of Eton, Shelley's active resistance to the system of fagging imposed on the younger boys earned him admiration, as well as considerable bullying. His later years, when he was one of the upper boys, seem to have been happier. His letters in 1809 to James Tisdall, an Eton friend, exhibit the normal interests of a gregarious schoolboy whose greatest trial is that he cannot enjoy the company of his school friends during the winter and Easter vacations.[5]

I Early Writings and Wanderings

In the spring of 1810, during his last term at Eton, Shelley published a Gothic novel entitled *Zastrozzi: A Romance*. Between the fall of 1809 and the spring of 1810 he wrote a second romance, which appeared in December, 1810,[6] while he was at Oxford, as *St. Irvyne: or, The Rosicrucian*. Besides whatever interest they may have as illustrations of the worst features of the then-popular Gothic tale of horror—their plots are impossibly bad and far too complex to summarize here—these two works show the miscellaneous character of Shelley's ideas and inspiration before the central determining event in his life, his expulsion from University College, Oxford.

In spite of abominable writing and Gothic clap-trap, *Zastrozzi* has some interest in that it presents ethical and psychological dilemmas that were to figure prominently in Shelley's poetry. Matilda, the anti-heroine, is condemned throughout for the "anarchy" of her soul, her inability to control her illicit passions. Verezzi, the hero, is long saved from Matilda's blandishments by his ideal conception of Julia. Zastrozzi has been corrupted by the injustice of Verezzi's father. Here in their incipient forms are the themes that appear in *Prometheus Unbound*, *Alastor*, and *The Cenci*.

In *St. Irvyne*, as in *Zastrozzi*, the thematic suggestions are more interesting than the plotting or the writing. The epigraph to Chapter XII is a quotation from Scott's *Lay of the Last Minstrel* that had earlier appeared as one of the epigraphs to Chapter IX of *Zastrozzi*: "For love is heaven, and heaven is love." The thematic pattern of *St. Irvyne* seems to play off the Wolfstein-Megalena plot (in which selfish lust destroys the two principals) against the innocent, self-effacing love of Eloise and Fitzeustace. Ginotti, during the confession of his past to Wolfstein, indicates that his desire for knowledge and his selfish grasping for immortality have poisoned his life and prevented him from thinking of love. His evil power can destroy Wolfstein, but not Wolfstein's sister, Eloise, who is protected by her innocent trust in other people and by her refusal to wither up within selfish fears and desires. Both the incoherence of *St. Irvyne* and Shelley's letter to Graham of April 1, 1810, suggest that he originally projected this work as a three-volume novel, but he eventually put his scattered materials together into a single volume.

At the same time that Shelley made this abortive effort to construct a three-decker novel, he was also composing poetry—both shorter pieces of a miscellaneous nature, some of which were published (with five poems by his sister Elizabeth) in a slim volume called *Original Poetry by Victor and Cazire*, and, more ambitiously, a poem in four cantos (145 lines) entitled "The Wandering Jew."[7] The shorter poems are largely imitative or worse; John Stockdale, Shelley's publisher, persuaded the youthful author to suppress the edition when he discovered that one of the poems was plagiarized from M. G. ("Monk") Lewis' *Tales of Terror* (London, 1801). Since then readers have noted other plagiarisms or close imitations of Chatterton, Byron, and William Smyth. It seems likely that *Original Poetry* was meant to be a practical joke, its title calling attention to the joke's point. Shelley was not skillful enough to parody the bad poetry of the day, but he certainly knew when he was plagiarizing wholesale.

Shelley was unable to find a publisher for "The Wandering Jew," a more serious effort; it appeared in print only in garbled versions after Shelley's death (excerpts in 1829 and in a different version in 1831). The poem is written in the irregularly rhymed tetrameter verse of Scott's poetic romances. Once again the plot is the work's weakest feature, but perhaps a summary justifies itself by showing how, in this early phase, Shelley viewed the legend of the Wandering Jew. In Canto I, Paulo, a mysterious stranger, carries off the novice Rosa when she breaks away in terror during the ceremony of investiture for the convent. Paulo declares his eternal love for Rosa, and she becomes his mistress. In Canto II, Victorio, a young nobleman, visits Paulo and Rosa and finds them deeply in love with each other. During the visit Paulo is suddenly moved to tell his history to his beloved and his friend. Canto III is Paulo's revelation that he is the Wandering Jew and contains an account of Christ's curse and the outcast's sufferings, which have *not*, however, persuaded Paulo to league himself with the Devil. In the final canto, Victorio, who is also passionately in love with Rosa, accepts from a witch a love potion that is supposed to win Rosa to him; in reality, it is a poison that kills Rosa, leaving Paulo inconsolable. "The Wandering Jew," immature and worthless though it is as poetry, marks Shelley's first effort to construct a long poem and shows certain characteristic traits including an allusiveness and tendency to suggest rather than state intervening events in the plot. The poem concentrates on mood-creating descriptions and on moral and metaphysical observations.

The thrust of these earliest publishing efforts by Shelley was toward low-grade entertainment in the Gothic tradition of sensationalism, but the youthful poet's ethical and metaphysical concerns interfered; the ideas in these early works are too inchoate to be taken seriously for their own sake and, by warping the plots, succeed in dissipating any value the works might have had as light reading.

Soon after taking up residence at University College, Oxford, in October, 1810, Shelley began a friendship with Thomas Jefferson Hogg, a fellow student. Hogg's accounts of Shelley at Oxford emphasize the young poet's interest in experimental sciences, his wide reading, and his penchant for literary larks. Shelley is thought to have written, and perhaps published, several works during his five-month stay in Oxford, but only two are known to be his—*Posthumous Fragments of Margaret Nicholson* and the ill-fated *Necessity of Atheism*. The first, containing six poetical fragments (purportedly written by the insane washerwoman who had tried in 1786 to kill King George III and had been confined in Bedlam ever since), was published in November, 1810.[8] These fragments were supposedly edited by Margaret Nicholson's nephew John Fitzvictor, a pseudonym that follows in the tradition of the *Victor and Cazire* volume.

According to Hogg's account, Shelley originally intended to publish the poems as serious efforts; but Hogg, finding the quality low, persuaded Shelley to alter them for the worse and to publish them as burlesque verse. Scholars have disputed Hogg's story, and it seems likely that the poems were intended seriously enough. Although they are of the same low quality that characterizes the *Victor and Cazire* verse and the lyrics in *St. Irvyne*, the *Margaret Nicholson* poems deal more directly with social and political injustices. For example, the second fragment, "supposed to be an Epithalamium of Francis Ravaillac [1578–1610] and Charlotte Corday [1768–1793]," praises these two political assassins for their tyrannicides. (They had assassinated King Henry IV of France [Henry of Navarre] and Jean Paul Marat, respectively.) The most interesting lines show Shelley's idealistic bias at this early point in his metaphysical thinking:

> Congenial minds will seek their kindred soul,
>   E'en though the tide of time has rolled between;
> They mock weak matter's impotent control,
>   And seek of endless life the eternal scene.
>
>   (42–45)

Another poem of interest in the volume, "Melody to a Scene of Former Times," seems to reflect the unhappy termination of Shelley's first love affair, his presumed engagement to his cousin Harriet Grove. Harriet (and her parents) became alarmed at the growth of Shelley's radical opinions; the breaking of the engagement in 1810 in the name of Christian orthodoxy hardened Shelley's opposition to "bigotry" and thus helped precipitate his subsequent alienation from his family.[9]

The crisis in the conflict between Shelley's opinions and those of his elders came in February, 1811, when the young man, perhaps with Hogg's connivance, printed anonymously a seven-page pamphlet entitled *The Necessity of Atheism*. As Newman White has remarked, "Except for the title and the signature to the advertisement ('through deficiency of proof, an Atheist') there was no atheism in it." Rather, it follows the skeptical reasoning of David Hume and is agnostic; the Advertisement says: "As a love of truth is the only motive which actuates the Author of this little tract, he earnestly entreats that those of his readers who may discover any deficiency in his reasoning, or may be in possession of proofs which his mind could never obtain, would offer them, together with their objections to the Public. . . ."

Shelley gave Christian spokesmen every opportunity to enlighten him, sending copies of the tract to professors and heads of colleges at Oxford and Cambridge (all, of course, Anglican clergymen) and to the bishops of the Church of England. He had also surreptitiously left a number of copies of the pamphlet in the shop window of the Oxford printers and stationers, Munday and Slatter (publishers of *Margaret Nicholson*); upon receiving a protest from a fellow of New College, Munday and Slatter agreed to destroy the copies and burned them in the kitchen fire. Not until the outraged Reverend Edward Copleston, Professor of Poetry and Fellow of Oriel, forced the issue did the officials of University College take action. On March 25, 1811, the authorities expelled both Shelley and Hogg "for contumaciously refusing to answer questions proposed to them, and for also repeatedly declining to disavow a publication entitled *'The Necessity of Atheism.'*" Shelley and Hogg left for London, and from there they negotiated with their parents about their future.

As great a shock as the expulsion was to the two young men, it shocked their fathers more. Timothy Shelley attempted to force his son to abject penitance; and, by remaining adamant (partly on the advice of William Whitton, his solicitor), he threw his son more and more upon his own resources. Hogg's father, on the other hand, by asking a less overt capitulation, brought his son once again under parental influence. Their relative success may, in part, be assessed by noting that Hogg became a lawyer of the most conservative principles, while Shelley became an increasingly eloquent opponent of authoritarian power.

Shelley, alone in London, began seeing a Miss Elizabeth Westbrook and her younger sister, Harriet, a school friend of his sister Hellen. The Westbrook girls' father, a prosperous retired vintner and coffeehouse owner, belonged to the merchant class for whom Shelley usually had little sympathy; but, in his isolation from his own family, he seems to have become a familiar in the household. Eliza Westbrook (thirty years old) apparently threw her sixteen-year-old sister and Shelley (now eighteen) together as often as she could and was rewarded when this heir to a wealthy baronetcy eloped with Harriet. They traveled immediately to Edinburgh, where they obtained a license and were married on August 29, 1811. Hogg soon joined them in the Scottish capital, where the three remained through the end of September. Early in October they went to York, and from there Shelley set out for Sussex a few days later to see his family, leaving his wife and his friend together.

When Shelley returned to York, he had been preceded there by Eliza Westbrook. She lived with the Shelleys until their final separation, dominating Harriet and sometimes even keeping the communal household funds. Within a week after Shelley's return to York, he, Harriet, and Eliza left for Keswick, Cumberland (not far from the northern seat of the Duke of Norfolk). This precipitous departure was occasioned by Harriet's revealing that, in Shelley's absence, Hogg had tried to seduce her. Shelley and Hogg, in the long, agonized correspondence that followed, tried unsuccessfully to find a solid basis for restoring Hogg to the group.

II Political Activist

After visiting the Duke of Norfolk at Greystoke, Shelley cultivated an acquaintance with Robert Southey, who saw in the young radical "my own ghost. . . . He is just what I was in 1794." Southey discussed literature, philosophy, and politics with the young man and allowed him the use of his extensive library. There was not, however, complete sympathy between them because Southey condescended to Shelley's radicalism as a passing adolescent phase: "I tell him that all the difference between us is, that he is nineteen, and I am thirty-seven."[10] As long as Shelley remained in Keswick, all was amicable between him and Southey, but in later years the difference between the two poets widened into an open breach.[11]

While at Keswick, Shelley initiated a correspondence with William Godwin, the author of *Enquiry Concerning Political Justice* (1793) and other radical works. In this early phase of their relationship, Godwin warned Shelley against rushing into writings or actions that were hasty and ill-conceived. But the young man was not in the mood to heed his elders—whether Southey, the Duke of Norfolk, or even Godwin, the author of books that had strongly influenced Shelley's radical principles—and he hurried to Ireland to assist the cause of reform there.

Before leaving England, Shelley had written in a simple style and diction *An Address to the Irish People,* which was printed as a pamphlet soon after he reached Dublin on February 12, 1812; and he distributed most of fifteen hundred copies by March 18. A second pamphlet, *Proposals for an Association of . . . Philanthropists,* Shelley wrote in his "natural style" for the upper classes. Both pamphlets not only advocate Catholic emancipation and repeal of the Legislative Union Act (1800) that merged the Irish parliament with the British but also urge the Irish to re-examine the entire fabric of their society. Both tracts are republican in politics, egalitarian in economics, and free-thinking in theology ("all religions are good which make men good"). The *Proposals for an Association* is forcefully and clearly written, a marked advance over Shelley's earlier prose and infinitely superior to his poems and letters of the same period. On February 28, 1812, Shelley spoke at an Irish nationalist rally at the Fishamble Street Theatre, Dublin, where his expression of solidarity with the Irish people and their sufferings was well received, according to three contemporary newspaper accounts.[12]

While in Dublin, Shelley also had printed a broadside entitled *Declaration of Rights,* which sets forth in thirty-one articles Shelley's political credo. He wrote that "Government has no rights; it is a delegation from several individuals for the purpose of securing their own" (I); "No man has a right to disturb the public peace, by personally resisting the execution of a law however bad. He ought to acquiesce, using at the same time the utmost powers of his reason, to promote its repeal" (IX); "A man has a right to unrestricted liberty of discussion, falsehood is a scorpion that will sting itself to death" (XII); "No man has a right to do an evil thing that good may come" (XVII); "No man has a right to monopolize more than he can enjoy . . ." (XXVIII). The broadside concludes with an appeal to "Man" to "think of thy rights" and, finally, with a quotation from Satan's invocation to the fallen angels in Milton's *Paradise Lost,* Book I: "Awake!—arise!—or be for ever fallen."

Having made his presence felt briefly among the Irish nationalists and received his first public eulogies and attacks in the Dublin press, Shelley sailed for Wales to attempt to stimulate interest in his proposed Association of Philanthropists. With Harriet and Eliza, Shelley landed in north Wales on April 6, 1812, and soon thereafter settled on a farm that he hoped to make his home. He wrote to his father asking for five hundred pounds to rent the farm and buy furniture and equipment, but he was refused. The household moved once more, this time to

Lynmouth, Devon, where Shelley wrote and had printed locally his *Letter to Lord Ellenborough,* an eloquent plea for freedom of the press that was elicited by the Lord Chief Justice's sentencing an elderly printer named Daniel Isaac Eaton to eighteen months in prison for republishing the Third Part of Thomas Paine's *Age of Reason.* The *Letter,* too strongly worded for the repressive atmosphere of 1812, was not published; and only about fifty copies (out of a printing of one thousand) escaped being burned by the alarmed printer.[13] About this time Shelley's Irish servant, Daniel Hill (or Healy), was arrested for distributing the *Declaration of Rights.* Unable to raise two hundred pounds for Hill's fine, Shelley paid the jailer fifteen shillings a week to purchase privileges for Hill in prison before he himself departed in September, 1812, for Wales.

While at Lynmouth, Shelley's household had been joined by his constant correspondent since June, 1811, Miss Elizabeth Hitchener, a spinster schoolteacher of Hurstpierpoint, Sussex, who was ten years Shelley's senior, whom he found intellectually congenial, and whom he wished to save from the drudgery of daily labor so that she could develop her powers as a liberal writer. Such misguided philanthropy was characteristic of Shelley throughout his early years; not considering that introducing a talkative, opinionated blue-stocking into the same house with his child bride and her domineering sister could lead to nothing but disaster, he had encouraged Miss Hitchener from the time of the Irish adventure to give up her teaching post and join the indigent band of warriors against oppression. Quite naturally the arrangement did not prove satisfactory; Elizabeth Hitchener left the household four months later. Just beginning to learn the dangers of tampering with the lives of others, Shelley wrote to Hogg: "She was deprived by our misjudging haste of a situation, where she was going on smoothly. . . . certainly she is embarrassed and poor, and we being in some degree the cause, we ought to obviate it."[14]

While this domestic crisis was fermenting, Shelley was busily engaged at Tremadoc in North Wales. About five thousand acres that had been reclaimed from the sea by means of a large dike were threatened when the cost of repairing extensive storm damage outran the resources of the project's originator, William Alexander Madocks, M.P., a hero of English liberals for his recent efforts on behalf of parliamentary reform (1809). Shelley's enthusiastic canvassing for contributions helped to reactivate local interest in the work.[15]

When late in September, 1812, Shelley went to London in an attempt to raise additional money for the Tremadoc embankment (and to relieve his own pecuniary embarrassment), he first met William Godwin, whom he visited frequently during a stay of six weeks or more in London. At this time Shelley also saw Thomas Hookham, a free-thinking publisher; and he met Hookham's friend Thomas Love Peacock, a struggling poet. These three men were to be important to his future.

After Shelley returned to Tremadoc, he lived about three-and-a-half months in "Tanyrallt," a mountain-side house owned by Madocks. There he continued his efforts on behalf of the embankment and wrote poetry (*Queen Mab* and perhaps some of the poems in *The Esdaile Notebook*). Near the end of February, Shelley's party fled the house as the result of an incident that is one of the difficult cruxes of his biography. Shelley said—and Harriet wrote to Hookham[16]—that on the night of February 26 someone tried to murder him by firing through a window when he was going to investigate a noise. The Shelley's left Tremadoc immediately and, by writing in panic to Hookham and other friends, obtained enough money to go to Ireland.

Mr. Leeson, a prominent resident of the neighborhood who had no love for Shelley, afterward said that Shelley had invented the attack and had fled Wales to avoid paying large debts that he had accumulated. In the most cogent account of the evidence, Cameron argues that Shelley, who wished to leave Wales to continue his writing and hoped to have money when he came of age in August to repay the debts he had incurred, probably staged the incident (for the benefit of Harriet, Eliza, and the servants) so that his party would have a viable excuse for their hasty departure. Other scholars hold different views: some, that the attack was a real one (though perhaps exaggerated by Shelley in his accounts of it); others, that although there was no attack, Shelley suffered a hallucination that made him believe there had been one.[17]

Upon leaving Tremadoc, the Shelleys went once more to Ireland. In Dublin, Shelley seems to have recovered manuscripts of poems—some of those later copied into the "Esdaile Notebook"—that he had left there with a printer named Stockdale (not to be confused with the London publisher of the same name). After a hasty trip to the lakes at Killarney caused them to miss Hogg, who had come to Dublin on their invitation, Shelley and Harriet returned to London, arriving about April 5, 1813. In the capital Shelley saw *Queen Mab* through the press and attempted to bring about a mutually satisfactory financial settlement with his father before his twenty-first birthday (when he would be able to raise money, at exorbitant interest, by borrowing on *post obit* bonds). This effort was unsuccessful because Timothy Shelley insisted that his son should retract his heretical religious views, and Shelley refused to make such a declaration against his conscience.

III Another Pamphlet and *Queen Mab*

Early in 1814 Shelley had printed an anonymous pamphlet entitled *A Refutation of Deism: in a Dialogue.*[18] The dialogue is between Theosophus, a Deist who attacks Christianity, and Eusebes, a Christian who attacks Deism. According to the preface, "the object of the following Dialogue is to prove that the system of Deism is untenable. It is attempted to shew that there is no alternative between Atheism and Christianity . . ." (Julian, VI, 25). A casual reader might suppose that the work defends Christianity, but such is not the case. It shows the influence both of the French atheistic materialists like Diderot, D'Alembert, and Holbach, whom Shelley had been reading and translating in 1812, and of Cicero's *De Natura Deorum,* Hume's *Dialogues Concerning Natural Religion,* and a dialogue in Sir William Drummond's skeptical *Academical Questions.*

The two disputants of *A Refutation of Deism* punch holes in each other's arguments: Eusebes shows the intellectual untenability of the Deistic position while Theosophus scores the Christian churches' record of persecutions and anti-intellectualism. Both positions are effectively destroyed, but whether Shelley intended to reduce the reader to atheism (as an ironic reading of the Preface would suggest) or merely to academical skepticism (an agnostic position) remains problematical. His earlier correspondence with Elizabeth Hitchener and Godwin shows that Shelley had already abandoned his discipleship to French materialism.[19] He probably hoped that the tract would be purchased by intellectual Christians who, expecting to find arguments against Deism, would find their own faith undermined by the arguments of Theosophus. The work is notable as a companion piece to *Queen Mab* because it displays the subtlety and indirection lacking in that poem's attacks on religion. As with the *Address to the Irish People* and the *Proposals for an Association,* Shelley tried to reach two distinct audiences with *Queen Mab* and *A Refutation of Deism.*

Queen Mab, Shelley's first major poem, was printed for Thomas Hookham but never published because of the fear of prosecution. During Shelley's lifetime about seventy of the two-hundred-fifty copies were distributed privately to friends and known liberals. In 1821 a radical London bookseller named William Clark published a pirated edition of *Queen Mab*; and, though he went to prison for his act, the poem continued to be reprinted and circulated among the radicals throughout the nineteenth century.[20]

The poem consists of a dedication "To Harriet" and nine cantos totaling 2,305 lines. Blank verse forms the staple, but interspersed are lengthy passages in an irregular, unrhymed lyric verse derived from Southey's heroic poems. Following the poem are long explanatory notes—many of them are full essays which include supporting quotations in Greek, Latin, French, and English from a broad range of poets, philosophers, and historians. (In the original edition of 1813 the poem occupies the first 122 pages and the notes run through page 240.)

Shelley has been accused of failing to structure his poems rationally. Actually his sense of form manifests itself increasingly during his career as a poet, but it was strong from nearly the very beginning. *Queen Mab* illustrates an almost mechanical structure. In Canto I the soul of sleeping Ianthe (watched over by her lover Henry) is awakened by Mab, the Fairy Queen, who takes the Soul in her chariot far beyond the bounds of the solar system to the Hall of Spells (II.42). The journey fulfills two thematic functions: it depicts the duality of body and soul, asserting the superiority of the latter; and, in its descriptions of the vastness of the universe and multiplicity of the solar systems and other worlds, it tends to dwarf the Earth and to deflate man's exalted opinion of his own importance in the universe.

In Canto II Mab takes up the theme of human pride by pointing to the vanity of past human achievements: the glory of past civilizations persists only in the memory of man and in decaying ruins that testify to human transience and to the folly of glorying in material creations. At the beginning of Canto III the Spirit of Ianthe points out the uses of history ("I know / The past, and thence I will assay to glean / A warning for the future . . ."), and declares that virtue is its own reward: "when the power of imparting joy / Is equal to the will, the human soul / Requires no other Heaven" (III.11–13). The Fairy Queen then shows the evils of monarchy, or any form of society where some are masters and others must serve; for he "whom courtiers nickname monarch" is "a slave / Even to the basest appetites":

> The man
> Of virtuous soul commands not, nor obeys.
> Power, like a desolating pestilence,
> Pollutes whate'er it touches; and obedience,

Bane of all genius, virtue, freedom, truth,
Makes slaves of men, and, of the human frame,
A mechanized automaton.

(III.174–80)

The "Spirit of Nature" makes no distinctions among men; its "essence throbs / Alike in every human heart" and its power makes a mockery of distinctions raised by human selfishness and pride. The opening three cantos declare that, before the vastness of the universe and the impersonality of the Spirit of Nature, all human inequalities of power, wealth, or honor lose their significance, except that such inequities poison the happiness both of those who possess and those who lack the superfluity. Shelley, in Cantos IV–VI, attacks the chief manifestations of erring human pride: war (IV), commerce—really capitalism (V), and religion (VI). Canto VII is a systematic attack on the Judeo-Christian tradition, part of it spoken by the phantom of Ahasuerus, the Wandering Jew. Moses is portrayed as a murderer and Jehovah as a sadistic projection of human pride and sin.

Cantos VIII and IX depict the glorious future that is open to men if they will abandon their evil ways and live according to the laws of reason and love: the polar caps, deserts, and tropical jungles are made habitable; as in Isaiah's prophecy, "the lion now forgets to thirst for blood" and the nightshade, "like passion's fruit . . . poisons no more the pleasure it bestows" (VIII.124–30). Man, like the lion, becomes vegetarian: "no longer now / He slays the lamb that looks him in the face, / And horribly devours his mangled flesh" (VIII.211–13). "Man has lost / His terrible prerogative, and stands / An equal amidst equals . . ." (VIII.225–27).

With the demise of "Falsehood" (read "Religion"), human reason and passion are free and innocent, unified in seeking human happiness without infringing on the rights of other men. Freed from the fear of Hell and from the selfish quest for Heaven, death loses its terrors, old age its infirmities, and youth its doubts and rebelliousness (IX.57–75). Marriage, which had been attacked earlier ("Even love is sold," V.189), no longer exists to hinder "the kindred sympathies of human souls"; "dull and selfish chastity" no longer interferes with the natural expression of human affection; and "prostitution's venomed bane" no longer poisons "the springs of happiness and life" (IX.76–88). The ruins of palaces, cathedrals, and prisons—having no significance in the egalitarian human society—become scenes of innocent childhood play.

After Mab's admonition to Ianthe's soul ("Let virtue teach thee firmly
to pursue / The gradual paths of an aspiring change" [IX.147–48]),
the poem closes with the Spirit's return to Ianthe's sleeping form,
which awakes to behold

> Henry, who kneeled in silence by her couch,
> Watching her sleep with looks of speechless love,
> And the bright beaming stars
> That through the casement shone.
>
> (IX.237–40)

Queen Mab is a rhetorical poem, the rhetoric of the verse itself rein-
forced by the essays on astronomy, economics, philosophical Necessity,
and on the evils of religion, of marriage, and of the eating of animal
flesh. But, though the poem operates more on the literal level and less
through symbolic indirection than do Shelley's later major poems,
Queen Mab is of a piece in doctrine with *Prometheus Unbound* and "The
Triumph of Life"; and such symbolism as Shelley does introduce as an
adjunct to his open declarations prefigures that in later poems.

IV The Esdaile Poems

Hookham arranged for the printing of *Queen Mab,* but he declined
to publish a volume of shorter poems of a much more personal and
autobiographical nature; to these Shelley added a few more and gave
Harriet the notebook in which they were transcribed. Harriet retained
this copybook after Shelley's elopement with Mary Godwin, and it
passed to her heirs through her daughter Ianthe Shelley Esdaile. The
so-called "Esdaile Notebook," though transcribed by Edward Dowden,
who published portions of it in his biography of Shelley, remained for
the most part an unknown quantity until 1964, when Kenneth Neill
Cameron's edition appeared.[21] Thus, exactly a century and a half after
it was intended for publication, Shelley's first important body of
shorter poetry became available.

The collection is interesting and significant in several respects: first,
it shows that Shelley's apprenticeship in poetry was longer and more
varied than most critics had realized, and thus makes more easily un-
derstandable the marked superiority of *Alastor* and other poems of
1815–17 over the earlier published lyrics. For example, two poems in
the Spenserian stanza, "On leaving London for Wales" (written in No-

TECH...
LEARNING RESOURCES CENTER ... THE LOWCOUNTRY
POST OFFICE BOX 1288
BEAUFORT, SOUTH CAROLINA 29901-1288

vember, 1812) and "Henry and Louisa" (an anti-war poem), foreshadow
Shelley's later development in the use of the stanza in *The Revolt of
Islam*; and "Zeinab and Kathema," a poem of 180 lines in a six-line
stanza, is a thematic precursor of *The Revolt*.[22]

A number of poems in *The Esdaile Notebook* are interesting in their
own right as poetry. In "The Retrospect" (published in part by Dowden), Shelley at Cwm Elan in 1812 looks back over the year that has
passed since he visited his cousins, the Groves, in the summer of 1811,
just before his elopement with Harriet Westbrook. The 168 tetrameter
lines utilize the best aspects of the topographical-reflective poem re-
created by Wordsworth in "Lines composed a few miles above Tintern
Abbey. . . ." Shelley compares his present happiness in Harriet's love
with his distraught, almost suicidal state during the previous visit—a
condition produced by the combination of (1) unrequited love (his re-
jection by Harriet Grove); (2) a disdain of the mortal world (based on
a belief in a spiritual reality contrasting with "the chains of clay"); and
(3) a dearth of true friends to share his revolutionary ideals. Using the
couplet, in which his control is much surer than in some of the more
intricate stanzaic patterns, he achieves a tone of calm, reasonable reflection that has more of Wordsworth than most of his passionate out-
pourings of these early years, which generally suggest Southey or the
rhetorical Coleridge. The same restrained tone is also present in a
blank-verse poem addressed "To Harriet" beginning "It is not blas-
phemy. . . ." Here verbal echoes of Wordsworth abound; the apprenticeship leading to *Alastor* had begun by 1812.

In the poems added to the Esdaile copybook after Shelley had abandoned thought of publishing it, one sees the later deterioration of the
relationship between Shelley and Harriet. No single factor provides an
adequate explanation for this rift. In the first place, Harriet had her
own interests that, in part, reduced her dependence on Shelley: her
sister Eliza was a friend and confidante, and the sisters doubtless grew
closer in their war against Elizabeth Hitchener; the birth of Shelley's
daughter Eliza Ianthe (June 27 or 28, 1813) gave Harriet still another
role to add to that of wife and sister; at Bracknell (thirty miles from
London, where the Shelleys settled in July, 1813) and later on a trip
to the Lake Country and Edinburgh (to escape creditors), Harriet found
a congenial spirit in Peacock, whose classical skepticism gave him more
distance from Shelley's enthusiasms than had other members of the
Bracknell circle, which Peacock later burlesqued in *Nightmare Abbey*
(1818).

Shelley, on the other hand, was for the first time amid kindred souls, personal friends like Hogg and Peacock (whose intellects he admired in spite of differences in temperament) and fellow enthusiasts in the circle gathered around John Frank Newton (a vegetarian) and his sister-in-law Mrs. Boinville, English widow of Lafayette's *aide-de-camp*. While Harriet ceased to pursue her studies, Shelley was increasing his reading of empirical philosophy and the Classics and taking up the study of Italian literature. Shelley also saw William Godwin frequently during trips to London and was engaged in raising money for him. At Godwin's house, Shelley, even as he began to lose his initial awe of the author of *Political Justice,* found himself idolized by Mary Wollstonecraft Godwin, sixteen-year-old daughter of the philosopher and Mary Wollstonecraft (author of *A Vindication of the Rights of Woman* [1792] and other feminist and radical works who had died at the birth of her namesake [1797]). Shelley's alienation from Harriet can be traced in his flirtation at Bracknell with Mrs. Cornelia Turner, daughter of Mrs. Boinville and inspiration of Shelley's fine lyric, "Stanzas.—April, 1814" ("Away! the moor is dark beneath the moon"). But in June, 1814, Shelley and Mary Godwin declared their mutual love, bringing to an end not only the union with Harriet but also—though indirectly—Shelley's career as an activist reformer. In the years to follow, he turned more and more to literature as the medium through which he could best make his influence felt.

Chapter Two
Student to Poets

After June 26, 1814, when Shelley and Mary first declared their love to each other, William Godwin did everything he could to separate his daughter and Shelley (who had by this time gone deeply in debt to give money to Godwin). A frenzied month culminated when Shelley—torn between his duty to Harriet and his passion for Mary—took an overdose of laudanum in an attempted suicide. When he recovered, he and Mary determined not to be kept apart any longer; accompanied by Clara Mary Jane Clairmont (daughter of the second Mrs. Godwin), they eloped to France on the night of July 27. Their journey across France to Switzerland, down the Rhine Valley to Holland, and thence back to England is recorded in Mary's journal as published in *History of a Six Weeks' Tour* (1817). Neither constant lack of money, bad accommodations, warnings of bandits, incivility by the war-ravaged populace, sundry difficulties in buying and hiring transportation, nor (least of all) concern for the feelings of Harriet or the Godwins kept Shelley, Mary, and Jane from enjoying the scenery and, indeed, the very adventure of the improbable tour.

In Switzerland, Shelley began a prose romance called "The Assassins," based on sketchy information on that sect garnered from Tacitus and Gibbon. In this fragment of less than four full chapters he does not praise institutional Christianity, but he portrays the beneficial effects of Jesus' teachings within an isolated sect in Lebanon. Beginning with a pure, primitive Christianity based on mutual love and service, the Assassins developed through the centuries a purer religion of intellectual love and philanthropy. Against this background, Shelley began to construct a story in which Albedir, a young man in the secluded valley paradise of the Assassins, discovers a stranger (who, it is clear, is the Wandering Jew) impaled on a branch of a cedar tree and takes him into his humble cottage. Before the fragment ends, the persecuted stranger begins to learn that, in the idyllic seclusion of the Assassins' valley, man and nature are reconciled, for harmful snakes play peacefully with Albedir's children. Shelley was developing in "The Assassins" a vision of the ideal harmony between nature and regenerate human society like that portrayed earlier in *Queen Mab* and later in *Prometheus Unbound*.

Returning to London on September 13, 1814, Shelley, Mary, and Jane found themselves almost completely ostracized by their former society: Godwin remained aloof and tried to prevent his household from holding any communication with them (though Charles Clairmont, Jane's brother, and Fanny Imlay, Mary's half-sister, eventually broke Godwin's prohibitions). The Boinville circle cut them off, as did Mary's best friend, Isabel Baxter (soon to be Mrs. David Booth). Only Hookham and Peacock saw them at all frequently, and once even Hookham was suspected of planning to turn Shelley over to his creditors. Shelley, convinced of his own virtue and of the ingratitude of others, waged a war of wits against the bailiffs who tried repeatedly to arrest him for debt.

Shelley had tried to persuade Harriet that, although he did not love her in a passionate sense, he was still her best friend and that she ought to come live with him and Mary, not as his wife but as his sister. Harriet, quite naturally, had not acceded to this plan. On November 30, 1814, she gave birth to Shelley's first son, whom she named Charles. Shelley visited his wife and son, but Harriet learned at last that she must give up her hopes of winning back her husband.[1]

Apart from Mary's journal, which is greatly expurgated, there are few documents that give information about Shelley from December, 1814, through July, 1815. When Sir Bysshe Shelley died on January 5, 1815, Shelley's father, in order to protect his own interests in the entailed estates, came to financial terms with his wayward son, paying off the greater part of his debts and agreeing to allow Shelley an annuity of one thousand pounds (two hundred pounds to go directly to Harriet). This arrangement gave him the first financial security he had known since his expulsion from Oxford.

In January and February, 1815, Shelley apparently encouraged an experiment in free love among Mary (then pregnant), Hogg, Jane Clairmont, and himself. How far this situation went beyond gallantry is problematical, the chief evidence being a series of letters from Shelley and Mary to Hogg.[2] On February 22, 1815, Mary's first child was born; this daughter (two months premature) died about two weeks later. When in May, 1815, Jane "Claire" Clairmont left the household, Mary wrote in her journal, "I begin a new Journal with our regeneration" (page 47). During the months immediately following, Shelley probably cooperated with an Irish radical named George Cannon, who edited under the name "Erasmus Perkins" a short-lived periodical entitled *The Theological Inquirer, or Polemical Magazine*; this journal reprinted *A Refutation of Deism* and almost a third of *Queen Mab.*[3]

Early in August, 1815, Shelley and Mary moved into a cottage near Bishopsgate, one of the eastern entrances to the Great Park of Windsor, on the northwestern edge of Surrey. After a brief period of solitude, Shelley and Mary joined Peacock and Charles Clairmont in a boat excursion up the Thames River to its source, a trip that materially improved Shelley's health and spirits.[4] On his return he began the sustained writing that resulted in the publication in February, 1816, of a slim volume entitled *Alastor; or, The Spirit of Solitude: and Other Poems.* This first volume of poetry that Shelley published with his name on the title page marks the beginning of his public career as a poet.

I *Alastor*

Alastor, Shelley's first major effort in the symbolic mode of poetry that was to remain his forte, follows the implications outlined in its Preface. It shows the destruction through his "self-centered seclusion" of a potentially good young poet because of his vain search to find an ideal mate corresponding to the vision in which his imagination had embodied "all of wonderful, or wise, or beautiful, which the poet, the philosopher, or the lover could depicture." Although the poem has its autobiographical aspects, it should be read primarily as Shelley's warning to men not to abandon their social concerns. One must be willing to accept the "choicest gifts" of "the spirit of sweet human love"—his own imperfect, human mate and his friends—rather than pursue a perfect being of his own imagining.

"Alastor," a Greek word meaning "evil genius," refers to the "spirit of solitude" that avenges itself on the deluded youth who is nameless throughout the work. The opening lines of the poem (1–17) are an invocation addressed by Shelley's own persona to "earth, ocean, air, belovèd brotherhood"; Shelley here speaks as the spirit of fire,[5] the fourth cardinal element and the one that in Shelley's symbolic universe represents spiritual vitality.

Throughout Shelley's poetry the four elements of ancient physical science have consistent symbolic values: *earth* (often referred to as *dust*) symbolizes inert matter, deprived of all vitality; *water* represents natural mortal vitality—earthly generation; *air*—between the earth and waters, on the one hand, and the fires of heaven (sun, moon, and stars) on the other—symbolizes the realm of ideas and abstractions, the world of human thought. The ultimate source of fire, or spiritual energy, in Shelley's universe is the sun. On the cosmic level it represents the divinity (however Shelley might define it at a given moment) and, on the human level, imagination, which embodies both the warmth of love and the light of reason. Rationality devoid of love is symbolized in the moon, cold reflector of sunlight; but love separated from reason[6] is often represented by Venus, the evening star.

In *Alastor,* following the invocation to the brotherhood of the sublunar elements, there is a second invocation to the "Mother of this unfathomable world" (18–49). Shelley says that, although this unknown power has never unveiled its "inmost sanctuary," even when his "heart ever gazes on the depth / Of thy deep mysteries," he has understood enough from "incommunicable dream," "twilight phantasms," and "noon-day thought" to await confidently the breath of the "Great Parent" like a lyre waiting for the wind. Lines 50–66 summarize the theme of the poem: a poet wasted his life because "he lived, he died, he sung, in solitude" (60); he left behind no friends, but "strangers" (61), no wife, but "virgins" (62). Because he attempted "to exist without human sympathy," he perished, in the words of the Preface, "through the intensity and passion of [his] search after its communities." In other words, because he refused to accept the natural outlet for his human social instincts, they were distorted into a monomania.

Following this recapitulation of the theme, the Poet describes the birth and education of the Youth.[7] In his infancy and early boyhood the Youth had the advantage of pleasant natural surroundings, as well as books and educational opportunities ("the fountains of divine philosophy"); but he later left "his cold fireside and alienated home / To seek strange truths in undiscovered lands" (76–77). In his allegorical journey the Youth pursues the secrets of nature (81–106) and those of human civilizations (106 ff.)—he studies both sciences and humanities. At last "he saw / The thrilling secrets of the birth of time" (126–28).

While the Youth has been pursuing knowledge, he has neglected the living world around him. An Arab maiden loves him so much that she has "brought his food, / Her daily portion"; but such self-sacrifice is lost on the Youth, who takes no notice of the girl, and she must return "to her cold home / Wildered, and wan, and panting," a victim of the Youth's lack of sympathy for his fellow human beings. Although the Youth has been ignoring the love offered him by the Arab maiden, he has come to desire love; in the words of the Preface, "his mind . . . thirsts for intercourse with an intelligence similar to itself." His imagination coalesces all the beauty, truth, and love that he has read about or imagined during his pursuit of knowledge into the idea of a beautiful woman, who appears to him in a dream and with whom he imagines that he consummates his love (140–87). Immediately afterwards "night . . . swallowed up the vision" as "sleep . . . / Rolled back its impulse on his vacant brain" (188–91).

Having lost the dream-vision who had promised to be his ideal love, the Youth finds the next morning that the beauties of nature seem flat, stale, and unprofitable; he seeks his vision "beyond the realms of dream" and is doomed to disappointment. In despair, he wonders whether he could find the dream-vision beyond the grave, and during the first day (192–222) the Youth contemplates suicide. He is soon overcome, however, by a fierce passion that drives him over the world in a frantic search for the lost vision (222–54). Everywhere he goes, the humble people treat him kindly, calling him "with false names / Brother, and friend," names that are false because he has voluntarily withdrawn from the human community (254–71).

The Youth's journey has carried him generally backward through the history of human civilizations (109–16) and then eastward across Arabia, Persia, and the Hindu Kush mountains to the "vale of Cashmire," the site of his dream-vision (140–51). Cashmire had earlier been the scene of the innocent youth of the lovers in "Zeinab and Kathema" (The Esdaile Notebook, pp. 148–51); later, in Prometheus Unbound, Asia awaits Prometheus in "a lovely Vale in the Indian Caucasus" and the two retire to a cave in the same general area. In Shelley's day the region of the Indian Caucasus and the nearby Vale of Cashmire was regarded as the probable site of the origin of human civilization and, perhaps, of the race itself.[8] Thus the Youth's retreat to the Vale of Cashmire and, later, back into the heart of the Indian Caucasus parallels the retreat to a secular Eden that had appeared in "The Assassins" and was to be embodied through one of Plato's myths in Prometheus, where Asia passes from "Age's icy caves" through Manhood, Youth, and Infancy, "through Death and Birth, to a diviner day" (II.v.97–110).[9]

This background contributes to an understanding of Alastor (272–468). After his wandering, the Youth pauses "upon the lone Chorasmian shore" (the Aral Sea). Seeing a swan, he is reminded of the vast disparity between man's state and that of other living things. The

swan, a merely natural creature, can fulfill its destiny within existing creation; the Youth asks, "And what am I that I should linger
here / . . . wasting these surpassing powers / In the deaf air, to the
blind earth, and heaven / That echoes not my thoughts?" (285–90).
Whereas the Poet addresses his opening invocation to "earth, ocean,
air, beloved brotherhood," the Youth has become so deluded by the
desires of his own heart that everything seems inert and unreal except
himself and his own imaginings. Queen Mab had warned Ianthe not
to suppose that the universe was dead:

> How strange is human pride!
> . . . .
> I tell thee that those viewless beings,
> Whose mansion is the smallest particle
> Of the impassive atmosphere,
> Think, feel and live like man . . . .
> (II.225–34)

The Youth in *Alastor,* like Coleridge's Ancient Mariner, has committed
this sin of pride by despising his fellow creatures. In his pride the
Youth again reasons that, if man can find no fulfillment within this
life, perhaps he should seek his destiny beyond the grave. "Startled by
his own thoughts," he suspects that he is being tempted to evil; but,
seeing "no fair fiend near him," he finds a little shallop and follows "a
restless impulse . . . to embark / And meet lone Death on the drear
ocean's waste . . ." (304–5).

The description of the voyage that follows is in the mode of "The
Rime of the Ancient Mariner." In the afternoon of a fair day the sea
remains tranquil; but, as in the Mariner's homeward voyage, a mysterious wind drives the boat along (308–20). Next a whirlwind sweeps
the boat through stormy waters, while the Youth calmly steers (320–
33). As night comes on, the boat still sails safely, "as if that frail and
wasted human form, / Had been an elemental god" (333–51). The
symbolic pattern of the passage has emphasized the difference between
man and water, the element of merely mortal generation on which he
navigates in the journey of life, for physical dangers stimulate rather
than cow the human spirit. At midnight, the dark night of the soul,
the moon rises, showing the "ice summits" of the Caucasus; examined
by human reason, the source of life appears foreign and inimical to
human aspirations. The sight fails, however, to daunt the Youth:

"'Vision and Love!' / The Poet cried aloud, 'I have beheld / The path of thy departure. Sleep and death / Shall not divide us long!'" (366–69).

At dawn the boat, which has moved mysteriously upstream *against* the current,[10] reaches a whirlpool formed by a waterfall that plunges from an immense height. The eye of the whirlpool is described as "a pool of treacherous and tremendous calm," "reflecting, yet distorting every cloud" (385–86). This reflection of the realm of air in the water signifies the Youth's tendency to attribute his own thoughts and desires to the natural world. (A cloud, as we shall see, is Shelley's recurring symbol of the human mind.) As the boat rises on the outer ridges of whirling waters, a gust of the west wind catches the sail and carries it to the calm edge of the pool, a cove lined with narcissuses, "yellow flowers" that "gaze on their own drooping eyes, / Reflected in the crystal calm" (406–8). The Youth longed to make a circlet of the narcissuses, "but on his heart its solitude returned, / And he forbore" (412–15).

Finally, at noonday (symbol of the closest conjunction between the divine and the human, when the sun's rays are least distorted by the earth's atmosphere), the Youth wanders through the forest, seeking "in Nature's dearest haunt, some bank, / Her cradle, and his sepulchre" (429–30); that is, he hopes to trace human existence back to its source, to discover the meaning of life, and in that discovery to die. In his search, the Youth finds another pool in which a "Spirit seemed / To stand beside him," but it proves to be only the reflection of his own "two starry eyes, hung in the gloom of thought" (490). Shelley likens the Youth's experience to "the human heart / Gazing in dreams over the gloomy grave," and seeing "its own treacherous likeness there" (472–74). The Youth's quest for the source of human life thus ends in failure; he finds no answer except his own narcissistic conceptions, and he is unable to penetrate the mystery of the world's origins.

In the final major section of the poem, the Youth seeks to answer the other ultimate question—What is the end and purpose of human existence? Once again he traces a river, but this time *from* its source rather than *to* its source (and from East to West). The symbolism here becomes explicit: "O stream! / Whose source is inaccessibly profound, / Whither do thy mysterious waters tend? / Thou imagest my life. . ." (502–5). This stream progresses from dancing "like childhood laughing as it went" (499), through a maturity bordered by "the forest's solemn canopies" (525), to an old age beside "nought but gnarled roots of ancient pines / Branchless and blasted" (530–31), where it descends "with its wintry speed" (543) until finally "the broad river . . . Fell into that immeasurable void" (567–70).

This allegory of human life again points up its ultimate mystery. The lone, "solemn pine" (561 ff., 571) at the edge of the precipice symbolizes life's persistent struggle to maintain itself in a hostile environment[11] and thus is a sign of hope to the now aged man in his final bewilderment, suggesting the possibility of some survival for human beings beyond the grave. But, unsatisfied in his search for answers to life's two supreme questions, the Youth dies just as two tips of the horned moon, like two stars or the eyes of the dream-vision, disappear behind the jagged hills on the horizon.

The concluding lines of *Alastor* are the lament of the Poet for the lost young man. But, still more, they are the human outcry of pity and fear at the fact of death. The Poet is not sentimentalizing the Youth when he laments that "many worms / And beasts and men live on . . . but thou art fled" (691–95); he is echoing the cry of Lear: "Why should a dog, a horse, a rat have life / And thou no breath at all?"—the cry against the destruction of the exceptional individual. The Poet's admitted sympathy for the Youth's extraordinary potentialities does not constitute sympathy with his course of action, for the Youth abandoned his associations with his fellow men as friend, lover, father, citizen of the world, and benefactor of his country.

Of the three classes of men that Shelley mentions in the Preface, the worst are those with neither human love nor vision; the best are those who combine a vision of the ideal with a compassion for limited human beings. The first class could be the subjects only of satirical literature, and the latter were to be treated by Shelley in his next major effort, *The Revolt of Islam*. The middle category, those men with vision who allowed their private search for truth to carry them away from their public duty, were proper subjects for tragic literature, for their greatness was flawed; unlike Prometheus, they brought no fire from Heaven to mankind.

Included in the volume with *Alastor* were a number of shorter poems: revised versions of two portions of *Queen Mab*—part of Canto I under the title of "The Daemon of the World" and Canto VI, 72–102, called "Superstition"; a lyric beginning "Oh! there are spirits of the air," the theme of which relates closely to that of *Alastor* and which, according to Mary Shelley, was written with Coleridge in mind; "Stanzas.—April, 1814"; a poem entitled "Mutability" that asserts the power of change over all human activities; lyrics on death and religion; a sonnet to Wordsworth and one on Napoleon's fall; and translations from Moschus and Dante, the first fruits of Shelley's studies in Greek and Italian literature. The volume as a whole shows Shelley stabilizing his views on man's nature and destiny and, at the same time, broadening and deepening his intellectual and esthetic foundations.

II Switzerland and the Poems of 1816

A son was born to Shelley and Mary on January 24, 1816, and named William. The subsequent winter and spring found Shelley happy enough in his family life and in his intellectual activities with Hogg and Peacock; but the unhealthy climate of England and financial complications, especially with Godwin, continued to harass him. In May, therefore, Shelley, Mary, the baby, and Claire Clairmont sailed from Dover for the Continent.

Claire, who had by this time become the mistress of Lord Byron, persuaded Shelley to change the destination of the party from Italy to Geneva, for which Byron had already departed.[12] Shelley's party actually arrived at Geneva ten days before Byron. An excursion by boat around Lake Geneva the last week in June—in part a literary pilgrimage to the scenes of Rousseau's *Julie, ou la Nouvelle Héloïse*—evoked Shelley's long literary letter to Peacock of July 12, 1816, and "Hymn to Intellectual Beauty," one of Shelley's finest poems. The same trip inspired Byron to write "The Prisoner of Chillon" and several passages in Canto III of *Childe Harold's Pilgrimage.*

Late in July, Shelley, Mary, and Claire traveled to the Valley of Chamouni to see Mont Blanc, Europe's highest mountain. There Shelley wrote "Mont Blanc," his second important poem of 1816, and described the scene in another long letter to Peacock (July 22–August 2). This letter and poem conclude *History of a Six Weeks' Tour.* "Mont Blanc" consists of 144 irregularly rhymed pentameter lines, divided into five unequal parts. The argument of the poem is as follows: In Part I (1–11), impressions of the "universe of things" (external nature, the world outside the human mind) flow through the passive universal mind, as a great river flows through a ravine; the stream is fed by two active forces, of which the "source of human thought" (not the human mind, but some unknown source of its thoughts) is to the great "universe of things" as a "feeble brook" (7) is to a "vast river" (10).

In Part II (12–48), the ravine of the River Arve descending from Mont Blanc is compared to the universal mind, and the River Arve itself to the "universe of things." When the poet thinks about his own existence, he realizes that it passively receives and then (just as passively) mirrors "fast influencings, / Holding an unremitting interchange / With the clear universe of things around" (34–40). Still addressing the "Ravine of Arve" as "thou" (12), Shelley equates his own mind ("my own separate fantasy," 36) with "one legion of wild thoughts" (the two phrases are in apposition). This "legion" constitutes the self-consciousness that can view objectively its own existence ("float above" the "darkness" of the ravine) and can seek "some shade" of the universal mind ("thee") "in the still cave of the witch of Poesy," which contains images, "ghosts" of all existing things. Basically, in the first two sections of the poem Shelley has described the state of the universe as one in which *active* impressions impinge on a *passive* universal mind that includes all sensate creation. Out of the interaction between mind and matter has arisen a third quality, the *human* mind, self-consciously questioning its own nature. But, being so feeble and limited, the human mind's only method of delving into the secrets of its nature is to plunge back into the unconscious pool of the universal mind. These depths are the source of poetic inspiration, as Shelley explains at length in his "Defence of Poetry."

In Part III (lines 49–83), the poet, now inspired, is not sure whether the "veil of life and death" has been lifted by an unknown god, or whether he is caught up in a dream where the inspiration of the universal mind (or collective unconscious) can illuminate his individual mind. But he sees for the first time the *meaning* of Mont Blanc. On the peak all is "still, snowy, and serene," frozen, "a desert peopled by the storms alone"—save for an occasional inquiring spirit ("eagle," 68), pursued by its own vision of evil (the "wolf," 69). What is the history and destiny of this mountain and valley scene that has become an emblem of all creation? "None can reply—all seems eternal now" (75).

But the very blankness of this wilderness does convey a message: It teaches either awe-filled ("awful") doubt—reverent skepticism as opposed to cynicism—"or faith so mild" (a non-dogmatic piety) that "but for" (except for) this faith, man could be perfectly reconciled with nature. The mountain has a voice "to repeal / Large codes of fraud and woe," such as fideistic religions and authoritarian rulers who claim divine sanctions. The voice is "not understood / By all," but "the

wise . . . interpret" it; the "great . . . make [it] felt"; and the "good
. . . deeply feel" it (82–83). The mountain's message is stated in Part
IV of the poem (84–126).

All sublunar creatures—fields and lakes, lightning and rain, earthquake and hurricane, "the works and ways of man"—are subject to
mutability: "All things that move and breathe with toil and sound /
Are born and die; revolve, subside, and swell" (94–95). But "Power"
(a term that means "First Cause," or "God" in the terminology of eighteenth-century philosophy) is *not* mortal and is *not* subject to change:
"Power dwells apart in its tranquillity, / Remote, serene, and inacces-
sible" (96–97). And *"this"* is what the "mountains / Teach the adverting mind" (99–100): that God is *not* simply a very big man, that there
is an unbridgeable gulf between everything that man experiences
within natural creation and the originating "Power" that exists beyond
the limits of human cognition.

At the top of Mont Blanc "Frost and the Sun in scorn of mortal
power" have created a "city of death"—but even to use the term "city"
is to anthropomorphize abstract, impersonal forces—"not a city, but a
flood of ruin" from which glaciers creep down, destroying all living
things in their paths. The glaciers are not solely destructive, however;
they are also the source of the River Arve, which is "the breath and
blood of distant lands" (120–26). The cycle of necessity is perpetually
changing; it oscillates between destroying and revivifying, creating
and obliterating. This cycle of mutability is what earth's creatures,
including man, constantly experience.

As Part IV showed the encounter of the cycle of necessity (symbolized by the glaciers and by the River Arve) with human life, so Part V
examines the source of that cycle, epitomized by the unseen top of
Mont Blanc. "The power is there" that is the ultimate *source* "of many
sights, / And many sounds, and much of life and death" (127–29); but
the top of the mountain itself has neither "sights" ("none beholds
them," 132) nor "sounds" ("Winds contend / Silently there . . . silently," "voiceless lightning," 134–39). The hidden source of "things,"
both governs "thought" and "is as a law" to "the infinite dome / Of
Heaven" (139–41), an unmoved mover far beyond concern for human
beings and their petty problems. The final three lines, however, ask a
rhetorical question that puts the poem back into the human perspective. If "silence and solitude were vacancy" to the "human mind's
imaginings," man would feel so overwhelmed by his isolation in a

foreign and inimical universe that he could not go on. The prismatic human imagination, however, has the ability to reflect and refract the cold blank whiteness of benighted snow into the beautiful colors of the rainbow, giving joy to men during their lives and hope for a survival beyond the grave.

Such power of the human imagination is the subject of "Hymn to Intellectual Beauty." This poem of seven twelve-line stanzas consists of three parts: Stanza I asserts that men are visited by "the awful shadow of some unseen Power" that comes and goes, bringing moments of inspiration and then vanishing. We should note that Shelley does not claim that man is visited by the "Power," but rather by its "shadow," which is itself "unseen" (2). Nevertheless the poet reverences the unknown god and addresses it in the subsequent stanzas in its function, not as "Mother of this unfathomable world," but as "Spirit of BEAUTY." Stanzas II–IV identify the Spirit as unknowable but necessary to *human* life (as distinguished from merely natural, animal existence); if the Spirit would remain with man, he would be "immortal and omnipotent" like an anthropomorphic god. The poet petitions the Spirit not to depart, "lest the grave should be, / Like life and fear, a dark reality" (47–48).

In the final three stanzas the poet recounts the stages of his life: he tells of his boyhood quest for knowledge and his dedication to the service of the Spirit of Beauty (Stanza V); in Stanza VI he declares that he has fulfilled this vow in his young manhood; and in Stanza VII he asks that the Spirit bless his maturer years with its continued inspiration. The three parts thus describe the nature of the Spirit of Intellectual Beauty, the Spirit's relation to mankind in general, and the Spirit's relation to one representative man (the poet) through three stages of his life—ones not unlike those described in Wordsworth's "Tintern Abbey" (1798) and "Ode: Intimations of Immortality" (1807).

The poems of 1815–16 embody the high-water mark of Wordsworth's influence on Shelley, but the influence is discernible in two opposing directions. On the one hand, man is seen as an integral part of nature, sharing with animate, vegetative, and perhaps even nonliving creation a vital creative principle that requires of man a reverence for life and humility before that undergirding creative Spirit. On the other hand, only men are self-conscious and able, therefore, to respond to this vital principle and become co-workers with it in its task of creating a significant universe out of chaos. Thus human destiny is at once exalted and humble: every man is both a child of the "Mother of this unfathomable world" and a brother of the inert elements. Because the creative imagination is involuntary, a gift lent momentarily by an unknown Power, man has no cause to boast of it; but that creative force is man's one hope of shaping and directing the blind power of the immanent will which, remorseless as a potter's wheel, crushes and shapes the universe of things. Shelley believed that without human participation, the potter's wheel lacked a potter; only an upsurging of the creative force in self-aware human imagination and human love could provide the necessary moral direction to the cycle of blind necessity.

Chapter Three

A Hermit at Marlow

At the end of August, 1816, Shelley's party left Geneva to return to England. They lived first at Bath, where Claire's pregnancy with Byron's child could be kept from their London acquaintances, with Shelley visiting London to complete financial arrangements with his father. On the night of October 9, Fanny Imlay (daughter of Mary Wollstonecraft by Gilbert Imlay before she had married Godwin) committed suicide by taking an overdose of laudanum in a hotel room in Swansea, Wales. Fanny's letters to Shelley and Mary during their sojourn in Switzerland and afterward show that she was driven to despair by her feeling of complete financial dependence on Godwin, whom she knew to be deeply in debt.[1] The sorrow of this tragedy was somewhat lifted for Shelley when, on a visit to London early in December, he first met Leigh Hunt and Horace Smith, two men who were to become his close, dependable friends. On his return to Bath, however, he received a letter from Hookham informing him of Harriet Shelley's suicide.

Harriet had left the Westbrook household early in September and rented the second floor of a house in London; she disappeared from these lodgings the evening of November 9, leaving behind a suicide letter. On December 10 her body was found in the Serpentine, in which she had drowned herself. A newspaper account in *The Times* of December 11 described her as "a respectable female far advanced in pregnancy," but White adds that there is no medical testimony to substantiate the statement, which may have been based on the suspicions of her landlady and on the condition of the water-saturated body.[2] From her suicide letter it seems clear that Harriet's melancholia arose in large part from her reflections on Shelley's betrayal of her. Long before their separation, however, she had talked to many of her friends about suicide as an attractive alternative to unhappiness.

In her suicide letter Harriet had asked that "Bysshe" honor her final wish by allowing Ianthe to remain with Eliza Westbrook; she assumed that Shelley would take Charles, his legal heir, only warning him: "As you form his infant mind so will you reap the fruits hereafter."[3] Neither

31

Shelley nor the Westbrooks chose to honor Harriet's last request, for Shelley was determined to have custody of both his children, and the Westbrooks responded by challenging in a suit in the Court of Chancery his fitness to rear either one. Before these affairs were far advanced, however, Shelley strengthened his claim to his children by legalizing his connection with Mary Godwin. On December 30, 1816, Shelley and Mary were married in a quiet church wedding with Mr. and Mrs. Godwin acting as witnesses. Apparently the ceremony was all that was needed to reconcile Godwin—once a vigorous advocate of free love— with Shelley and Mary; a letter to his brother shows him smugly self-congratulatory: "You will wonder, I daresay, how a girl without a penny of fortune should meet with so good a match."[4]

In the custody case Harriet's father and sister asked the Court of Chancery to appoint them or some other "proper persons" to be guardians of Ianthe and Charles on the grounds that Shelley, by virtue of his opinions on religion, government, and marriage, was unfit to take custody. They presented in evidence copies of *Queen Mab*, the *Letter to Lord Ellenborough*, and ten letters written after the separation—nine to Harriet and one to Eliza Westbrook—that show Shelley at his self-righteous worst. Lord Eldon, the Lord Chancellor, was known to be an unwavering Tory supporter of the *status quo*. After a lengthy deliberation he ruled on March 27, 1817, that Shelley could not be deprived of his children *simply* because he held unconventional and unpopular views, nor *simply* because he had deserted his wife to live with another woman. But, because he both advocated *and* practiced what the court regarded as immoral conduct, he was denied custody of his children; the Westbrooks' qualifications as guardians were also cast in doubt by the trial; and they, too, were denied custody. Finally, Dr. and Mrs. Thomas Hume, friends of Shelley's solicitor P. W. Longdill, were appointed to educate and care for Ianthe and Charles. Shelley never exercised his right to visit his children because by the time the Lord Chancellor officially approved the arrangements on July 25, 1818, Shelley, Mary, and their two children William and Clara Everina (born September 2, 1817), together with Claire and her daughter Alba (later named Allegra), had left England; only Mary and Claire were ever to see England again.

The period that intervened between the beginning of the Chancery action in January, 1817, and Shelley's departure from England on March 12, 1818, was fruitful so far as Shelley's intellectual and esthetic development was concerned. While in London pursuing the Chancery case, Shelley deepened his friendships with Leigh Hunt and Horace Smith (as well as meeting Lamb, Keats, Hazlitt, and others of their circle). He also renewed a more nearly normal relationship with Godwin. After moving to Great Marlow, Buckinghamshire, in February, 1817, Shelley continued to see many of these London friends on visits.

I Two Political Pamphlets

Neither frequent houseguests nor days of reading and walking with their neighbor Peacock prevented the Shelleys from continuing their writing. Mary was finishing *Frankenstein* (destined to be a critical and commercial success upon its publication in 1818 by Lackington). Early in 1817 Shelley published (under the pseudonym "The Hermit of Marlow") a pamphlet entitled *A Proposal for Putting Reform to the Vote Throughout the Kingdom* and on November 11–12, 1817, he wrote under the same pseudonym *An Address to the People on the Death of the Princess Charlotte*. The first work proposes that the leading advocates of reform meet and remain in session until a group of canvassers shall have circulated petitions to all adult men and women in Great Britain and Ireland asking them to sign a statement calling for the reform of Parliament. If a majority sign it, Shelley wrote, then the leaders of reform should *require*, not petition, that the House of Commons be reformed and the electorate broadened. If, on the other hand, the people do not wish to support reform, it behooves the reformers to cease their agitation until conditions change. At the end of the pamphlet Shelley states his own, relatively moderate view of electoral reform:

It appears to me that Annual Parliaments ought to be adopted as an immediate measure. . . . The securest method of arriving at such beneficial innovations, is to proceed gradually and with caution; or in the place of that order and reform which the Friends of Reform assert to be violated now, anarchy and despotism will follow. . . .

With respect to Universal Suffrage, I confess I consider its adoption, in the present unprepared state of public knowledge and feeling, a measure fraught with peril. I think that none but those who register their names as paying a certain small sum in *direct taxes* ought, at present, to send Members to Parliament. . . . nothing can less consist with reason, or afford smaller hopes of any beneficial issue, than the plan which should abolish the regal and the aristocratical branches of our constitution, before the public mind, through many gradations of improvement, shall have arrived at the maturity which can disregard these symbols of its childhood. (Julian, VI, 67–68)

An Address to the People on the Death of the Princess Charlotte was written for another audience and in another mood.[5] The title page contains a variant of the famous statement from Thomas Paine's *The Rights of Man*: "We Pity the Plumage, but Forget the Dying Bird," and the *Address* is a rhetorical reproach to the people of England for publicly mourning the death of Princess Charlotte while ignoring the execution of three Yorkshire workmen for the revolutionary activities to which they were incited by government spies posing as fellow workmen. The death of the only daughter of the Prince Regent, "the last and the best of her race," is indeed sad, Shelley writes, but how much more horrible were the deaths of Brandreth, Ludlam, and Turner, "shut up in a horrible dungeon, for many months, with the fear of a hideous death and of everlasting hell thrust before their eyes; and at last . . . brought to the scaffold and hung." In his peroration Shelley calls upon the people of England to mourn in solemn black:

A beautiful Princess is dead. . . . LIBERTY is dead. Slave! I charge thee disturb not the depth and solemnity of our grief by any meaner sorrow. If One has died who was like her that should have ruled over this land, like Liberty, young, innocent, and lovely, know that the power through which that one perished was God, and that it was a private grief. But *man* has murdered Liberty. . . . Let us follow the corpse of British Liberty slowly and reverentially to its tomb: and if some glorious Phantom should appear, . . . let us say that the Spirit of Liberty has arisen from its grave . . . , and kneel down and worship it as our Queen. (Julian, VI, 75–76, 82)

This *Address* was obviously written to arouse the British public to support reform, rather than to argue in logical order what practical steps ought to be taken to implement reform. Shelley's readers have too often neglected to distinguish between those poems and essays designed simply to move the inert public to *desire* something better than the *status quo* and those of his prose tracts that set forth practical programs—the ways and means of achieving a better society.

II *The Revolt of Islam*

Between writing the two "Hermit of Marlow" tracts, Shelley composed his longest poem, designed to test (he says in his Preface) "how far a thirst for a happier condition of moral and political society survives . . . the tempests which have shaken the age in which we live."

Shelley received his first answer to this question from his printer Buchanan McMillan and his publishers Charles and James Ollier, who objected to certain attacks on religion and to the incest between the poem's two chief characters. After negotiations, Shelley made minimal revisions (which were inserted by means of twenty-six cancel leaves); the poem was finally published, not under its original title *Laon and Cythna; or, The Revolution of the Golden City: A Vision of the Nineteenth Century,* but as *The Revolt of Islam; a Poem, in Twelve Cantos.*

The poem is an idealized account of what, Shelley believed, the French Revolution should have been—a bloodless overthrow of the king by the combined resistance of a whole people dedicated to ending tyranny by direct action but without vengeance for past wrong. The perfidious king calls other tyrants to his aid and bloodily crushes his people. The noble example of love and forbearance exhibited by Laon and Cythna and other patriot-revolutionaries is more glorious, even in defeat, than is the cynical and brutal victory of the kings and their priestly allies. The poem calls liberals from despair at the aftermath of the Congress of Vienna, assuring them that the struggle between good and evil has been waged since the birth of self-consciousness and that good, though sorely wounded, can never be destroyed and will be victorious in succeeding struggles.

In the Preface Shelley outlines his views on several important political, historical, philosophical, and literary questions. Noteworthy are the following points: "The panic . . . during the excesses consequent upon the French Revolution, is gradually giving place to sanity," because at a distance one realizes that it was impossible for men who had been abject slaves for generations to be suddenly endowed with the capacity for temperate self-rule. Unfortunately, at the time of the Revolution "the sanguine eagerness for good overleaped the solution of these questions," and "many . . . worshippers of public good have been morally ruined" because their expectations were unrealistically high.

That Wordsworth and Coleridge were among those so "ruined" becomes clear from Shelley's allusions to them in the next paragraph: "I do not presume to enter into competition with our greatest contemporary Poets. . . . Nor have I permitted any system relating to mere words[6] to divert the attention of the reader, from whatever interest I may have succeeded in creating, to my own ingenuity. . . ." Two paragraphs later Shelley returns to the theme of his relations with his contemporaries: "there must be a resemblance, which does not depend upon their own will, between all the writers of any particular age. They cannot escape from subjection to a common influence which arises out of an infinite combination of circumstances belonging to the times in which they live. . . ." The next paragraph begins: "I have adopted the stanza of Spenser. . . ." Clearly Shelley alludes to *Childe Harold's Pilgrimage,* the most notable poem of its day using the Spenserian stanza, the third canto of which he had seen Byron composing in Switzerland and had carried back in manuscript to John Murray.[7]

Some of the extremes of vice and virtue portrayed in *The Revolt of Islam* can be understood in light of the following passage by Sir William Drummond, whom Shelley praises in a footnote:

If you wish to make men virtuous, endeavour to inspire into them the love of virtue. Show them the beauty of order, and the fitness of things. . . . Represent vice, as indignant virtue will always represent it, as hideous, loathsome, and deformed. . . . will cannot be changed, while sentiment remains unaltered. There is no power, by which men can create, or destroy their feelings. Sensation alone overcomes sensation. (*Academical Questions* [1805], pp. 20–21)

The ideas reflected here are those of the British empirical school, which saw the human mind as basically passive. From the viewpoint of the modern reader, trained by another school, Shelley's poetry—especially when he portrays vice with righteous indignation—suffers from his adherence to this view of human psychology.

Shelley's poetic Dedication, "To Mary—— ——," is one of his most self-revealing poems. Here he recounts (as in "Hymn to Intellectual Beauty") his experience of dedication to the service of others and how he armed himself to war against vice and error by gathering "knowledge from forbidden mines of lore" (Stanza v). In the sixth stanza he tells how he found that love was "a blight and snare / To those who seek all sympathies in one!—" until the arrival of Mary, "whose presence on my wintry heart / Fell, like bright Spring." Unsure whether he is but striking "the prelude of a loftier strain" in *The Revolt of Islam,* or whether he will die before he achieves more, Shelley declares that, even if the truths he presents and the love he feels for his fellow men meet with no response, he and Mary can "look from our tranquillity / Like lamps into the world's tempestuous night,— / Two tranquil stars, while clouds are passing by. . . ."

Canto I of *The Revolt* contains a moral allegory outlining the major themes of the poem. The persona of the Poet, despairing at the failure of the French Revolution, sees an emblem of the cosmic struggle between Good and Evil in an aerial battle between an eagle and a serpent. Shelley consistently used the eagle as a symbol of the good—the aspiring soul of a man of imagination—and the serpent as a symbol of evil. Here a woman whom the Poet meets on the shore explains that when Evil ("a blood-red Comet") first won ascendancy in the human heart, it drove out the Spirit of Good, changing it "from starry shape" (of the Morning Star) "to a dire Snake, with man and beast unreconciled" (I.xxvi–xxvii). This image echoes Dante's use, where Guido del Duca says of the Arno Valley, "virtue is driven forth as an enemy by all, even as a snake" (*Purgatorio* xiv.37–38).

The woman tells her story: her "heart was pierced with sympathy" for the troubles of others, "woe / Which could not be mine own" (I.xxxv); and a "dying poet . . . , a youth with hoary hair—a fleeting guest / Of our lone mountains,"[8] gave her books and inspired her ideals. When she continues that she "loved; but not a human lover!" and describes her dream-vision encounter with a "wingèd youth" who wore "the Morning Star," we see another example of how the ideal, a projection of the human imagination (to be described in *Epipsychidion* as the "soul out of my soul"), takes the form of the opposite sex. After dreaming of her ideal lover, the woman first went to the shore "to muse and weep; / But as I moved, over my heart did creep / A joy less soft, but more profound and strong / Than my sweet dream" (I.xliii). This joy caused her to leave her isolated musing and return to the city to serve her fellow human beings.

Having recounted her past history, the woman takes the Poet and the wounded serpent across the sea to a land crowned with "mountains of ice, like sapphire" and to a domed temple beyond the descriptive power of "painting's light, or mightier verse, / Or sculpture's marble language" where "there sate on many a sapphire throne, / The Great, who had departed from mankind, / A mighty Senate" (I.liv). Here she assumes her rightful place on an empty throne, and the serpent returns to its true nature as the Morning Star. Then one of the great departed spirits of men (Laon) begins to tell his story, which extends through cantos II–XII.

Laon tells in the second canto of his childhood and youth. Unlike the protagonist in *Alastor,* Laon does appreciate human friendship; but his closest friend disappoints him (as Hogg did Shelley). He then communes with the great spirits of past ages—"deathless minds which leave where they have passed / A path of light . . ." (xx)—and with Cythna, a young orphan (his sister in the original version), who becomes his disciple and joins him in plans to struggle for freedom. Because she shares his feelings, Laon is spared the disappointments of the isolated Youth in *Alastor,* for she "endued / My purpose with a wider sympathy" (xxxvi).

In Canto III, when marauding soldiers looking for slave girls seize Cythna, Laon stabs three of them before he is overcome and chained atop a column. There, in a fit of madness he imagines that, driven by extreme hunger and thirst, he has eaten the flesh of Cythna's corpse. Just as he is about to die, he is rescued by an old Hermit, who carries him off in a small boat to an island covered with pines and myrtles (symbolic of hope and love, respectively).

In Canto IV the Hermit takes Laon, who is unable to distinguish between dream and reality, to his tower, "a changeling of man's art, nursed amid Nature's brood" (IV.i), where he cures Laon's madness. The Hermit had first gained inspiration "in converse with the dead, who leave the stamp / Of ever-burning thoughts on many a page"; but, valuing human society, his "deep thirst for knowledge" led not to desert wastes, but "through peopled haunts, the City and the Camp" (viii). Disillusionment because of the power that fate held over men had eventually caused him to withdraw to the solitary island, but news of Laon's active resistance to tyranny had roused the old man to go immediately to his aid.

Seven years pass before Laon returns to full sanity; during this time the Hermit has been educating the people by writing revolutionary tracts that have improved the climate of opinion, and now, because of the persuasive preaching of an unknown young woman, the people of the empire are assembling on a great plain outside the Golden City; though not threatening violence, they boldly demand their rights. At the Hermit's urging, Laon sets out for the capital, hoping that the unknown maiden will prove to be Cythna.

Canto V recounts the story of the patriots. Arriving at the camp, Laon encounters the young man who had once been his close friend, and they are reconciled. The same night the soldiers of the king, brutalized by their profession almost beyond humanity, attack and slaughter many sleeping citizens; but the soldiers flee after Laon rallies the mass of assembled patriots. When the citizens surround the soldiers, Laon persuades the angry crowd not to avenge blood with more slaughter and thereby sink to the level of their oppressors. Instead, he urges the soldiers to throw down their arms and, forgetting past guilt, to act benevolently toward their fellow men in the future. Soldiers and citizens then march together to the Golden City, whose people joyfully open their gates to the new brotherhood. Othman, the king, abandoned by all his courtier-slaves, remains unattended except by an innocent little girl who genuinely loves him. The people are about to lynch the fallen monarch when Laon once more intervenes, asking which of them is so pure that he has never wished to harm another: "the chastened will / Of virtue sees that justice is the light / Of love, and not revenge" (V.xxxiv).

The people assign the bitter king a home where he is to live a retired life in peace, and they then celebrate their new-won, guiltless freedom. In their midst they raise, spontaneously, a huge marble pyramid called "the Altar of the Federation" upon which are carved three statues: a giant child crushing "sceptres and crowns"; a woman nursing both "a human babe and a young basilisk"; a winged youth, gazing on the sun as he tramples "faith, an obscene worm" (V.xlix–l). Atop the pyramid a mysterious maiden, high priestess of the new religion of light and love, sings a hymn celebrating these symbols of, first, powerful Wisdom; second, the eternal Spirit who is, like the Spirit of Intellectual Beauty, a loving mother of all living creatures; and third, the "eldest of things, divine Equality," represented by the winged youth who responds to both the sun's light (wisdom) and its warmth (love), thus epitomizing the brotherly, non-dogmatic religion (similar to that "faith so mild" taught by Mont Blanc).[9] When the maiden in her hymn calls upon free men never again to pollute their meals with the "blood of bird or beast," the people respond by sharing a vegetarian love-feast of "an overflowing store / Of pomegranates, and citrons, fairest fruit, / Melons, and dates, and figs, and many a root / . . . and brown corn set / In baskets." Instead of wine, they drink from "pure streams" (V.lvi).

In Canto VI, while Laon and his long-estranged friend are "weaving swift language from impassioned themes," the armies of allied kings attack the patriots, slaughtering them without check until the citizens recover their courage and put to use "a bundle of rude pikes, the instrument / Of those who war but on their native ground / For natural rights" (VI.xiii). Even then the patriots are massacred almost to a man. Both Laon's youthful friend and the old Hermit, who had recently arrived, are cut down before his eyes.

At the last minute "a black Tartarian horse of giant frame" bearing one "like to an Angel, robed in white" (VI.xix), rescues Laon; the giant horse carries the pair beyond all pursuit to a rocky seacoast. There, in a ruin, Laon discovers that the maiden who has rescued him is Cythna, and that she was, indeed, the mysterious priestess who, under the name of Laone, had roused the people to their peaceful revolution. Having lost their hope for an early victory for their ideals of love and reason within the social context, Laon and Cythna embrace and physically consummate their love, the union signalized by a meteor overhead (VI.xxxii–xxxiv).

In the original, Laon and Cythna had been presented as brother and sister; what function had this use of incest? In the final paragraph of his original Preface, Shelley had written: "I have . . . endeavoured to strengthen the moral sense, by forbidding it to waste its energies in seeking to avoid actions which are only crimes of convention. It is because there is so great a multitude of artificial vices, that there are so few real virtues. Those feelings alone which are benevolent or malevolent, are essentially good or bad."[10] In the poem itself, just before sexual union, Laon declares, in the words of St. Paul, "To the pure all things are pure!" (VI.xxx).[11]

In the next three cantos (VII–IX) Cythna tells Laon her adventures during the seven years of their separation. When the king violated her in the seraglio, she went mad, as Laon had done during his sufferings (Canto III). Because her madness precipitated resistance to the monarch's tyranny, Cythna was spirited off by two slaves and imprisoned in a cave with a small opening in the domed ceiling through which daily there flew a sea-eagle that had been trained to bring food to inmates of the strange prison. (Pliny's *Natural History* records a similar story of a sea-eagle feeding a girl.[12])

Symbolically, Cythna's cave complements the tower in which Laon recovered from his sufferings. As Laon under the tutelage of the Hermit turned outward, studying the creations of the great spirits of the past, so Cythna turned inward, examining her own mind to learn the secrets of the universe. But, even in her enforced isolation, Cythna's image of the ideal took on a social form inspired by love rather than a selfish quest for personal fulfillment. As Laon had, during his first insanity, imagined himself eating Cythna's flesh, so Cythna tells Laon that in her madness, "the sea-eagle looked a fiend, who bore / Thy mangled limbs for food" (VII.xv). Immediately after this hallucination Cythna imagined that she had conceived a child who was born and grew up to girlhood, fostered by her love.

The child, she now realizes in retrospect, though physically the result of the king's rape of her in the seraglio, was spiritually the offspring of her own mind—a *beau idéal* comparable to the dream-vision in *Alastor,* conceived by the interaction of two loving minds. The significance of Laon's and Cythna's hallucinations about cannibalism seems to be that their earlier love for each other fed and sustained them through their most soul-wrenching tortures. But when Cythna's child was carried off by the slave who had first brought Cythna into the cave, she—like all Shelley's idealists—was thrown back on her own resources with the problem of how to live in a phenomenal world from which the visionary ideal had disappeared. She examined her own mind, seeking to discover from her representative human nature the limits of man's powers and imitations of his destiny:

> "My mind became the book through which I grew
> Wise in all human wisdom, and its cave,
> Which like a mine I rifled through and through,
> To me the keeping of its secrets gave—
> One mind, the type of all. . . ."
>
> (VII.xxxi)

At last, when she has created "a subtler language within language / . . . / The key of truths" (VII.xxxii), an earthquake frees her from her prison; and she is rescued by a passing ship.[13]

Cythna's adventures in Canto VII parallel those of Laon in cantos III and IV. In Canto VII and Canto IX.i–xviii Cythna tells how she freed men from their former prejudices by her persuasive rhetoric and by her clear presentation of the facts of human existence: All men are created free and equal; no person knows—or can know—the answers to the ultimate questions of man's origin and destiny; love can make human life not only bearable but beautiful; men should not remain enslaved by feelings of guilt for their past sins: "Reproach not thine own soul, but know thyself, / Nor hate another's crime, nor loathe thine own" (VIII.xxii).

First, she converts the officers and crew of the ship that rescues her so that they release the captive maidens whom they were carrying to the slave market. When the ship, decked with green boughs to signal its regeneration, arrives at the Golden City, Cythna and her followers vanquish the priests in open debate. Following Canto IX.xix, Cythna assures Laon that, in spite of the present reversals, their efforts have not been in vain; for "the blasts of Autumn drive the wingèd seeds" that in the spring will bring forth "flowers on the mountains, fruits over the plain" (IX.xxi). Stanzas xxi–xxv outline the conception to which Shelley later gave more powerful expression in "Ode to the West Wind" and Stanza xxxv contains the germ of "The Cloud." Laon and Cythna are the "chosen slaves" of Virtue, Hope, and Love, sacrificing themselves that human beings may in the future lead more fruitful lives. The example of "the good and mighty of departed ages" who leave their conceptions of "hope, or love, or truth, or liberty . . . To be a rule and law to ages that survive" (IX.xxviii) gives courage to assure Cythna that virtue is alive with power of self-renewal, whereas evil is not vital but inert, a mere absence of good.

In Canto X Laon once again takes up the story. When the plague terrifies the tyrants' armies, the superstitious people are led by an "Iberian Priest" (of whom it is said, "fear of God did in his bosom breed / A jealous hate of man" [X.xxxiv]); he urges them to propitiate their angry god by capturing and burning Laon and Laone. "The maniac multitude" construct a second pyramid, a pyre of torture-sacrifice, sharply contrasting with that in Canto V. At the patriot's victory, all men had shared a feast unstained by any blood, whereas in the latter, famine and universal misery have driven men to become bloody beasts themselves. In Canto XI Laon leaves Cythna and gives himself up to his enemies after extracting a promise, bound by an oath, that they will permit Cythna to go unharmed to America—the last, best hope of freedom. In Canto XII, as Laon is tied to the stake and Cythna's child, sole friend of the king, now pleads for the young man's life, Cythna rides up on a giant Tartary horse, kisses the steed, and sends him away.[14] The king, on the insistence of the priest, breaks his oath and, instead of freeing Cythna, burns her with Laon.

The last twenty-five stanzas of the poem describe the voyage of the spirits of Laon and Cythna, guided by the child that was born to Cythna in the cave, "a wingèd Thought" (such as those that will mourn Keats in *Adonais*). They travel from an earthly paradise (XII.xix) much like the gardens of Milton's Paradise and Coleridge's "Kubla Khan" to the Temple of the Spirit, the realm of thought where the benefactors of humanity sit as the unacknowledged legislators of the world.

The Revolt of Islam is not a good poem, but it is an important one in Shelley's development. Like Keats's *Endymion,* which may have been written in friendly rivalry with it,[15] *The Revolt* contains within its overextended bulk the materials that Shelley was to rework during his Italian sojourn into truly great poetry. I have suggested how certain passages look forward to "Ode to the West Wind," *Adonais,* and other poems. A major conception of *Prometheus Unbound*—the complementary nature of Prometheus and Asia and the importance of their reunion—is prefigured in the separation and reunion of Laon and Cythna. Cythna, the feminine member, embodies the power of knowledge and reason, whereas Laon embodies forgiving love. Cythna convinces men through her irrefutable arguments of the need to overthrow the old order and their ability to do so; Laon dissuades them from using their new-found power to corrupt themselves by exacting vengeance or even cold, unforgiving "justice." Cythna's knowledge of the human mind has shown her man's power; Laon's familiarity with the humanistic tradition and his association with the benevolent Hermit teach him to temper justice with mercy.

The Revolt of Islam fails as a poem because Shelley tries unsuccessfully to fuse didactic-expository passages, a romance narrative, and mythic or symbolic passages (that sometimes descend to unsophisticated allegory). *Alastor,* "Mont Blanc," and "Hymn to Intellectual Beauty" are better poems because they attempt to do less at one time. Shelley never again tried to synthesize such large quantities of disparate material into a single poetic conception. Critical selectivity enabled him later to write *Prometheus Unbound* and *The Cenci* almost simultaneously and to keep each true to its essential nature.

III. "Essay on Christianity"

Sometime before Shelley left England, and very likely during the summer of 1817, he wrote a fragmentary "Essay on Christianity"[16] that puts into perspective his mature attitude toward Jesus and toward institutional Christianity. Like other reformers before and since, Shelley asserts that the teachings of Jesus had been distorted and perverted by followers who lacked His "comprehensive morality." Shelley views, amid the accretions and mistakes of those who recorded Jesus' life and words, the doctrines that "God is some universal being, differing both from man and from the mind of man" (page 229), that this "Universal Being can only be described or defined by negatives" because "where indefiniteness ends idolatry and anthropomorphism begin" (page 232). Jesus, he declares, never taught a system of rewards and punishments: "Jesus represents God as the fountain of all goodness, the eternal enemy of pain and evil" (page 235). Shelley weaves these apparently diverse points together artfully even in the often-interrupted progression of the fragments we possess.

The "otherness" of God, his dissimilarity to human nature, explains why He makes the sun to shine upon the just and the unjust; but men "have not failed to attribute to the universal cause a character analogous with their own" (page 238), vengefully eager to reward friends and punish enemies. After speculating on the extent to which Jesus has been misunderstood because He, like all reformers, "accommodated his doctrines to the prepossessions of those whom he addressed" (page 242), Shelley lays down in one terse sentence a complete moral (and political) doctrine that, he believed, he held in common with Jesus of Nazareth: "The only perfect and genuine republic is that which comprehends every living being" (page 245). This concept is very close to Albert Schweitzer's "reverence for life," and many of Shelley's other statements—apparently thought so radical that Mary Shelley never published this essay—sound equally commonplace in the context of twentieth-century liberal and neo-orthodox theology.

Chapter Four
Green Isles

Shelley had, at the time of his second trip to Switzerland in the summer of 1816, contemplated a long sojourn in Italy, the art and literature of which he admired and the climate of which had been recommended to him for his health. His resolve to live abroad was strengthened, first, by the necessity of putting Claire's daughter Allegra under the care of the child's father, Byron; by the fear that, with the negative results of the Chancery case as a precedent, he and Mary were in some danger of losing custody of their children William and Clara; and, finally, by the debilitating financial negotiations arising from Godwin's importunities. On February 7, 1818, Shelley left Marlow for good.

After a month in London, seeing friends and winding up affairs, Shelley's party left for the Continent on March 11. They traveled overland from Calais via Lyons, Chambéry, and Turin to Milan. After a brief visit to Lake Como, Shelley wrote to Byron from Milan, inviting him to come to take his child. But Byron wanted nothing to do with Claire, and Shelley had misgivings about sending Allegra into Byron's licentious Venetian establishment. In the strained exchange of letters that followed, Shelley tactfully mediated between Claire and Byron, eventually arranging for Allegra to go to Venice in the care of Elise, the Swiss nurse.

Shelley, Mary, and Claire then proceeded to Pisa, waiting there until they heard of the safe arrival in Venice of Elise and Allegra. They next moved to Leghorn (Livorno), where they presented a letter of introduction from Godwin to Maria Gisborne, the former Mrs. Reveley to whom Godwin had once proposed marriage. Enjoying the congenial society of Mrs. Gisborne, her husband John, and her son Henry Reveley (an engineer trying to develop a steamboat), the Shelleys remained in Leghorn for a month. On July 11, 1818, they went into the Apennines to Bagni di Lucca, where they lived in the Casa Bertini for nine weeks.

I First Writings in Italy

Unable to begin new poetry, Shelley read, walked, and went horseback riding with Mary, and he completed *Rosalind and Helen,* which he had begun at Marlow.[1] He also translated Plato's *Symposium,* wrote a prose fragment published posthumously under the title "On Love," and drafted a longer fragmentary "Discourse on the Manners of the Ancients . . ." designed to explain "the cause of some differences in sentiment between the antients & moderns" on the subject of love. In "On Love" (which may have been a false start on the essay explaining the handling of love in the *Symposium*[2]), Shelley says that love is "that powerful attraction towards all that we conceive, or fear, or hope beyond ourselves" when we find a void within ourselves and require a community of sympathy to echo our own thoughts, imaginings, and feelings. Here Shelley articulates clearly in prose the conception underlying *Alastor*—that when one refuses to accept the sympathy of other living creatures, one falls in love with his own ideal of perfection, which is his own inner nature idealized and purified.

In the longer essay, Shelley, after praising Periclean Athens as both the fountainhead and high point of Western civilization, speculates that the homosexuality of the society resulted from the Greek degradation of women, which made them unattractive intellectually to men and, therefore, unsatisfactory objects of love, since love requires an object either actually or supposedly superior to the lover. In the elevation of women and abolition of slavery alone has modern Europe surpassed ancient Athens. Shelley, unlike Byron, never idealized the submissive, unintellectual child of nature, but rather the woman who could take her place as man's equal in intellectual attainments.

Rosalind and Helen: A Modern Eclogue was inspired by the broken friendship of Mary Shelley and Isabel Baxter Booth. Shelley began the poem at Marlow, probably in September, 1817, before the final breach between himself and both William Thomas Baxter, Isabel's father, and David Booth, her husband. But the poem was altered and lengthened in Italy before Ollier published it in 1819. The story concerns two English women, once friends but long estranged, who meet unexpectedly on the shore of Lake Como; having agreed to forget past differences, each tells her unhappy story. Rosalind was prevented from marrying the man she loved because at the last minute her father revealed that the youth was her half-brother; she then made a conventional loveless marriage with a hard-hearted miser. Three children cheered her life, but on the death of her husband neither she nor the children could feel any grief. The dead husband, however, had his revenge; for in his will he charged her (falsely) with adultery and heresy and demanded that she leave her children, or else all the property would go to another heir. Knowing the burdens of poverty, Rosalind went away so that her children could inherit their rightful patrimony.

Helen enjoyed the love of a good man, Lionel; but, because they were unable to marry, they lived in an unsanctioned union. Lionel himself was persecuted for his religious and political beliefs; when released from prison, his health broken, he wasted away and died. Helen then temporarily lost her reason and was nursed by Lionel's mother. Shortly after this good woman died, Helen recovered her sanity and cared for her child Henry. Having heard one another's stories, Rosalind and Helen reunite their fortunes and live together in Helen's cottage. Eventually Rosalind's daughter is allowed to join her, and this child and Henry grow up to love one another and to marry happily. Rosalind dies young but is buried on a mountain-top and mourned by Helen and others; Helen dies years later "among her kindred." Both women have been blessed by their mutual love.

Interwoven in the tale of the two women are lengthy symbolic descriptions involving myrtle, owls, nightingales, a domed temple "To Fidelity," and the like; but the poem moves more or less in the realm of realistic narrative—much more so than *The Revolt of Islam,* with which it has strong thematic affinities. In calling it "a modern eclogue," Shelley was no doubt thinking of its domestic, personal quality as opposed to the romantic-epic sweep of his earlier long poems; *Rosalind and Helen* is, in fact, the prototype of a *genre* that Tennyson was to develop in poems like *Enoch Arden.* It shares the limitations of its mode. In addition, it involves more undigested—or unidealized—biographical elements than usually characterize Shelley's poems, and the tone is overly shrill.

In short, the domestic idyl proved too fragile a vehicle to elevate personal disappointments into cosmic or even social issues. Wordsworth was able to achieve proper esthetic detachment by distancing his experiences through time, "emotion recollected in tranquillity"; Coleridge, Shelley, and Keats all achieved their most successful transmutations of fact into poetry by embodying their ideas and experiences in symbolic or mythic patterns. As the works of Dante and Milton readily demonstrate, an artist sounds—and is—less egotistical and self-centered when he expresses his personal ideas and feelings through the greater literary forms than when he writes a letter on the same theme. For the very discipline of shaping the larger conception distances the individual's expression and molds it in a traditional way, thus giving it more universal significance.

II A Tragic Journey

The Shelleys originally intended to go south from Bagni di Lucca to winter at Naples, but Claire, made uneasy by Elise's letters, persuaded Shelley to accompany her to Venice so that she could see her child. On August 17, Shelley, Claire, and a servant named Paolo Foggi left Bagni di Lucca, arriving in Venice at midnight, August 22. The next day Shelley and Claire were cordially received by the British consul Richard Belgrave Hoppner and his Swiss wife, who were keeping Allegra (with Byron's full agreement) so that the fifteen-month-old child would not have to live amid the confusion of Byron's *palazzo* which was filled with "caged wild animals and uncaged mistresses."[3] When Shelley visited Byron that afternoon, they enjoyed the ride on the Lido and conversation that inspired the opening of "Julian and Maddalo."

To avoid telling Byron that Claire had come expressly to see Allegra, Shelley said that Mary, Claire, and the children were then at Padua; when Byron offered to lend Shelley a villa at Este, Shelley wrote (August 24) urging Mary to hurry there in order to maintain his fiction. She did so, but on the tiring journey (August 31–September 5) Clara Shelley, already upset from teething, contracted dysentery; and, after a long illness and ineffectual treatment by a physician in Padua, was rushed to Venice, where she died September 24, 1818. Clara's death seems to have shocked Mary very deeply, and Shelley's apparent willingness to jeopardize the comfort and even safety of his own family to assist Claire (and others) probably became a cause of friction between Mary and him.

III Two Venetian Poems

In spite of these domestic troubles, the conversation of Byron and his circle in Venice apparently stimulated Shelley to begin three important works at Este: *Prometheus Unbound* (which is discussed in the next chapter), "Lines written among the Euganean Hills," and "Julian and Maddalo." The latter two poems, though shorter than *Rosalind and Helen,* are—like "Hymn to Intellectual Beauty" and "Mont

Blanc"—intrinsically far more important and successful works, the first flowering of Shelley's genius in Italy. Both exhibit a disciplined arrangement of their parts that again reminds us of Shelley's architectonic skill.

"Lines written among the Euganean Hills"[4] consists of thirteen verse-paragraphs of varying lengths, but it divides itself into three major parts, with the middle one of these again divisible into three: three verse-paragraphs (89 lines); three paragraphs (77 lines); one paragraph (39 lines); three paragraphs (79 lines); and three paragraphs (89 lines). This symmetrical structure supports narrative and symbolic patterns that are also symmetrical: the first paragraph (1–44) describes the human predicament but postulates the existence of "many a green isle" amid the "sea of Misery." The second paragraph, the most difficult in the poem, mentions "a solitary heap, / One white skull and seven dry bones," "on the beach of a northern sea." These "seven dry bones" represent the seven years between Shelley's expulsion from Oxford (March, 1811) and his final departure from England (March 1818); Shelley was describing his past life as dead but unburied, in that its consequences were carried on by the tempest-winds of necessity.

"Lines written among the Euganean Hills," though outwardly a moralizing topographical poem in the vein of Pope's *Windsor Forest,* actually turns on the central motif of death and rebirth, the pattern being repeated in each of the three major sections of the poem. In the first part, the cycle of death and rebirth is a personal one: the Poet must free himself from feelings of guilt and regret associated with his past life if he is to experience psychological and moral regeneration. In the third and final paragraph of the movement (66–89), the sun rises, like an infusion of imaginative inspiration; and a flock of rooks, like "night's dreams and terrors,"[5] flee, leaving the Poem on one of those green isles where "all is bright, and clear, and still."

The second major movement (90–284) progresses from personal to social death and rebirth. The first subdivision (90–166) pictures Venice as a city of sin; once "Ocean's nursling," it has, like Minos, so misused the gifts of the sea as to sink into bestiality and become "a peopled labyrinth"; now its sins are rapidly leading it to destruction and "Amphitrite's destined halls" will soon sink beneath the waves of the Adriatic:

> Sun-girt City, thou hast been
> Ocean's child, and then his queen;

> Now is come a darker day,
> And thou soon must be his prey. . . .
>   (115–18)

The subdivision ends with the thought that "if Freedom should awake," even corrupt and dying Venice and a hundred sister cities, now in degrading bondage to Austria, "might adorn this sunny land, / Twining memories of old time / With new virtues more sublime; / If not, perish thou and they!—" (157–60).

The seventh verse-paragraph (167–205), central to the second movement and to the poem, praises Lord Byron as the ideal poet, "a tempest-cleaving Swan" who is able to fly against the winds of necessity and who, when his "sunlike soul" is freed from its overclouding personal guilt, will give life to Venice in his writings (as the art of Homer preserves "Scamander's wasting springs") even though the city itself may be obliterated; he will, like Shakespeare and Petrarch, fill the world with the light of reason and the warmth of love.

The third subdivision of the second movement (206–84) centers on Padua, once a great center of learning but now symbolically dead—a "peopled solitude" (216) as Venice was "a peopled labyrinth." Though the "lamp of learning" is now extinguished in Padua, sparks from it had earlier kindled new flames throughout Europe, and this spread of imaginative knowledge symbolized through the lamp-sun imagery will ultimately bring the downfall of the present tyranny. Of this overthrow, Shelley has no doubt, but he is not happy with the prospect of "destruction's harvest-home"; rather, he wishes that imaginative men like the idealized Byron would be able to prevent men from repeating the cycle of provocation and retribution by teaching them through "love or reason" to avoid taking vengeance for past wrongs:

> Men must reap the things they sow,
> Force from force must ever flow,
> Or worse; but 'tis a bitter woe
> That love or reason cannot change
> The despot's rage, the slave's revenge.
>   (231–35)

The poem's final movement (285–373) begins at noon, that hour symbolic of the closest proximity of the divine and the mundane, the eternal and the temporal. At this point the Poet feels himself in harmony with all natural creation; all "living things" "interpenetrated lie /

By the glory of the sky." True to his skeptical epistemology, Shelley refrains from stating categorically whether his mood was created by an explicable physical or psychological stimulus ("love, light, harmony, / Odour"), by an objective metaphysical reality ("the soul of all / Which from Heaven like dew doth fall"), or by his own active imagination ("the mind which feeds this verse / Peopling the lone universe" [310–19]). After the joyful, silent harmony of this interchange, the spirit of delight soon fades into the light of "Autumn's evening." The sun, uniting both light (reason) and heat (love), gives place to the new moon and the evening star (Venus), which represent in isolation the two elements embodied in the symbolic sun. In the Poet's voyage of life, the "ancient pilot, Pain, / Sits beside the helm again" (333–34).

But, as the Poet metaphorically passes once more from noontide life into the dark night of the soul, the memory of this day among the Euganean Hills reminds him that "other flowering isles must be / In the sea of Life and Agony," and he hopes that someday the spirits will guide him

> To some calm and blooming cove,
> Where for me, and those I love,
> May a windless bower be built,
> Far from passion, pain, and guilt. . . .
> (342–45)

In that island of peace within their own souls, he and his loved ones might form the nucleus of a redeemed society, overcoming the maenadic rage of "the polluting multitude" with their own "mild brotherhood"; instead of being torn to pieces like Orpheus, they might transform the society into another Golden Age: "Every sprite beneath the moon / Would repent its envy vain, / And the earth grow young again" (371–73).

"Lines written among the Euganean Hills" was composed, Shelley says in his prefatory Advertisement to the *Rosalind and Helen* volume, "after a day's excursion among those lovely mountains which surround what was once the retreat, and where is now the sepulchre, of Petrarch." One can actually see the panorama it describes from near the top of Monte Rua', and the poem seems firmly grounded in Shelley's actual experience. This probability makes more poignant the opening passage, lines that Shelley says were left in the poem "at the request of a dear friend, with whom added years of intercourse only add to my apprehension of its value, and who would have had more right than any one to complain, that she has not been able to extinguish in me the very power of delineating sadness." Beautiful as is the opening verse-paragraph, that Mary Shelley did not wish it erased shows that she did not comprehend its implications. For in it Shelley says that, were it not for infrequent moments of inspiration, death would be preferable to life; even if there is no personal immortality, man can never dream "to find refuge from distress / In friendship's smile, in love's caress" (32–33).

In the Dedication and text of *The Revolt of Islam,* love between Shelley and Mary (or Laon and Cythna) had been enough to counteract all the evils of mortal existence. But, from the period at Este onward, love no longer conquers all for Shelley. The date given in the printed text of "Lines written among the Euganean Hills," October, 1818, is significant; for it marks the first aftermath of Clara Shelley's death and the incipient emotional estrangement of Shelley and Mary.

Newman Ivey White saw this estrangement reflected in the long speech of the maniac in "Julian and Maddalo," which was also begun at Este.[6] In one sense, this contention is easily demonstrable. But, as others have shown, the maniac's situation also resembles that of Tasso (whose life Shelley had recently read).[7] Shelley's Preface appeals to the universality of the maniac's experience: "His story, told at length, might be like many other stories of the same kind: the unconnected exclamations of his agony will perhaps be found a sufficient comment for the text of every heart." When we examine the maniac's role within the larger context of the poem, it can be seen that his monologue merely adds a dimension to the more significant foreground story of Julian and Count Maddalo.

The theme of the poem unfolds most clearly if we divide it into its main structural elements and then, somewhat more arbitrarily, subdivide these. The first part (1–140) recounts the pastimes and discussions of Julian and Maddalo during and immediately following their ride on the Lido. In the early lines (1–35), Julian identifies himself with the desolate natural setting (14–17, 21–27) and, even more, with his friend (19–21, 28–32). But, on turning home, the "talk grew somewhat serious," and Julian and Maddalo argued (36–52). Within the account of their debate is an allusion to Book II of Milton's *Paradise Lost* that is to prove important for Shelley's theme:

> —'twas forlorn,
> Yet pleasing, such as once, so poets tell,

The devils held within the dales of Hell
Concerning God, freewill and destiny:
Of all that earth has been or yet may be
All that vain men imagine or believe,
Or hope can paint or suffering may achieve,
We descanted. . . .

                                                    (39–46)

Shelley had earlier pictured Cythna as attacking the folly of human beings who attempted to answer the ultimate questions, and he had shown the destruction of the Youth in *Alastor* who had devoted himself to a search for those answers; part of his point in "Julian and Maddalo" is that the debate concerns unanswerable questions. This emphasis appears clearly, though subtly, in the remainder of the poem's first part. In lines 53–85, Julian describes the beautiful natural setting in the "Paradise of exiles, Italy!" All nature is at peace, and the implication is that man alone disturbs this harmony. For amid the tranquillity of nature, Maddalo uses the beautiful sunset to silhouette and emphasize "in strong and black relief" a madhouse, emblem to the proud Count of "our mortality" (85–140). At the end of Maddalo's outburst, the entire city of Venice has sunk into a deep gloom, both literally and figuratively, for Julian.

The second major part (141–299) concerns the experiences and discussions of the next day. At first (141–57) Julian plays with Maddalo's child, a thing of natural beauty but possessing, in addition, "eyes . . . With such deep meaning, as we never see / But in the human countenance." When the Count appears, however, Julian cannot resist using the little girl to support his side of the argument, to which Maddalo replies in kind by citing the example of a madman who once talked as idealistically as Julian: "his wild talk will show / How vain are such aspiring theories" (200–1). Julian answers that he hopes "to prove" that a lack of a "true theory . . . has thus bowed / His being" (202–6). For, he continues, some men are patient in the face of all reverses except unrequited love; but succumbing even to this disillusionment "is not destiny / But man's own wilful ill."

The maniac's soliloquy does not fully support either Julian or the Count. Although the madman admits that he may owe his sufferings to himself "in part," he suspects that some "Power delights to torture us" (320–22). But he has not lost his idealistic integrity: unlike Byron,[8] he will not "infect the untainted breast / Of sacred nature" (352–

53) by venting hatred and scorn on the world. Nor will he "sanction tyranny" even by remaining silent, nor succumb to the popular service of "gain," "ambition," "revenge," coldness of heart, or (again unlike Byron) "avarice, or misanthropy or lust" (361–68).

He says, in fact, his weakness is that he was too sensitive to accept calmly the scorn of one whom he loved. She has, he laments, told him "with many a bare broad word" her wish that he "like some maniac monk" had emasculated himself so that they could never experience a passionate union which ends in revulsion (420–35). Earlier the maniac had warned his friends: "There is one road / To peace and that is truth, which follow ye! / Love sometimes leads astray to misery" (347–49). Now he declares that he, who has "loved and pitied all things"—"who am as a nerve o'er which do creep / The else unfelt oppressions of this earth" (442–50)—suffers extremely from his unrequited love. Because he will take no action to harm his beloved (not even his own suicide, which might cause her regret), her only punishment will be to know the misery she has caused him (482–83).

The maniac's case certainly does not lend strong support to Julian's hopes for humanity, but his refusal to allow his sufferings to crush his integrity and his admission of partial guilt lend no aid to Maddalo's arguments for a deeply pessimistic view of the human condition. No longer does either Julian or Maddalo, however, try to use the poor demented man as merely a case-study to bolster his side of the argument—to point a moral or adorn a tale. Maddalo had earlier shown his essential benevolence by fitting up the maniac's rooms with "busts and books and urns for flowers . . . And instruments of music" (252–56); now he and Julian again show their humanity by forgetting their ego-centered debate. Both men agree on the single generalization to come from the maniac's case: "Most wretched men / Are cradled into poetry by wrong, / They learn in suffering what they teach in song." This aphorism (ending the opening section of part four) suggests, that, because suffering leads to creativity, some good comes directly out of evil. But this statement is not meant to be taken as a full answer to the question of evil.

Mundane duties call Julian back to London. Though he would like to stay at Maddalo's palace amid books, pictures, statues (like those that surround the maniac) and to enjoy Maddalo's conversation, his sense of responsibility prevails. Years later he returns to Venice to find that Maddalo's little girl, for whom he held such high hopes, has, indeed, grown up to be "a wonder of this earth, / Where there is little of transcendent worth,— / Like one of Shakespeare's women" (590–92). She, who provides a moral standard that the reader can trust, first attempts to turn aside Julian's restless queries about the fate of the maniac and his cruel mistress, requesting him to respect the privacy of the unfortunate lovers: "Ask me no more, but let the silent years / Be closed and cered over their memory / As yon mute marble where their corpses lie" (613–15). Julian "urged and questioned still"; but, after she told him "how / All happened," he ends his account: "the cold world shall not know" (617), thereby implying that Maddalo's daughter was right in wishing to allow the personal lives to remain private.

Shelley had earlier wished to publish the record of his inmost thoughts, but, as he implies in the opening of the fragmentary essay "On Love," he had come to realize that most people were not interested in the ideas or feelings of others and to wear one's heart on the proverbial sleeve was to expose oneself far more to misunderstanding than to sympathetic concern. In "Julian and Maddalo" the danger of prying into another's privacy forms a domestic counterpart to the larger theme that questions the efficacy of ignorant humans arguing about "God, freewill and destiny." The maniac's soliloquy certainly reflects—though it may not directly treat—Shelley's marital troubles; contrary to the doctrine underlying *Alastor, The Revolt of Islam,* and *Rosalind and Helen,* love is not regarded as a sufficient or even necessarily a safe goal for human ideals. The maniac is repelled by sexual love and warns others that only truth, not love, is an unalloyed good.

Insofar as the presentation is concerned, the poem's form reflects its theme; for, in dramatizing his own ideas through at least three characters, Shelley avoids the danger of falling into a confessional-didactic style. "Julian and Maddalo" marks a major shift in Shelley's thought, for its complementary themes are both that there is no ideal love in this world that can solve human problems and that human feelings are more important than theories about life. "Julian and Maddalo," though probably begun late in 1818, was not completed until the summer of 1819, after the death of William Shelley had driven Mary Shelley into a serious depression that deepened the estrangement between her and Shelley. In its completed text, then, it reflects the end of Shelley's hopes of finding a fully satisfactory love relationship within the realm of mutability and mortality.

Chapter Five
Roman Scenes

On October 31, 1818, the Shelleys left Venice, after having entrusted Allegra to the care of the Hoppners, and on November 5 the entire party started south from Este. In a series of brilliant letters to Peacock, Shelley described the highlights of their journey to Rome along the historic Via Æmilia and Via Flaminia and—after sightseeing there—to Naples, which they reached by December 1, 1818. From Naples he wrote glowing descriptions of the Bay of Naples, Mount Vesuvius, Pompeii, and the sculptures in the national museum, but the months there were lonely ones for the Shelleys and remain for us the least documented of their Italian sojourn.[1]

White, while studying the so-called "Hoppner scandal," discovered three documents relating to "Elena Adelaide Shelley." On February 27, 1819, Shelley registered a child, named Elena Adelaide Shelley, whom he declared to be the lawful child of himself and his wife, Mary Godwin Shelley, and to have been born on December 27, 1818. The child was also baptized on February 27, 1819. The state archives in Naples contain the certificate of death of "Elena Schelly," dated June 10, 1820, stating that she died the previous day, aged fifteen months and twelve days (which, if true, would place her birth February 27, 1819, instead of December 27, 1818; but the date may result from a misreading of the birth certificate).[2] Shelley alluded to the death of his "Neapolitan charge" in a letter to John and Maria Gisborne.[3]

These facts prove the existence of such a child and that Shelley claimed her as his and Mary's. But it is unlikely that they would have left a child of theirs behind in the care of working-class Neapolitans. Later Elise, the Swiss nurse, told Mrs. Hoppner that the child was Claire's by Shelley and that Mary knew nothing of it—a story that is not credible for a number of reasons. Scholars have suggested that the child may have been the daughter of Elise and Paolo Foggi, the daughter of Elise and Shelley, or an orphan adopted by Shelley to comfort Mary by replacing her infant daughter who died at Venice. There are difficulties with each of these theories, but they need not detain us.[4]

Although we may never know the truth underlying the "Hoppner scandal," we can judge that the months in Naples mark the beginning of one of Shelley's most productive periods. During 1819 he completed "Julian and Maddalo" and "Euganean Hills," he wrote the last three acts of *Prometheus Unbound, The Cenci,* and several fine short poems published with *Prometheus,* and he drafted "A Philosophical View of Reform" and, probably, "On Life"—as well as other, lesser pieces. The critic who would do justice to this material within a relatively short space must necessarily emphasize some works to the diminution of others. This chapter will treat *Prometheus Unbound* and *The Cenci,* leaving other works for briefer comment in Chapter 6.

I *Prometheus Unbound*

Prometheus Unbound exhibits a structure that is classically simple and symmetrical; Act I, though not divided into scenes, has three movements. The first section (1–305) portrays Prometheus' self-examination, his wish to hear his curse again, and the change of heart that enables him to repent his blind hate; the section ends: "I wish no living thing to suffer pain." In the second movement, Prometheus is tortured by the Furies at the instigation of Mercury. As Mercury, a slave to the despotic power of Jupiter, represents the threat of external force to Prometheus' free will, so the Furies, "ministers of pain, and fear, / And disappointment, and mistrust, and hate" (452–53), emblem the threat of Prometheus' own unruly passions to that same freedom. Now that he has, however, renounced his hatred, the Titan can truly say that he is king over himself (492–94). Finally comes the threat of despair when he is shown the betrayal of the French Revolution, the greatest human effort to throw off the bondage of unjust social conditions (the tyranny of external power), and the perversion in Christianity of the teachings of Jesus, mankind's greatest example of a self-controlled spirit (who though overcome in the crucifixion by external power, resisted the temptation either to hate or to capitulate to his enemies). At the end of this section, Prometheus routs the Furies by freely accepting the torture that comes to those who honor fragile and transitory human virtue: "Thy words are like a cloud of wingèd snakes; / And yet I pity those they torture not" (I.632–33).

The third part of Act I begins with Prometheus' speech (634–45). When the Titan has objectified his own greatest fears and doubts, Earth sends "to cheer [his] state . . . those subtle and fair spirits, /

Whose homes are the dim caves of human thought" (657–59). At last Prometheus can say that, although "most vain all hope but love," Panthea loves (808, 824), and thus she can transmit Prometheus' needs to Asia, the greater, unseen power of whom Panthea is the shadow. The pattern of the first act (I–305; 306–634; 635–833) corresponds closely, as we shall see, to the tripartite structure of Act IV.

In the first of the five scenes in Act II, Panthea transmits her two dreams to Asia. In the dream that Panthea can remember, Prometheus "grew radiant with the glory of that form / Which lives unchanged within" (II.i.64–65), and Prometheus' soul merged into Panthea's. As Asia gazes into Panthea's eyes so that she might read the dream, a second shape with "rude hair" appears between her and Panthea. This figure, the other dream, urges Asia to "Follow! Follow!" This "thing of air" is, as later develops, a vision of one of the Spirits of the Hours that will chariot Demogorgon and Asia to their unions with Jupiter and Prometheus, respectively. Asia and Panthea respond to the call of the dream of Echoes to "Follow, follow!" In Scene ii a chorus of Spirits tells of the operation of "Demogorgon's mighty law" and two Fauns explain the significance of the chorus. *Prometheus* II.ii repeatedly echoes Milton's description of Paradise before the fall and the description of the region through which Asia and Panthea travel on their way to Demogorgon's cave evokes reminiscences of the pre-lapsarian state of man.[5]

At the end of the same scene, the second Faun describes the hydrogen cycle (70–82). The Fauns suppose that the Spirits who sing are, like hydrogen, found embodied in many forms—like Shelley's "Cloud," they change, but they cannot die. This discovery leads the first Faun to ask, "if such live thus, have others other lives . . . ?" to which the second Faun replies affirmatively, and then closes the scene with an allusion to Silenus and to the carefree Classical Golden Age in which the Fauns are themselves living. Thus Asia and Panthea must pass, in terms of space, through the region of earthly paradise variously denominated in Christian and Classical myth. Historically, they are returning through the origins of human civilization and even human self-awareness.

The next scene (II.iii) finds them at the *physical* source of existence, a region of both volcanic vitality and mountain snow, combining images drawn from Mont Blanc and Vesuvius, the two manifestations of natural power that Shelley found most impressive. Here at Demogorgon's threshold, amid the amoral forces of nature, Panthea and Asia comment on the relationship between power and the will for good. Panthea, whose eyes are focused primarily on the world of human beings, first describes the "chasm, / Whence the oracular vapour is hurled up" that causes "lonely men . . . in their youth" to "uplift . . . the voice which is contagion to the world" (II.iii.3–10).

These men, like the misguided young idealist in *Alastor,* dissipate their energies in a vain frenzy that can be as dangerous to true inspiration as was the Maenads' madness to Orpheus. Shelley was always a poet of social regeneration. The individualistic course of "silence, exile, and cunning" that might seem to a post-Romantic like Stephen Dedalus a viable alternative to social reform was seen as a tragic waste by Shelley, who modified his Enlightenment humanitarianism with the ideals of fifth-century Athens and Renaissance England—both cultures of the greatest social cohesion.

To Panthea's observation on the destructive power of the "oracular vapour" emanating from Demogorgon's realm, Asia adds that the earth itself is beautiful and that if the earth is "the shadow of some spirit lovelier still, / . . . and it should be / Like its creation, weak yet beautiful, / I could fall down and worship that [Spirit] and thee [Earth]" (II.iii.12–16). Again Shelley has proclaimed nature good and only man's use of it evil. At the end of the scene, as the Spirits carry Panthea and Asia into the deep, far beyond such antinomies as death and life, "where the air is no prism" (that is, where human limitations no longer distort the radiance of knowledge into its prismatic colors), the Spirits urge the two oceanides not to resist their own helplessness in being bound and guided by the servants of Demogorgon; for there is strength in "meekness" to unleash the force of that "mighty darkness / Filling the seat of power."[6]

In Act II, Scene iv, Asia provides the mythical metaphysics and history that give shape to the verse drama; Demogorgon himself gives only equivocal answers characteristic of an oracle. As Asia finally realizes, "my heart gave / The response thou hast given; and of such truths / Each to itself must be the oracle" (II.iv.121–23). Perhaps the best gloss for this dialogue is "Mont Blanc," 76–83. Demogorgon personifies the force occupying the throne of Power (or necessity), emblemed by that "great Mountain," from which issued endless cycles of destruction and regeneration. To understand the unbridgeable chasm between the One and the many, between Power and humanity, between the Eternal and "all things that . . . / Are born and die; revolve, subside, and swell" ("Mont Blanc," 94–95) is "to repeal / Large codes

of fraud and woe," because this understanding removes the divine sanction from temporal evils.

To comprehend the amorality of nature (which is governed by what
men call "necessity") is to be motivated to change human institutions
for the benefit of human beings. The "voice" of the "great Mountain"
that proclaims the message of nature's amorality is not understood by
all, but the *wise interpret* it, the *great make* it *felt* through their actions,
and the *good deeply feel* it ("Mont Blanc," 81–83). Asia, Panthea, and
Ione roughly correspond with modified emphases, to the "wise,"
"great," and "good" in "Mont Blanc"; but they look forward even more
strikingly to the roles played by Sun, Moon, and Comet in *Epipsychidion*. Asia, the Spirit of Intellectual Beauty whose shadow Shelley in-
voked in his "Hymn" and who corresponds to the sun in later poems,
is associated with the power of imagination, which embodies both love
and reason. Panthea, who can "make felt" to Prometheus the influence
of Asia and to Asia the Titan's response, is both the "shadow of [that]
unseen Power" and an analogue of reason, the discursive mode by
which the power of feelings is communicated, as a manifestation of
love, she embodies intellectual love. Ione, who is farther removed from
the divine power, has only the knowledge available through sensory
impressions, and her love is limited to her proximity. She can *deeply
feel* but cannot communicate; she senses needs but can provide no
solutions.

To Asia's question of who created the "living world" and "all / That
it contains"—"thought, passion, reason, will, / Imagination"—Demogorgon gives two answers: "Almighty," "merciful" God made all
the good things of creation. But when Asia asks "who made terror,
madness, crime, remorse" and all other *evil* things, Demogorgon replies only, "He reigns." Asia then recounts the mythic history of human life (II.iv.32–109, an account paralleled in "Ode to Liberty"). She
says that from the action of Light and Love (purpose and energy) on a
pre-existent Heaven and Earth came forth Saturn and his realm.
Though Saturn's reign saw the introduction of time as a meaningful
category, moral innocence remained; yet accompanying the lack of
moral discrimination was man's lack of knowledge in other areas, for
Saturn denied men

> The birthright of their being, knowledge, power,
> The skill which wields the elements, the thought

> Which pierces this dim universe like light,
> Self-empire, and the majesty of love. . . .
>
>   (II.iv.39–42)

Then Prometheus, the mythic representation of the creative power of the human mind, gave "wisdom, which is strength, to Jupiter" (who embodies man's false self-idealization as proud, triumphant ruler). Under the reign of Jove, however, men became conscious of their unfulfilled desires and the same imaginative power that had abstracted a deity like Jupiter from isolated phenomenal experiences of power and pride now generalized other abstractions—"famine," "toil," "disease," "strife, wounds, and ghastly death unseen before" (II.iv.50–52). Having identified abstract evils amid the data of experience, men began to take arms against their newly-conceived troubles in ways consonant with Jupiter, their primitive self-conception:

> in their desert hearts fierce wants he sent,
> And mad disquietudes, and shadows idle
> Of unreal good, which levied mutual war,
> So ruining the lair wherein they raged.

But the imaginative power that, in its early attempts created unsuitable ideals, could create the antidotes to its own ills; Prometheus sent "the legioned hopes" to "hide with thin and rainbow wings / The shape of Death"; he sent Love to bind up again the broken strands of the human community; he tamed fire, creating arts and sciences through which men could supply their physical deficiencies and which shook the "thrones of earth and heaven," undermining the original, limited ideals and self-conceptions. Finally, Prometheus created "speech, and speech created thought," and "the harmonious mind" created poetry and then the plastic arts. With the growth of civilization, however, the originating Prometheus had been more and more trapped within the systems of his own earlier creations; thus Prometheus, the creative spirit who should have continued to improve man's conception of himself, was now confined and tortured by the older, more limited ideals of which he was himself the author; for the very arts and sciences that protected men from despair at the ravages of nature and time tended both to ossify and to perpetuate the old order: "Such, the alleviations of his state / Prometheus gave to man, for which he hangs / Withering in destined pain . . ." (II.iv.98–100).

Thus, by the time Asia asks "who rains down / Evil?" she has already clearly eliminated Jupiter. Demogorgon answers that "Jove is the supreme of living things," that "the deep truth is imageless," and that it would do no good to seek information about the hidden ultimate reality from "Fate, Time, Occasion, Chance, and Change," to which "all things are subject but eternal Love." In other words, the imaginative creation called "God" rules as long as it remains man's dominant idealization; the image is, however, subject to mutability and only the benevolent creative desire—the "eternal Love"—that brought forth the conception can withstand the powers of change. Jupiter, like other living things, is subject to mutability; and, as a creation of Prometheus, he is, in a sense, removable at the pleasure of that creativity that Prometheus represents.

But from the view of human mythologies, Prometheus is the rival of Jupiter for man's loyalties: Will men worship a self-ideal of static omnipotence or one of creative egalitarianism? Creativity working through the human mind has in the past destroyed one ideal of omnipotence (the Pope, for example) to replace it with another of the same character (national kings). Mutability assures, in any case, that Jupiter shall fall, and Asia's next question is the pragmatic one: "When shall the destined hour arrive?" (II.iv.128). In answer, Demogorgon says only, "Behold!" and points to the chariots of the Hours. One of these takes Demogorgon to his destined rendezvous with Jupiter, and the subsequent one carries Asia and Panthea to their reunion with Prometheus.

The fifth scene of Act II—the central scene of the drama—makes clear Asia's role as the personification of beauty and the goal of love, the anthropomorphic form of the abstract principle that, Shelley believed, underlies all the creativity of the universe. Panthea, necessary here as elsewhere as a chorus character to comment on the significance of the action, tells how Asia had first appeared in the form of Venus: "Within a veinèd shell, which floated on / Over the calm floor of the crystal sea, / Among the Ægean isles . . ." (II.v.23–25).

Asia replies that "all love is sweet"—that it is sweet to inspire love, as Panthea has said Asia does, but that it is more blessed to feel love for others, as she hopes soon to do. After a spirit voice has addressed Asia as "Life of Life," "Child of Light," and "Lamp of Earth" (the sequence tracing the descent of her beauty from beneficent abstract principle to benevolent practical reality), Asia sings of the voyage of her soul back through time to the fountainhead of being.[7] Thus, in this keystone scene in the drama Shelley portrays Asia, the principle of beauty, at the same time drawing near to earth in a moment of direct revelation and returning through "Age's icy caves," Manhood, Youth, Infancy, and "Death and Birth, to a diviner day." At the end of "Lines written among the Euganean Hills," Shelley had hoped that the Earth might "grow young again"; in *Hellas* he would envision a new beginning of "the world's great age." The cycles of history, as Shelley viewed them, would seem to resemble in their operation the incessantly spinning double-spools of Yeats's gyres. But *Prometheus Unbound* owes its structure, and, indeed, its very reason for being, to Shelley's hope that men could stop the moral cycle of decay and rebirth, preserving an ethical springtime with which to compensate for the inevitable physical winter.

Act III begins with Jupiter, in his moment of hubris, expecting a final victory through a child, a "strange wonder" that he has "begotten." When the car of the Hour arrives, Demogorgon (operative as necessity, the principle of cause and effect) tells puzzled Jupiter, "I am thy child, as thou wert Saturn's child" (III.i.54). Commentators have made unnecessary difficulties here by asking how Jupiter can be said to have begotten Demogorgon. Clearly every action within the realm of being begets consequences, and Jupiter's actions have begotten a reaction that can conveniently be personified as Demogorgon. In a sense, Demogorgon is everyone's child, even though, as Moira, Fate, Necessity, he is prior to and more powerful than any god. Shelley has underlined the exact nature of Jupiter's crimes in the tyrant's first speech, for Jupiter tells how he violated Thetis against her wishes ("God! Spare me!"). Jupiter is self-seeking, unwilling to treat others as anything but toys for his own pleasure; and his treatment of Thetis contrasts sharply with the mutuality of the love relationship between Prometheus and Asia.[8]

What is the relationship between Prometheus' decision to retract his curse in Act I and Jupiter's downfall in Act III? Jupiter, subject like all other living things to the amoral operations of "Fate, Time, Occasion, Chance, and Change," would someday have fallen. What is important is that Prometheus, by choosing to take no vengeance against the old order, keeps himself from becoming another Jupiter. As Shelley had seen in the course of the French Revolution, when the oppressed lack the capacity to love and forgive, they soon turn into new oppressors who are basically indistinguishable from the old. Prometheus' decision to turn from self-centered hatred to outgoing love marks the moment in human history that breaks the old meaningless cycle of oppression and retribution—"the despot's rage, the slave's revenge"—and introduces a new order based on forgiveness and equality. Prometheus becomes an ideal far different from a vengeful rebel, a Jupiter-out-of-office; he becomes a purified symbol of human creativity, offering men something to emulate that will change their conceptions of what they are and what they can and ought to become.

In Demogorgon's cave, Asia had recognized that Jupiter himself was but a slave both to evil and to the cycle of mutability, and this perspective justifies Prometheus' act of forgiveness. Indeed, this relationship between the action of Act I and that of Act II plays an important part in the structure of *Prometheus Unbound,* for only by understanding the thematic alternations can one comprehend fully the function of Act IV. In Act I Prometheus, embodying the imaginative, creative, and moral power of the human mind, decides to cast aside his hatred, as being mean and petty compared to the enormity of his own and mankind's sufferings. The tortures, representing two threats to human moral autonomy—external power and the anarchy of internal passions—are essentially psychological and are answered by hopes likewise generated within the mind. Asia represents an objective, metaphysical reality with which the human imagination is consonant.

Act II recounts Asia's inquiry into the relationship between "power" and "will for good," between the desire and the capacity for moral amelioration: If man wishes to improve his lot and to live a more nearly perfect life, is this desire a realistic, attainable one within the world as we know it? Demogorgon, the supreme ground of being, the basic principle of cause and effect and natural law, replies that love is, in fact, the only reality that is self-sustaining and regenerative; all other things are subject to mutability. Thus Act II gives metaphysical support to the moral decision of Act I. The same relation holds, as we shall see, between acts III and IV: the third articulates the social order that should follow the moral revolution in individual hearts and the fourth act (in which Prometheus and Asia do not appear) delineates the metaphysical implications of Act III. Act IV may have been an afterthought, but it was an inevitable one, for it completes both the symmetrical structure and the thematic development of the drama.

The conversation between Ocean and Apollo (III.ii) parallels the chorus of Spirits and the conversation of the Fauns in II.ii, but in Act III the commentary concerns the moral future rather than the metaphysical character of the natural universe. After man's regeneration, neither the sun nor the ocean will be obscured and stained by the crimes of man, who, no longer the outcast stepchild of nature, will recognize the harmony between his own temporal, physical being (symbolized in Shelley's poems by water) and his eternal, creative character (symbolized by fire and, more specifically, by the sun).

In the third scene Hercules, the strength attendant on virtue, releases Prometheus, who descends to the social level of humanity (not into the bowels of the earth as Asia and Panthea had in the corresponding scene in Act II). Unlike Jupiter, Prometheus has no intention of reigning *above* mankind, inasmuch as to do so would violate the principle of equality and self-control that stands at the center of Shelley's moral vision.[9] Each man is to govern himself, aided by the arts through which society voices its collective moral wisdom. Prometheus, man's creative imagination, will act as an unacknowledged legislator through "the progeny immortal / Of Painting, Sculpture, and rapt Poesy, / And arts, though unimagined, yet to be" (III.iii.54–56). He will rule, in other words, not through power but through creative example.

Once he has made this decision (which really sanctifies Jupiter's fall and assures the new order), Prometheus can send the Spirit of the Hour to sound the "curvèd shell, which Proteus old / Made Asia's nuptial boon," to usher in the new society. "Mother Earth" next raises the issue of death by assuring Prometheus that, in the new harmony between man and nature, death will no longer seem to be a threat but "shall be the last embrace of her / Who takes the life she gave, even as a mother / Folding her child, says, 'Leave me not again'" (III.iii.105–7). Asia, who, like the Witch of Atlas, hates the "name of death," wishes to know whether those who die cease "to love, and move, and breathe, and speak." Earth replies that, since Asia and Prometheus are immortal, "it would avail not to reply"; but she does answer through a figure: "Death is the veil which those who live call life: / They sleep, and it is lifted . . ." (III.iii.113–14).

Shelley, not claiming omniscience, limits his speculations on immortality to this ambiguous answer by Earth, who in Act I showed her limited character by believing that, when Prometheus withdrew his curse, he was capitulating to Jupiter. Such are the uses of dramatic characterization; from the sublunar perspective, as Shelley makes quite clear in his essay "On a Future State" (Julian, VI, 205–9), there is no evidence for personal immortality. And Earth quite consistently feels that the perpetuation of beauty by means of the human creative faculty (Prometheus) and its allied cosmic principle (Asia), in addition to its perpetuation in recurring cycles of the natural world, ought to be enough. That Shelley did not feel completely satisfied by this answer can be seen in his second note to *Hellas* (OSA, pp. 478–79).

Earth directs Prometheus, and the oceanides to a cavern, apparently the same one which Asia and Panthea described in II.iii, "whence the oracular vapour is hurled up." Earlier, under the reign of Jupiter this vapor had been dangerous, driving men mad; but its "breath now rises, as . . . / A violet's exhalation," feeding luxuriant flowers and "inspiring calm and happy thoughts, like mine, / Now thou art thus restored" (III.iii.124–47). Earth calls the Spirit of the Earth, personified as a male cherub, to guide them to the cave and its accompanying temple, which was once sacred to Prometheus and is now to return to its proper function as the seat of worship of the best potentialities of the human mind.

In the fourth and final scene of Act III, the Spirit of the Earth calls Asia "mother, dearest mother," though Panthea admits that "whence it sprung it knew not, nor do I" (III.iv.23). While retaining his skepticism, Shelley suggests mythically that Asia—the universal, creative force that inspires human imagination—is also the source of natural creative energy; in other words, Asia is a kind of Platonic demiurge underlying the vital powers of the entire active universe. In a beautiful speech, the Spirit of the Earth describes how he saw "all things . . . put their evil nature off," a reversal of the growth of evil following man's fall that Milton describes in *Paradise Lost*. Then the Spirit of the Hour re-enters and, in the long concluding speech of the act, gives an account of the changes he has observed in human society. Men (and women), now equal and fraternal, no longer see in "thrones, altars, judgement-seats, and prisons" their old, dread significance.[10] Men are no longer divided by arbitrary barriers of class, tribe, or nation; but each is "king over himself," kept from soaring beyond "the loftiest star of unascended heaven" only by the limitations of mortality—"chance, death, and mutability."

Act IV, like the first act, has three clearly definable movements: lines 1–181 contain songs by two choruses, interspersed with comments and questions by Panthea and Ione. The "unseen Spirits" who open the act later reveal themselves as "Spirits of the human mind" (IV.81), and the "train of dark Forms and Shadows" become the "Chorus of Hours." Sometimes singing together in a unified "Chorus of Spirits and Hours," they symbolize the new harmonious relationship between the human mind and time, its medium—a harmony that contrasts sharply and specifically with the corresponding section of Act I, where Prometheus had to undergo "three thousand years of sleep-un-sheltered hours" filled with torture and where the hours were described as "wingless, crawling hours" (I.12, 48). The lightness, rapidity, and joyfulness of the choruses in the last act of *Prometheus Unbound* are almost unique in English literature, and C. S. Lewis has rightly pointed to Dante's *Paradiso* as their inspiration.[11] The fourth act is Dantesque in spirit, as large portions of the first three acts are Miltonic, though the *Prometheus Bound* of Æschylus provided the structural and thematic basis of the drama.

After a short transition (IV.180–84), the second movement begins when Ione and Panthea hear "new notes arise," sounds which prove to be the music of the Spheres. Moon and Earth appear, each cradling within it an infant spirit. Moon and its spirit are cold and colorless, whereas Earth and its spirit are colorful and vital, though Earth is marred by the wrecks of lost civilizations and extinct species of animal life. Now the joyous animation of Earth penetrates the "frozen frame" of Moon, which bursts into life in response to Earth's love (358–69). Earth hymns the creative power of "Man," no longer a disparate collection of "men," but a "chain of linkèd thought" (394), who has now subordinated his will, "a spirit ill to guide, but mighty to obey" (408), to Love. Not only has Earth warmed and vivified Moon, but the "crystal accents" of the "gentle Moon," mingling with Earth's vitality, charm its "tiger joy, whose tramplings fierce / Made wounds" (499–502).

The second movement of Act IV thus records the interaction of passion and reason in a harmonious balance that perpetuates and implements the good efforts of Prometheus' self-control as that was demonstrated in the second movement of the first act. Now, as a counter-piece to the third movement of Act I, Demogorgon, the voice of destiny, speaks to the various elements of the universe—Earth, Moon, Spirits of the Stars (to reappear prominently in *Adonais*), the Dead, the "elemental Genii," living spirits, and Man. To them he addresses congratulations, a warning, and a formula: today "Conquest is dragged captive" and "Love . . . folds over the world its healing wings" (554–61); but, should the cycle of oppression and vengeance—the tyranny of false ideals—begin anew, he recommends a series of antidotes (expressed, appropriately, in timeless infinitives):

> To suffer woes which Hope thinks infinite;
> To forgive wrongs darker than death or night;
> To defy Power, which seems omnipotent;

> To love, and bear; to hope till Hope creates
> From its own wreck the thing it contemplates;
>   Neither to change, nor falter, nor repent;
> This, like thy glory, Titan, is to be
> Good, great and joyous, beautiful and free;
> This is alone Life, Joy, Empire, and Victory.
>
> (IV.570–78)

Prometheus Unbound thus portrays the power of man over himself and over external circumstances, insofar as these are used to excuse his own moral shortcomings. Though death, chance, and mutability cannot be overcome, if man-created evils were eliminated, men could reduce their tribulations to this residual minimum; and, by taking a less negative attitude toward death, they might reduce the evil effects of even it.

Prometheus is a masterpiece of symmetrical structure, the central scene (II.v) being the turning point in which the Spirit of Intellectual Beauty is transfigured so as to reveal itself to men and dwell among them. Thematically, there is a principle of alternation at work: acts I and III deal with man's moral growth, and acts II and IV recount the implications of this growing moral awareness for his metaphysical conceptions. If each man were at peace with himself, and all men with one another, the natural universe would seem to them harmonious. Practically speaking, man's moral regeneration redeems the universe.

II *The Cenci*

The Shelleys left Naples at the end of February, 1819, and went to Rome, where they saw more of both English and Italian society than they had elsewhere in Italy. Shelley, who was less involved in the social whirl than were Mary and Claire, wrote parts of *Prometheus Unbound* at the Baths of Caracalla—then an overgrown mass of vegetation beyond the limits of the inhabited city. He completed three acts of *Prometheus Unbound* by April. About this same time he saw the supposed Guido Reni portrait of Beatrice Cenci, and by mid-May he was composing his drama on the subject of the Cenci. A heavy blow fell on the Shelleys when their son William (ca. three and a half years old) became ill and died on June 7. They could not bear to remain in Rome, but hastened to Leghorn and by June 24 were ensconced in the Villa Valsovano outside the city on the road to Monte Nero. By July, Shelley was at work again on *The Cenci,* and he seems by August 8 to have finished it. On September 9, 1819, he sent a copy to Peacock, writing later that he had "printed in Italy 250 copies, because it costs, with all duties & freightage about half what it wd. cost in London. . . ."

As Shelley explained in his Dedication to Leigh Hunt, his earlier writings had been "visions which impersonate my own apprehensions of the beautiful and the just"; but in this drama he laid aside "the presumptuous attitude of an instructor" to paint, instead, "that which has been." The plot of *The Cenci* came not from his imagination, but from *Relation of the Death of the Family of the Cenci,*[12] a document purporting to be a historically accurate account written shortly after the events. The interest that the story continued to elicit in Rome more than two centuries after the event convinced Shelley that its appeal was universal enough to be the subject of great tragedy.

The Cenci, which was written in a style studiously different from his "ideal" poems, aimed at the popular market and was, indeed, the only poem by Shelley to go into an authorized second edition during his lifetime (and thus the only work in which he could correct printer's errors—fewer than usual even in the first edition, for which he read proof). At the same time, the author's characteristic ideas appear in a kind of mirror-image; for, by showing what was debilitating and evil in the society of sixteenth-century Rome, he implied that removing these conditions would ameliorate human life.

In Act I, Scene i, Cardinal Camillo, a childhood friend of Count Francesco Cenci, has arranged terms of settlement for the Count's latest crime—murder of a servant who had been a witness to another of his crimes. The Pope has agreed to exonerate Cenci in return for land "beyond the Pincian gate" that amounts to a third of his possessions. The Count speaks candidly to Camillo of his sadistic pleasures; once he had gained satisfaction from his physical lusts, then from physical sadism, but in his old age he has refined his taste so that now,

> I rarely kill the body, which preserves,
> Like a strong prison, the soul within my power,
> Wherein I feed it with the breath of fear
> For hourly pain.
>
> (I.i.114–17)

Cenci does not fear Camillo because the Cardinal has told people that he has "half reformed" the Count; therefore, Camillo's vanity will combine with his fear to keep him from exposing the evil old man. After Camillo leaves, Count Cenci in a soliloquy hints at his plot against Beatrice.

In the second scene Beatrice Cenci, planning to send a petition to the Pope by Orsino (a priest who claims to be in love with her), tells him that he has a "sly, equivocating vein" that she distrusts. Once she is offstage, Orsino proves her right by planning to get Beatrice completely in his power and to make her his mistress.

The third and final scene of Act I, the banquet scene, is the most dramatic in the play. In it Count Cenci demonstrates his power by openly thanking God for having blessed him by destroying two of his rebellious sons, Rocco and Christofano—"which shows that Heaven has special care of me" (I.iii.65). While the nobles and churchmen who are guests at the "celebration" are openly shocked, Beatrice deems it a propitious time to appeal to them for protection from her father for herself, Cenci's wife Lucretia, and the youngest son Bernardo. Many of the guests feel conscience-stricken, but fear keeps them from taking any action, though several say they "would second any one" who would take the initiative. Count Cenci has overborne all who approach him in power and prestige; only his daughter Beatrice, helplessly in his grip, has the boldness to defy him. At the end of the scene, Cenci drinks wine to prepare himself to break Beatrice's will by violating her.

In Act II the trap is closing on Beatrice. Orsino's servant informs her that the Pope has returned her petition unopened. (Actually Orsino never presented it.) Lucretia and Bernardo show how dependent they are on Beatrice's strength of will for protection from Count Cenci. Meanwhile, Beatrice herself is shaken by her premonitions of Cenci's evil intent. When Lucretia tries to calm her husband, he accuses her and his children of plotting to murder him. During the closing soliloquy, Cenci again alludes to his intention. In Act II.ii, Cardinal Camillo and Giacomo Cenci consult at the Vatican about Giacomo's legal recourse to obtain his rightful money from his father; he has no possibility of getting justice through the law. Orsino, entering as Camillo leaves, hints to Giacomo that Cenci ought to be murdered. When Giacomo, much shaken, exits, Orsino soliloquizes about his intention to use the evil of others for his own ends. Beatrice has shown him the dark side of his nature by pointing out his "sly, equivocating vein"; and he now plans to live up to this estimate of his character.

At the beginning of Act III, Beatrice enters, distraught to madness at having been incestuously violated by her father. Searching desperately for the means of redressing the wrong, or of at least preventing its recurrence, she rejects suicide as being contrary to God's law and, therefore, a gate to Hell. Orsino enters; but, when he gives no comfort, Beatrice concludes that Cenci must die:

> As I have said, I have endured a wrong,
> Which, though it be expressionless, is such
> As asks atonement; both for what is past,
> And lest I be reserved, day after day,
> To load with crimes an overburthened soul,
> And be . . . what ye can dream not. . . .
> (III.i.213–18)

Once she has decided that Cenci's death is the only means by which she, Lucretia, and Bernardo can save themselves, not only from physical destruction but also from moral corruption, she never wavers: She sees herself as God's minister of vengeance, and her view of the moral implications is thereafter simplistic. Orsino, who fears Cenci as an obstacle to his plans to seduce Beatrice, supports the plot to murder him, offering to engage two cutthroats for that purpose. Giacomo, entering with a new tale of Cenci's fiendish sadism, also agrees that the Count must die. In the next scene, however, Giacomo has second thoughts and conscience-qualms about the murder. When Orsino tells him that the first attempt has misfired but that another has been arranged, Giacomo weakly wishes that he had never been born.

In Act IV Cenci has decided not only to continue to have intercourse with his daughter, but to seduce her with the fascination of the abomination: he wishes her not only to submit but to consent to the liaison, for he is determined not only to pollute her body but also to kill her soul. When Beatrice twice refuses to come of her own volition, Count Cenci curses her with a blood-chilling anathema. In this moment of hubris he sees God as a father who will help him, another father, chastise his unruly children as God has, Cenci thinks, killed Rocco and Christofano in response to the Count's prayers. Already, however, Count Cenci is under the power of a sleeping potion that leaves him an easy prey for the hired assassins who soon enter (IV.ii).

Beatrice urges Olimpio and Marzio to perform the murder, but in IV.iii they return, being like Shakespeare's murderers too much under the power of conscience to kill a sleeping man. Though their reluctance is hardly "realistic," Shelley is underlining the corrupted feelings of other characters in the play by showing how the most hardened, un-imaginative men shrink from the cowardly slaying of a fellow human being. Beatrice, like Lady Macbeth, has lost her human nature in a dogmatic assurance of her rectitude, which matches Count Cenci's own megalomania. Each thinks he is fulfilling God's will. This dogmatic self-righteousness is one of the "codes of fraud and woe" that the healthy skepticism engendered by Mont Blanc was to repeal; and Bea-trice's submission to it marks the "pernicious mistake" that, according to Shelley's Preface, she has committed by resorting to vengeance. At the same time, of course, the change in Beatrice illustrates once again that oppressors who, like Cenci, sow the wind will reap the whirlwind by arousing in the oppressed a similar vindictiveness. Beatrice, assured of the righteousness of her cause, shames the two ruffians into return-ing to commit the murder; when they report their success, she and Lucretia go to bed.

The last scene of Act IV gives the murder its final thematic twist; in an incident that Shelley has added to his source, Savella, the Papal Legate, arrives with a warrant from the Pope for Count Cenci's "instant death." Thus, as Lucretia laments, "All was prepared by unforbidden means / Which we must pay so dearly, having done"(IV.iv.29–30). The Pope's sudden interest in destroying Cenci only underlines the moral capriciousness of the world in which Beatrice and her co-conspirators live. We can hardly term the order "justice," inasmuch as Cenci is to be killed without trial for unspecified crimes, perhaps those for which papal courts have already exonerated him; and, upon finding the Count dead by other means than his, Savella finds it necessary to bring charges against Cenci's victims, who had been driven to desperation by the long history of collusion between Count Cenci and the papal govern-ment. Fear and a troubled conscience break down Lucretia, who by her weakness and confusion betrays her guilt. Beatrice, however, has risen above all doubts and expects to be vindicated by God's vicar.

In Act V Giacomo, self-pitying and wavering, is betrayed by Or-sino, who has committed all his treacheries with open eyes and now begins to feel some compunctions for his actions. His conscience, we are led to believe, will make all his days restless, though he escapes immediate justice. In the second scene, Marzio under torture admits his guilt and implicates Giacomo, Orsino, Lucretia, and Beatrice; later, under the influence of Beatrice's forceful protestations, Marzio recants his confession and dies declaring Beatrice and all the others innocent. Camillo, by now convinced of Beatrice's innocence, stops the proceedings to intercede on her behalf with the Pope.

In the third scene Bernardo visits Beatrice in prison with the news that Giacomo and Lucretia have broken under the torture and confessed. Though Bernardo still hopes that the Pope will pardon them and though Lucretia says that after death God, not "they," will be their judge and will understand their situation, Beatrice continues to maintain that, if she is called guilty, the judge is really accusing God of permitting her to be tortured and degraded without allowing her any refuge or recourse except her father's death: Either she is innocent, or God and his representatives are equally guilty (V.iii.65–83). In her last speech of the scene, even after she is resigned to receiving injustice from the papal court, Beatrice still clings to her belief in the righteousness of her cause and in God's justice:

> Take cheer! The God who knew my wrong, and made
> Our speedy act the angel of His wrath,
> Seems, and but seems, to have abandoned us.
> Let us not think that we shall die for this.
>
> (V.iii.113–16)

Only in the play's final scene does the truth dawn on Beatrice that the Pope has, like Count Cenci and Beatrice herself (under provocation), lost all human sympathies and become, in Cardinal Camillo's words

> as calm and keen as is the engine
> Which tortures and which kills, exempt itself
> From aught that it inflicts; a marble form,
> A rite, a law, a custom: not a man.
>
> (V.iv.2–5)

In *Prometheus Unbound* the Phantasm of Jupiter was described thus: "Cruel he looks, but calm and strong, / Like one who does, not suffers wrong" (I.238–39). These and other descriptions of tyrants in Shelley's works reiterate the poet's essential vision of what happens to a human being when he assumes an abstract role and takes it more seriously than he does his own nature, whether that role be king, Pope, father, or minister of God's vengeance. Beatrice, who has so far corrupted herself that she has sent Count Cenci, Olimpio, Marzio, and now most of her family to their deaths without a qualm, awakens to the possibility that her role may have been a false one. But she is now unable to accept full responsibility for assuming the role: rather, pursuing the train of logic that she employed before the judges in the previous scene, she believes that if she is guilty, then God must have tricked her— that the ruling force of the universe may be only a cosmic amplification of her father's nature:

> If there should be
> No God, no Heaven, no Earth in the void world;
> The wide, gray, lampless, deep, unpeopled world!
> If all things then should be . . . my father's spirit,
> His eye, his voice, his touch surrounding me;
> The atmosphere and breath of my dead life!
> ·
>   . . . Even though dead,
> Does not his spirit live in all that breathe,
> And work for me and mine still the same ruin,
> Scorn, pain, despair? Who ever yet returned
> To teach the laws of Death's untrodden realm?
> Unjust perhaps as those which drive us now,
> Oh, whither, whither?
>   (V.iv.57–62, 69–75)

This vision of cosmic evil finally breaks through Beatrice's façade of self-possession and allows her to regain her common human sympathies. By refusing any longer to hope and by resigning herself to whatever unknowable fate may await her beyond the grave, Beatrice for the first time since her decision to kill her father shows affection and pity for Lucretia and her two brothers, and in this renewal of human sympathy lies the final heightening of her character requisite for effective tragedy.

The Cenci follows the five-act structure of Elizabethan drama. The rising action shows Count Cenci and Orsino laying nets for Beatrice, while she exhibits a firm determination to resist evil without resorting to it herself. In Act III, after Cenci has violated her, she brings the plot to its climax in her determination to strike back, to meet violence with violence. The main action is, then, the development of Beatrice's character, rather than the murder of Count Cenci and the destruction of his murderers. *The Cenci* thus forms a parallel opposite to the thematic movement of *Prometheus Unbound*. When Prometheus renounced hatred and vengeance, wishing "no living thing to suffer pain," the universe around him seemed to become benevolent and harmonious; when Beatrice Cenci, also pushed to the brink by circumstances, adopted the evil ways of her oppressors, the universe itself seemed to her increasingly malevolent.

Shelley's technical virtuosity enabled him to compose *Prometheus Unbound* and *The Cenci* in totally dissimilar styles. This ability to write in various forms and styles (while always articulating the same general themes) increased as time passed, but in no poems did Shelley demonstrate this virtuosity more than in his works of late 1819 and 1820.

Chapter Six
The Chameleon

The year from September, 1819, through August, 1820, marked Shelley's last serious attempt to write for a popular audience; for, by the end of this time, he had concluded that his talents and inclinations led him in another direction. The diverse works of this period seem almost the products of a second apprenticeship in which Shelley groped for the medium of self-expression that could communicate his vision to a wider audience than those who already saw life as he did. Except for the poems that grew directly out of the composition of *Prometheus Unbound,* nearly all those discussed in this chapter were occasional; most were written as direct responses to political events.

I "The Mask of Anarchy"

Shelley wrote "The Mask of Anarchy," for example, at Leghorn when he heard of the "Peterloo Massacre" (August 16, 1819), in which drunken mounted militiamen broke up a peaceful reform meeting in St. Peter's Field outside Manchester, England, by wielding their sabers and riding down unarmed men, women, and children.[1] On September 23, the poem, written in a simple, direct, and powerful style, was sent to Leigh Hunt for publication in *The Examiner.* Structurally, it shows less self-conscious symmetry than other poems that Shelley had written in Italy, but the thirteen stanzas describing slavery (xxxix–li) are, for example, balanced by thirteen describing its opposite, freedom (lii–lxiv). The opening stanza, which introduces the dream-vision, is followed by two-stanza sketches of Murder (Lord Castlereagh, the foreign minister), Fraud (Lord Eldon, the lord chancellor who had deprived Shelley of his children), Hypocrisy (Lord Sidmouth, the home secretary), and Anarchy. Shelley saw tyranny and anarchy as closely related, for one holding temporal rule who did not submit his will to the law of love is a slave to the anarchy of his own unchecked desires, and human achievements become subject to the historical anarchy of fluctuation between the despot's rage and the slave's revenge.[2]

Shelley hopes to forestall that revenge by inciting the people to take the initiative before their hatred and desperation can drive them to the state of mind he had just portrayed in *The Cenci*. He describes the apparent triumph of the reactionary powers only to show them overthrown by an armed giant, an emanation of Hope (stanzas xxii–xxxiii). Then the earth of England itself seems to speak to the people, urging them to rise up in defense of their rights, but warning them at the same time that "to feel revenge / Fiercely thirsting to exchange / Blood for blood" (193–95) is one of the signs of slavery. Beginning at Stanza lxv the people are urged to come from all walks of life, to assemble peacefully, as they did at St. Peter's Field, and to demand their rights in the name of the English constitution. If the soldiers of the tyrants attack, the people should not resist but by their calm courage should shame their fellow-Englishmen into abandoning the slaughter and joining the cause of freedom. United, they can be assured of victory, for they are many, their oppressors few.

The English nation was, in fact, outraged by the excesses of Peterloo. Shelley, who knew little of the popular reaction in England, was merely reiterating conceptions that had already appeared in *A Proposal for Putting Reform to the Vote* and *The Revolt of Islam*. Even if such pacific methods had not proved initially successful, he would have defended their ultimate value; for he saw clearly that those who use violence generate fear and hatred among others, thus weakening their power eternally, and, what was far worse, they themselves become the thing they previously fought against. For Shelley, the end did not justify the means; the means itself shaped the end.

During the following weeks, Shelley also wrote a series of shorter political poems. The most famous of these, beginning "Men of England, wherefore plough / For the lords who lay ye low?" later became the rallying-cry of English Communists (and was parodied as "Beasts of England" in George Orwell's *Animal Farm*). But neither these poems nor "The Mask of Anarchy" was published until after Shelley's death, for Leigh Hunt apparently felt that they were too inflammatory to appear in a paper that was at the time struggling to survive a drop in circulation and that stood under the threat of intensified government persecution.

II Four Odes

Parallel in sentiment to these "exoteric" poems, but written in a quite different style, are four odes, three published with *Prometheus Unbound* ("Ode to the West Wind," "An Ode, written October, 1819, before the Spaniards had recovered their Liberty," and "Ode to Liberty") and "Ode to Naples," written in August, 1820, published in the *Morning Chronicle*, September 26, 1820, and reprinted in a military publication in October, 1820.[3]

"Ode to the West Wind," written at Florence in the autumn of 1819, embodies the conflicting themes of the Poet's personal despair and his hopes for social renewal in images drawn from the seasonal cycle. In nature, the individual always dies; yet the species is always reborn in the spring. So the Poet prays that the wind of necessity, which he invokes as ruler of the vegetation of earth (Stanza i), air (ii), and water (iii), might make him its lyre. As Irene H. Chayes has pointed out,[4] however, the Poet really asks in the concluding stanza, not that he be enabled to merge his character with the wind's and become its instrument, but that it become him: "Be thou, Spirit fierce, / My spirit! Be thou me, impetuous one!" The Poet asks that Demogorgon fight his battles (which are those of Prometheus), destroy the old order, and carry (not seeds of the vegetation of earth, air, or water, but) sparks of spiritual fire. Though the fire of his individual thoughts may be dead and though his physical life is dying, he prays the wind to "Scatter, as from an unextinguished hearth / Ashes and sparks, my words among mankind!"

In the climactic position, however, stands a metaphor not of natural force but of artistic inspiration. The stanza began with a petition to the wind to *make* the Poet *its* lyre; now, true to the dramatic inversion of lines 61–62, the Poet demands that the wind shape its power to *his* will: "Be through my lips to unawakened earth / The trumpet of a prophecy!" The very choice of words for the final question, "*if* Winter comes" rather than "*when* Winter comes," implies that the analogy between the seasonal cycle and human affairs is not a perfect one, for the cycle of *moral* mutability can be stopped in its course. The conscious efforts of men of vision are required to turn the wheel past Winter to Spring; and it is possible, as *Prometheus Unbound* makes clear, to maintain moral springtime longer than has been customary in most of human history.

The fourth stanza would seem to present a problem, dwelling as it does on the Poet's weakness. If he retained the enthusiasm and illusions of his boyhood, "when to outstrip thy skiey speed / Scarce seemed a vision," he would not "have striven / As thus with thee in prayer in my sore need" (50–52). Shelley had learned the stubbornness of matter. He, like Dante, had been lost in the dark wood of our life and had been tangled in the vegetation governed by the force of necessity (stanzas i–iii). He fell "upon the thorns of life" and bled. The fires of imagination sometimes consume thorns, but only (as Shelley was to declare in "A Defence of Poetry") during a relatively few brief moments of inspiration. During the reflux of imagination, a poet is, like other men, subject to mortal limitations; and it is the Poet's realization of this condition that impels him to pray the wind to stir his ashes and fan the fading coal of imagination.[5]

"An Ode, written October, 1819," more stylized than "Song to the Men of England," also urges a bloodless rebellion. Although it expresses Shelley's premonition of civil struggle in England, it could be published with *Prometheus Unbound* without fear of censorship because it is ostensibly addressed to the Spanish people, who, because of their alliance with the British during the Peninsular Campaign, were very popular with the English of all classes. In the fourth stanza Shelley appeals to the people not only to conquer the "revenge, pride, and power" of their foes, but to ride "more victorious" over their own similar faults (26–28). The poem ends with an injunction to bind the victors' brows "with crownals of violet, ivy, and pine," which emblem "azure hope," "green strength," and "eternity," respectively, while warning against using the pansy, the flower that symbolizes memory (and thus reflection on past wrongs).

"Ode to Liberty" is one of Shelley's most important middle-length poems, on a par with "Mont Blanc," "Hymn to Intellectual Beauty," and "Lines written among the Euganean Hills." The poem is framed by stanzas (i and xix) that recount the beginning and end of poetic inspiration, comparing the Poet as he begins his flight of imagination to "a young eagle" soaring among the clouds and likening him after inspiration has faded to a "wild swan . . . When the bolt has pierced its brain," as well as to a bursting cloud, a fading candle, and a dying insect (273–80).

After two stanzas stating that truly human life is impossible without liberty, there begins an idealized history of liberty: its birth in Greece (iv–vi), its eclipse after the death of the Roman Republic and during the "Dark Ages" (vii–viii), its rebirth in Saxon England and in the Italian communes of the Middle Ages (ix), its growth through the Reformation and English Renaissance (x), and its bursting forth on the heels of the Enlightenment in the French Revolution (xi), which became, however, so perverted that Napoleon triumphed ("the Anarch of thine own bewildered powers"). In Stanza xiii Shelley turns from

past failures to present opportunities: Spain (in revolution in 1820)
calls England; the two peoples who together had fought Napoleon's
tyranny are now seen as "twins of a single destiny." If Spain can cast
off her chains, which were "links of steel," England can cast off her
"threads of gold." In the next stanza, Shelley appeals to "king-deluded
Germany" to emulate Arminius (victor over the legions of the Roman
Empire) and to Italy to "repress / The beasts who make their dens thy
sacred palaces."

These themes are taken up at greater length in xv and xvi, which
advocate the overthrow of kings and priests respectively: Human
thoughts should "kneel alone, / Each before the judgement-throne / Of
its own aweless soul, or of the Power unknown!" The "Power unknown," beyond the realm of fallible human cognition, that "taught
man to vanquish whatsoever / Can be between the cradle and the
grave / Crowned him the King of Life" (241–43). Though man has
created art, which now rules in the place of nature (its mother), he has
enslaved himself, as life has bred new wants and as desire to accumulate
wealth has left some people a surfeit while others are in need. Shelley,
therefore, in Stanza xviii calls upon Liberty to lead Wisdom "out of the
inmost cave / Of man's deep spirit" (256–57). Liberty will be itself
only when joined to "blind Love" (love that is no respecter of persons),
"equal Justice," "the Fame" of past good, and "the Hope of what will
be."

In "Ode to Naples" Shelley recalls standing in Pompeii and noticing
the rumblings of Vesuvius, which seemed to be the Earth speaking in
an undertone—a premonition of the approaching revolution. The second *epode* begins with the winds that literally drive the Poet's vessel
across the Bay of Naples and that also correspond to the "winds" of
change and those of inspiration that seize the Poet (51). In Strophe I
he hails Naples as "Metropolis of a ruined Paradise / Long lost, late
won, and yet but half regained" (57–58); Strophe II urges Naples not
to let her "high heart fail" in the struggle against the "Crowned Trans-
gressors." The first two *antistrophes* predict that the "blind slaves" of
Austria will see their own plight and, like Actaeon's hounds, turn on
their master to destroy the Austrian tyranny. Unlike Actaeon, who saw
too much when he witnessed Artemis bathing nude, the oppressors
have so cloaked the truth in veils of error that they themselves have
not foreseen the inevitable reaction to their tyranny. Now the people
are to "strip every impious gawd" from "Freedom's form divine, / From
Nature's inmost shrine."

The second two *antistrophes* call the other cities of "eternal Italy" to join Naples in gaining freedom: Genoa remembers Andrea Doria, its greatest hero; Milan throws off the heritage of the tyrannical Visconti family; Florence awaits freedom; Rome strips off the garments of ecclesiastical rule, thus regaining the freedom lost at Philippi (where Antony and Octavius Caesar defeated Brutus and Cassius, thus putting an end to the Roman republic). The final two *epodes* allude to the advance of Austrian armies: "The Anarchs of the North lead forth their legions / Like Chaos o'er creation, uncreating" (137–38).

In the last *epode* the Poet addresses as "Great Spirit, deepest Love!" the spirit of beauty that infuses Italy—identifiable with the Spirit of Intellectual Beauty that undergirds both nature and man. As in "Ode to the West Wind" (though with less personal reference) he prays for the success of the revolutionary movement and asks that the Spirit work its will through human agency: "Be man's high hope and unextinct desire / The instrument to work thy will divine!" (168–69). When this happens, the "Celtic wolves" (Austrian soldiers) will flee from the "Ausonian" (Italian) shepherds. Once again Shelley urges the need for solid first principles. Mere activity for its own sake is meaningless; only when revolutionary efforts are truly *radical* (striking at the roots of human evil) by reorienting human drives from egotism to altruism and from hate and pride to love and justice can there be meaningful progress.

III "A Philosophical View of Reform"

Late in 1819, Shelley began a prose treatise entitled "A Philosophical View of Reform." In the "Introduction," he sketches the history of the sentiment for liberty and equality since the end of the Roman Empire. This account parallels "Ode to Liberty" in discussing the contributions to liberty by the Italian communes, the Reformation, and the writers of the Renaissance and the Enlightenment. In the essay Shelley dwells at length upon the beneficial example of the American Revolution and the United States of America. After an analysis of the French Revolution (and its parallels with the English civil wars of the seventeenth century), the chapter comments on the possibilities for reform not only in the countries of Europe but also in India, China, Egypt, Persia, and other areas. At a time when there was almost no organized Zionism, Shelley speculates that "the Jews . . . may reassume their ancestral seats" and predicts a revival of culture in the Turkish domains, including Syria and Arabia, after the demise of the Ottoman empire.[6]

In England, the special focus of his attention, he sees in the revival of a vital literary tradition the chief sign that reform and greatness are at hand:

> The literature of England, an energetic development of which has ever followed or preceded a great and free development of the national will, has arisen, as it were, from a new birth. . . . ours is in intellectual achievements a *memorable age,* and we live among such philosophers and poets as surpass beyond comparison any who have appeared in our nation since its last struggle for liberty. . . . They are the priests of an unapprehended inspiration, the mirrors of gigantic shadows which futurity casts upon the present; the words which express what they conceive not; the trumpet which sings to battle and feels not what it inspires; the influence which is moved not but moves. Poets and philosophers are the unacknowledged legislators of the world. (Julian, VII, 19–20)

Though Shelley was later to plunder from this passage the peroration of "A Defence of Poetry," its meaning becomes clearer in the context of his social philosophy.

The next chapter, "On the Sentiment of the Necessity of Change," surveys the political history of England from the period of the Long Parliament in the mid-seventeenth century (which, Shelley believed, was the last Parliament with any claim to be thought of as representing the various classes of the English people). During the one-hundred-seventy-five-year interval English society had changed so basically that the government now required radical reform. Shelley, who had observed the relations between his grandfather and father and the Duke of Norfolk, recognized the influence exerted by the Lords on the House of Commons. He understood, moreover, that the ruling power preventing reform was not that of the monarchy or regency, but that of an oligarchy of landed and commercial interests: "The power which has increased therefore is the [pow]er of the rich. The name and office of king is merely the mask of this power, and is a kind of stalking-horse used to conceal these 'catchers of men,' whilst they lay their nets. Monarchy is only the string which ties the robber's bundle" (Julian, VII, 25).

Thus Shelley exposed the threat of the class of society from which he himself came and on which his future financial expectations and those of his heirs depended. (Here may be one reason for the Shelley family's failure to publish this pamphlet.) He was concerned with the burden imposed upon the laboring classes (who bore the brunt both of taxation on commodities and of inflated prices) because of 1) the national debt and 2) the government's policy of permitting banks to issue paper money. The national debt, in Shelley's view, had been created to finance "two liberticide wars" against the American and French people and was, therefore, not truly a *national* debt, "but a debt contracted by the whole mass of the privileged classes towards one particular portion of those classes."

Shelley's solution to end the double burden of taxation on the poor (who had to support not only the old landed aristocracy and the established church, but a new aristocracy of money-lenders and bond-holders who collected interest on the debt) is as simple as it is radical:

The property of the rich is mortgaged: to use the language of the law, let the mortgagee foreclose.—

If the principal of this debt were paid, . . . it would be a mere transfer among persons of property. Such a gentleman must lose a third of his estate, such a citizen a fourth of his money in the funds; the persons who borrowed would have paid, and the juggling and complicated system of paper finance be suddenly at an end. (Julian, VII, 35)

Shelley distinguishes between two kinds of property: that which results from "labour and skill is a property of the most sacred and indisputable right," but that which has descended from feudal estates, from appropriations of church property by the king's favorites at the time of the establishment of the Church of England, from trade monopolies given to royal favorites, from financial speculations, or from fraud has less definite rights. In ordinary times, the nation may not find it expedient or necessary to challenge citizens' rights to such property; but, in times of national crisis, such property can be appropriated for the public good. Shelley ends this chapter, however, by urging, not immediate enforcement of the doctrines he has just propounded but restraint and the gradual working out of justice through immediate though limited reform of the Parliament. Keeping the basic principles in mind, the reformed Parliament could relieve first the grossest inequities. Eventually education and experience in self-rule would extend the franchise and further reform the economy.

In the third and last chapter of the fragmentary tract, "Probable Means," Shelley pursues his distinction between the theoretical "rights of man" and the practical instruments of political regulation. Ideally, each man ought to have a direct voice in the government; practically, men elect representatives to exercise that right. So far as property rights are concerned, the "broad principle of political reform is the natural equality of men, not with relation to their property but to their rights. That equality in possessions which Jesus Christ so passionately taught is a moral rather than a political truth and is such as social institutions cannot without mischief inflexibly secure" (Julian, VII, 42). Haste and impatience lead to immature social reforms that bear no fruit. Shelley, therefore, advocates universal adult manhood suffrage, extending the franchise to women only if that step seems practical to others.

The entire burden of Chapter III is that revolution would distort rather than fulfill the impulse for reform. Instead of urging the people to violent measures, Shelley writes:

If Reform shall be begun by the existing government, let us be contented with a limited *beginning*, with any whatsoever opening; let the rotten boroughs be disfranchised and their rights transferred to the unrepresented cities and districts of the Nation; . . . we shall demand more and more with firmness and moderation, never anticipating but never deferring the moment of successful opposition, so that the people may become habituated [to] exercising the functions of sovereignty, in proportion as they acquire the possession of it. (Julian, VII, 46)

"A Philosophical View of Reform" demonstrates both Shelley's sanity in practical matters and the uses of his idealism. Because he kept always in his mind's eye the ideal goal toward which society ought to be steering, he became neither ecstatic at slight ameliorations in social conditions nor unduly depressed at minor reversals. He realized that not *all* changes in the existing system would be for the better, but only those that would contribute lasting rather than expedient temporary benefits. In his "ideal" poems like *Prometheus Unbound* and "Ode to Liberty" he examined the operations of universal laws of change in the moral-political realm; in "The Mask of Anarchy" he suggested immediate action that would not conflict with these distant goals. "A Philosophical View of Reform" elucidates these interrelations between the ideal and the practical, between the morally imperative "ought" and the politically possible "can be."

At the end of September, 1819, the Shelleys left Leghorn for Florence, where they hoped to put Mary under the care of Dr. John Bell, a well-known Scottish surgeon and medical writer who had attended William Shelley during his last illness. When the time arrived for Mary's confinement, however, Dr. Bell himself was seriously ill and had returned to Rome.[7] On November 12, 1819, Mary safely gave birth to a son, her fourth child and the only one to survive his parents. He was named for his father and the city of his birth—Percy Florence Shelley. The child's birth somewhat relieved Mary's depression following William Shelley's death, and his continued good health was one bright feature of the two and a half years before Shelley's death.

IV Shelley and the Urbane Style

Peter Bell the Third, Shelley's most successful attempt at comic verse, was composed October 1819 and sent to Hunt, who was to have it published anonymously.[8] (It first appeared in the second edition of Shelley's *Poetical Works* [1839].) The dedication of this work "To Thomas Brown, Esq." (a pseudonym of Thomas Moore, the Irish lyricist and friend of Byron) sets the tone. Though Shelley enjoyed Moore's writings, he knew that Moore was a popular poetical lightweight whose work could not be compared with the serious productions of the era. Hence, he addresses Moore in his role as "Thomas Brown," historian of *The Fudge Family in Paris,* and inserts this two-sentence paragraph: "Your works, indeed, dear Tom, sell better; but mine are far superior. The public is no judge; posterity sets all to rights" (OSA, p. 347). From the pen of "Miching Mallecho," the supposed author of *Peter Bell the Third,* these words seem humorous; when Shelley repeats their central idea in "A Defence of Poetry" we know that he is in earnest.

Shelley was prompted to write *Peter Bell the Third* by two reviews in Leigh Hunt's *Examiner.* Wordsworth wrote *Peter Bell* in 1798 but did not publish it until 1819, when he prefaced it with a pompous explanation (addressed to Southey) of why he had worked so long on the poem. Because Wordsworth had read *Peter Bell* to a number of friends and literary men, John Hamilton Reynolds (Keats's friend) was able to publish a parody entitled *Peter Bell, Lyrical Ballad* that actually came out before the original. *The Examiner* reviewed the two poems on April 25 and May 2 (Keats being the author of the review of Reynolds' parody), and from this information Shelley decided to write a third poem, this one treating the relation between the poetic career of Wordsworth and the age in which he lived. *Peter Bell the Third* handles a serious idea in a comic spirit.

In the "Prologue" Shelley distinguishes the three Peter Bells: Reynolds' "antenatal Peter" is an unfallen innocent ("Like the soul before it is / Born from *that* world into *this*" [29–30]); Wordsworth's Peter Bell has human moral qualities and must choose between good and evil; Shelley's own Peter Bell is, he says, eternally damned. What Shelley means is that Reynolds' poem is all in good fun, exposing only innocent foibles; Wordsworth's attempts to draw a moral lesson from human experience; and the third Peter Bell is a non-realistic distillation of negative "ideals": Shelley intends to show the subversive aspects of society that trap essentially good men and endanger their moral well-being.

The titles of the seven parts of the poem mark the stages of Peter's corruption: "Death," "The Devil," "Hell," "Sin," "Grace," "Damnation," "Double Damnation." As the poem begins, Wordsworth's Peter Bell has become a Christian of a nonconformist sect:

> His eyes turned up, his mouth turned down;
> His accent caught a nasal twang;
> He oiled his hair; there might be heard
> The grace of God in every word
> Which Peter said or sang.
>
> (6–10)

When he grows old and ill, however, his fellow churchmen, like Job's "friends," tell him that God has cursed him. He responds with an un–Job-like paroxysm of rage that drives everyone else out of his room and almost kills him. According to the local gossip, the Devil comes down in a cloud from Langdale Pike to carry off Peter, body and soul. What actually happened is revealed in "The Devil."

In Part the Second we are told that the Devil is just "what we are," an ordinary man who has so rationalized his behavior that he thinks he has been doing right when he has been participating in a corrupt society. This particular "Devil" had,

> 'Mid the misery and confusion
> Of an unjust war, just made
> A fortune by the gainful trade
> Of giving soldiers rations bad—
>
> (122–25)

He is a gentleman from Grosvenor Square who came to the Lake District "to see what was romantic there." He tells Peter that "he'd bring him to the world of fashion / By giving him a situation / In his own service" (139–41). The parallel between being "in the service" of the Devil and that of a London gentleman continues through the next part. "Hell," Shelley writes,

> is a city much like London—
> A populous and a smoky city;
> There are all sorts of people undone,
> And there is little or no fun done;
> Small justice shown, and still less pity.
> (147–51)

Throughout this section Shelley sketches human sins and follies with a concise precision unmatched in his poetry outside "The Triumph of Life." Parliament, for example, he describes as "a set / Of thieves who by themselves are sent / Similar thieves to represent" (163–65); and he summarizes the activities of the city in these words:

> Thrusting, toiling, wailing, moiling,
> Frowning, preaching—such a riot!
> Each with never-ceasing labour,
> Whilst he thinks he cheats his neighbour,
> Cheating his own heart of quiet.
> . . . .
> And this is Hell—and in this smother
> All are damnable and damned;
> Each one damning, damns the other;
> They are damned by one another,
> By none other are they damned.
>
> 'Tis a lie to say, "God damns!"
> . . . .
>
> Statesmen damn themselves to be
> Cursed; and lawyers damn their souls
> To the auction of a fee;
> Churchmen damn themselves to see
> God's sweet love in burning coals.
> (197–231, *passim*)

Finally, after recounting other ways in which men damn themselves,
Shelley's grim humor turns against himself and his fellow idealistic
reformers:

> And some few, like we know who,
>   Damned—but God alone knows why—
> To believe their minds are given
> To make this ugly Hell a Heaven;
>   In which faith they live and die.
>   (242–46)

In the next part, "Sin," Peter serves as "a footman in the Devil's
service" in Grosvenor Square. Here Peter suddenly shows a flair for
poetry, for

> his was individual mind,
>   And new created all he saw
> In a new manner, and refined
> Those new creations, and combined
>   Them, by a master-spirit's law.
>   (303–7)

But Peter was, from the first, "a kind of moral eunuch"; for he, unlike
Robert Burns, refused to look for the underlying significance of nature.
That is, Peter could have looked on Mont Blanc or on a field mouse
and failed to hear its great voice proclaiming that, in the sight of
nature and nature's God, all men are equal and brothers. Instead, he
continued to serve a patron who was a "heavy, dull, cold thing, / . . .
A drone too base to have a sting; / Who gluts, and grimes his lazy
wing, / And calls lust, luxury" (343–47).

In Part the Fifth, "Grace" comes to Grosvenor Square in the person
of "a mighty poet—and / A subtle-souled psychologist," an idealized
portrait of Coleridge (though with some of the ludicrous qualities attributed to him by Peacock in *Melincourt* and *Nightmare Abbey*).[9] When
this man's expansive talk inspires Peter to think about "the sweet,
strange mystery" of unseen things beyond the phenomenal world, Peter
seems about to emerge from his bondage to the Devil. But his doom
is sealed in Part the Sixth by the hostility of the reviewers, who attack
not only Peter's poetry but his private life: "Peter seduced Mrs. Foy's
daughter, / Then drowned the mother in Ullswater, / The last thing as
he went to bed"; "Is incest not enough? / And must there be adultery

too? / Grace after meat?" (470–72; 478–80). These lines refer not to attacks on Wordsworth, but rather to those that Shelley had just read against himself in a review of *Laon and Cythna* and *Rosalind and Helen* in *The Quarterly Review* for April, 1819. In a sense, then, Shelley sardonically identifies his own career as a poet with that of poor Peter Bell, who, when he is attacked by the critics, cries out,

> "What! . . . this is my reward
> For nights of thought, and days of toil?
> Do poets, but to be abhorred
> By men of whom they never heard,
> Consume their spirits' oil?"
> (493–97)

Shelley jokingly is warning himself (as Peacock had warned him in *Nightmare Abbey*) not to run off into abstruse German metaphysics or prose prefaces. Finally, Peter's despair at not finding public sympathy when he espoused the popular cause leads him unconsciously to compromise his principles. Then "the Reviews, who heaped abuse / On Peter while he wrote for freedom, / So soon as in his song they spy / The folly which soothes tyranny, / Praise him, for those who feed 'em" (619–23).

The upshot is that Peter, having in the sixth part suffered the "Damnation" of having his morals corrupted, in Part the Seventh, "Double Damnation," undergoes the second death of having his talent evaporate. He becomes "Dull—oh, so dull—so very dull!" that

> His sister, wife, and children yawned,
> With a long, slow, and drear ennui,
> All human patience far beyond;
> Their hopes of Heaven each would have pawned,
> Anywhere else to be.
> (713–17)

And, as in Book IV of Pope's *Dunciad*, the chaos of dullness repossesses the world from the creative power of genius until "Seven miles above— below—around— / This pest of dulness holds its sway" (768–69), as all living creatures are driven away or put to sleep by the uncreating power.

Shelley certainly did not think that William Wordsworth had arrived at such a pass. In *Peter Bell the Third* he combined and idealized his feelings toward late tendencies in the writings of Southey, Coleridge, and Wordsworth (and gossip about Wordsworth's political activities) with chagrin at the reviewer's abuse of himself and disappointment at not finding a larger audience for his poetry. To protect his self-esteem, Shelley chose two defenses: The first was a sincere contempt for the reviewers, a distrust of popularity, and a stated willingness to leave the final verdict on his writings to posterity; the second defense was an increasingly ironic attitude toward his own efforts to save the world.

His self-consciousness shows in the Preface to *Prometheus Unbound*: "Let this opportunity be conceded to me of acknowledging that I have, what a Scotch philosopher characteristically terms, 'a passion for reforming the world.' . . ."[10] Maddalo's worldly-wise experience acts as an antidote for the romantic idealism of Julian. The growth of Shelley's "urbanity" marks his increased awareness that not even Mary fully appreciated the works that he considered both his most important and most successful. The wit with which in *Peter Bell the Third* he treats the slanders against his private life—adultery after incest, "grace after meat"—shows how successfully he could objectify his problems by late 1819. Later self-portraits in *Adonais* and in "The Triumph of Life" are painted in more somber colors, but Shelley never again lost the power to distance himself from those portraits, and they become integral to the works of art in which they are embodied.

The verse "Letter to Maria Gisborne" was written July, 1820, while the Gisbornes were in England and the Shelleys were staying in their house at Leghorn. The easy pentameter couplets of the "Letter" show both Shelley's facility at poetizing everyday objects and events and his power to link the trivial to the cosmic. Most memorable are the thumbnail sketches of Godwin, Coleridge, Hunt, Hogg, Peacock, and Horace Smith (196–250)—intellectual companions who could, if they wished, form the nucleus of the ideal society he envisioned. Even in such heartfelt wishes, however, Shelley's wit does not abandon him, and "Letter to Maria Gisborne" is one of his least pretentious and, at the same time, one of his most pleasing poems. Familiar in tone, loose in structure, and clear and simple in diction, it has all the charm of genteel conversation; and it appeals to those who appreciate the role of decorum and civility in both poetry and social relations.[11]

In "The Sensitive Plant," written earlier in 1820 and published with *Prometheus Unbound*, Shelley had used something of the same urbane tone. The poem takes the form of a fable. Man (not Shelley personally) is cast in the role of a "sensitive plant," a kind of mimosa so named because it responds to touch. The world of nature is the garden in which the sensitive plant finds itself. Earl R. Wasserman, in a brilliant analysis of Shelley's poem,[12] has pointed out that all the other flowers mentioned in the poem—snowdrop, violet, windflower (anemone), tulip, narcissus, lily of the valley, hyacinth, rose—are perennials, whereas the sensitive plant is an annual. This distinction partially explains why in Part I the sensitive plant is called "companionless"; man is seen as separated from other natural creatures, and here (contrary to the doctrine in *Queen Mab*) the fable presumes that this isolation results from his inherent qualities and not because he has fallen from a preexistent harmony.

In Part I of the poem, the sensitive plant and the other flowers are harmonized by a spirit generated as "the Spring arose on the garden fair, / Like the Spirit of Love felt everywhere" (I. 5–6). The garden was an "undefilèd Paradise" (I.58) where the flowers "shone smiling to Heaven, and every one / Shared joy in the light of the gentle sun" (I.64–65). Springtime is the age of innocence, before the differences between man and other creatures become paramount. But even at this stage of life,

> the Sensitive Plant which could give small fruit
> Of the love which it felt from the leaf to the root,
> Received more than all, it loved more than ever,
> Where none wanted [lacked] but it, could belong to the giver,—
>
> For the Sensitive Plant has no bright flower;
> Radiance and odour are not its dower;
> It loves, even like Love, its deep heart is full,
> It desires what it has not, the Beautiful!
>
> (I.70–77)

Shelley follows Socrates' discussion of love in Plato's *Symposium*. Shelley's translation of "The Banquet" (*Symposium*) of Plato may be represented by the following quotation from Socrates' dialogue with Agathon: "'Love, therefore, and every thing else that desires anything, desires that which is absent and beyond his reach, that which it has not, that which is not itself, that which it wants; such are the things of which there are desire and love.'"[13]

Using the Platonic myth in his fable, Shelley attributes love to man rather than to other natural creatures. Man alone is unfulfilled within the natural sphere; he appreciates the beauty of natural creation, but cannot contribute to it. On the other hand, at the end of the day when all "the beasts, and the birds, and the insects were drowned / In an ocean of dreams without a sound" (I. 102–3), the sensitive plant heard "the sweet nightingale," "And snatches of its Elysian chant / Were mixed with the dreams of the Sensitive Plant . . ." (I. 108–9).

Part First, then, portrays the human mind in its springtime when man feels in harmony with nature but distinct from it. Part Second recounts the entry into this garden of a "Power" who "to the flowers . . . / Was as God is to the starry scheme" (II. 3–4). This beautiful lady who tends the garden "had no companion of mortal race," but she, too, had sweet dreams, "less slumber than Paradise." This Lady, an earthly manifestation of the ideal, is more a Panthea than an Asia. She is "an Eve in this Eden" (II. 2), a metaphor that conveys the Lady's limitations as well as her grace. Although she tends the garden ("that sublunar Heaven"), carrying away "all killing insects and gnawing worms," she herself, like all sublunar things, seems to be subject to mutability. At the end of Part Second, "she died."

In Part Third, first autumn and then winter come; blossoms and leaves fall, stalks wither, and weeds and parasites overrun the garden. By the next spring, "the Sensitive Plant was a leafless wreck," while "the mandrakes, and toadstools, and docks, and darnels, / Rose like the dead from their ruined charnels," like the perennials they were. Thus ends the narrative part of the fable, though we can presume that the rose, lily, and other perennial flowers also bloomed again. Tacked onto this tale is a "Conclusion" that, as Wasserman has pointed out, seems to be a *non sequitur*; the Poet, in spite of the evidence of his senses, "cannot say" whether the sensitive plant or the spirit within it "felt this change" or whether the "Lady's gentle mind" found sadness, where it left delight."

In this world of illusion and ignorance, continues the Poet, we may adopt a modest yet comforting belief that things are not what they seem, that we in the realm of decay and mutability have changed, not the Lady and the sensitive plant. Shelley suggests, then, that because the five senses and human reason are limited and fallible, the truth is beyond human apprehension or understanding:

> For love, and beauty, and delight,
> There is no death nor change; their might

    Exceeds our organs, which endure
    No light, being themselves obscure.

The symbolic pattern relating the flowers of the "sublunar Heaven" to the stars beyond earthly limitations gives coherence to the poem, subtly preparing the reader for the Conclusion, which is not "logically" but psychologically inevitable.

Shelley's Humean skepticism—the belief that man's knowledge was at best fragmentary—protected his hopes that, in the universe as a whole (if not within the limited range of his own experience), good was stronger than evil. Within the phenomenal world, the good and the beautiful were so transitory that they seemed unable to sustain human aspirations. The "modest creed" expressed at the end of "The Sensitive Plant" is Shelley's declaration that he is unwilling to accept as final the verdict of limited human senses and fallible human reason and that he intends to be guided by the premise that the Good and the Beautiful are ultimately True as well.

V "On Life"

The skeptical position is stated clearly and strongly in "On Life," an essay drafted in the same notebook as "A Philosophical View of Reform." In this brief fragment Shelley praises the "intellectual system" set forth in Sir William Drummond's *Academical Questions* (1805). But even Drummond's skeptical way of looking at experience does not offer solutions, for Shelley writes that "it establishes no new truth, it gives us no additional insight into our hidden nature, neither its action nor itself. Philosophy, impatient as it may be to build, has much work yet remaining. . . . it destroys error, and the roots of error. It leaves, what is too often the duty of the reformer in political and ethical questions to leave, a vacancy. It reduces the mind to that freedom in which it would have acted, but for the misuse of words and signs, the instruments of its own creation" (Julian, VI, 195).

Shelley asserts the primacy of the human mind over all flags, idols, and philosophical systems, which he declares to be merely instruments created by that mind. In "Mont Blanc," the voice of nature had taught the adverting mind that all systems seem equally limited in the face of the deep truth; in "On Life," Shelley asserts the superiority of experience over explanations of that experience. There is no contradiction in saying that human experience is both the ground of all philosophical and religious concepts and that human experience is untrustworthy as a final arbiter of what is true because Shelley is not trying to substitute a system of his own for other systems. He says that the "relations of *things,* remain unchanged, by whatever system"; and he includes in his definition of *things* "any object of thought"—both so-called external objects and ideas, when ideas become objects of other thoughts.

Ultimately, then, Shelley finds experience partial and self-contradictory, but he finds all human systems and explanations of experience limited and unable to account even for all experience. When a man assumes that his system is "true," he enslaves his mind to an arbitrary selection from the data of experience. Systems are at best, therefore, pragmatic constructs that come to terms with the most troublesome data of experience; and, when circumstances change, men must be willing to revise these schemes in the light of the new conditions.

VI *Swellfoot* and "The Witch of Atlas"

Two other long poems of this period, *Œdipus Tyrannus; or Swellfoot the Tyrant* and "The Witch of Atlas," show clearly how Shelley separated his attempts to reach a mass audience from the products of his idealizing imagination. *Swellfoot the Tyrant* was inspired by a scandal in the British royal family and by a chorus of grunting pigs whose noise outside Shelley's summer residence at the Baths of San Giuliano (near Pisa) disturbed his recitation on August 24, 1820, of one of his odes. The subject is the divorce trial of "Queen" Caroline, the ugly German princess who was married to the Prince of Wales in 1795, who had one daughter (the Princess Charlotte of Shelley's prose address), and who had gone her own way after the Prince (George IV to be) had returned to the arms of Mrs. Fitzherbert, his mistress. From 1814 onward, Princess Caroline had wandered about France and Italy; but, when in 1820 old George III died and the Prince Regent prepared for his coronation, his wife returned to England to claim her rights as queen. At this time, George began divorce proceedings on the grounds of adultery, a charge contested not only by Caroline herself but by the English Whigs, who saw another opportunity to discredit the reactionary monarch and his Tory supporters. Castlereagh, the Foreign Secretary, appointed the so-called "Milan Commission" to gather evidence against the would-be queen.[14]

Shelley's satire was published anonymously by J. Johnston, Cheapside; after a few copies had been sold, the remainder of the edition was suppressed on the threat of prosecution brought by a member of the Society for the Suppression of Vice.[15] The plot of the two-act burlesque is too slight to dwell on, but the modern reader can profit from knowing that the various characters are meant to represent certain celebrities. Swellfoot is, of course, George IV; Iona Taurina, Queen Caroline; "the Swinish Multitude," the English people; and the Minotaur (as he identifies himself), John Bull. Mammon is Lord Liverpool, the Prime Minister at the time; Purganax is a Greek-root translation of Castlereagh; Dakry (from Greek *dakru,* a tear) is Lord Eldon, the Lord Chancellor;[16] Laoctonos (Greek for "people killer") is the Duke of Wellington; the Leech, the Gadfly, and the Rat have been identified with the Vice-Chancellor Sir John Leach, William Cooke, and Lieutenant-Colonel Browne, respectively, all members of the Milan Commission;[17] Moses, the Sow-gelder, is Thomas Malthus, whose advocacy of birth control as a substitute for political reform was an anathema to Shelley and other reformers. The identifications of Solomon, the Porkman, and Zephaniah, the Pig-butcher, are less clear; since Moses, Solomon, and Zephaniah are all said to be Jews, David Ricardo and Nathan Meyer Rothschild might be intended—Ricardo, because Shelley distrusted his economic theories, and Rothschild, as a symbol of the new financial aristocracy that Shelley attacks in "A Philosophical View of Reform."

"The Witch of Atlas," written at the Baths of San Giuliano August 14–16, 1820, represents the opposite extreme of Shelley's art from "The Mask of Anarchy," but it shares the urbane tone of other poems of 1820 like "Letter to Maria Gisborne" and *Swellfoot,* and it shares with *Peter Bell the Third* certain reactions to Wordsworth's *Peter Bell.*[18] "The Witch" differs from all these, however, by returning to the mythopoeic mode of *Prometheus Unbound.* An examination of "To a Skylark" and "The Cloud" (two poems written earlier in 1820 and published with *Prometheus*) may serve as introductory to a consideration of "The Witch of Atlas."

"To a Skylark" has three main parts: in lines 1–30 the skylark (a bird that sings loudly while flying straight up in the air, often until it is lost to view in a haze or bright sunlight) is addressed as something more than a bird—"an unbodied joy" or "a star of Heaven," its song keen as the rays of that "silver sphere," the morning star. In the second part (31–60) the Poet, asserting that "we know not" what the symbolic bird is, tries to find the closest sublunar equivalent. He compares it in turn with poet, high-born maiden, glow-worm, rose, and showers—

in short, he moves from human life through lower animal, vegetable, and mineral creation.

This inverse order of comparison suggests again the unanswerability of the question and leads to the final section, in which the Poet ceases his questioning and accepts the value of the imaginative inspiration represented by the bird. "Teach us, Sprite or Bird" (whichever you are), the source of your inspiration: "What objects are the fountains / Of thy happy strain? / . . . What love of thine own kind? what ignorance of pain?" We men "look before and after, / And pine for what is not: . . . / Our sweetest songs are those that tell of saddest thought." Coleridge in "Kubla Khan" had promised that, could he revive within himself the "symphony and song" of his earlier visions, he would write poetry so powerful that men would be afraid of him; Shelley does not believe that poetic inspiration would separate him from other men but would attract them: "The world should listen then—as I am listening now."

A similar analogy underlies "The Cloud." At the first level, the poem presents a mythopoeic autobiography of a cloud. But for Shelley the cloud was an analogue of the human mind, and in this poem the unstated comparison is with the life-cycle of the human soul. Each stanza portrays an individual state of a cloud according to the best meteorology of Shelley's day;[19] and, at the same time, the interrelations between the cloud and other symbolic elements express various conditions of the human spirit. For example, the interaction between sun and cloud in the third stanza occurs at sunrise and sunset, when the sun's rays are most refracted and distorted, indicating that the human mind is illuminated only partially and imperfectly by the light of divine creativity. In the next stanza the moon (of reason) opens gaps in the cloud that enable the earth to see the stars (the spirits of the noble dead) and permit the mortal medium of water to reflect the moon and stars.

The fifth stanza alludes, once again, to the cloud's characteristic distorting and blotting of heavenly bodies from sublunar view. The cloud's "triumphal arch" is the "million-coloured" rainbow, which figures in several poems as the sign of limited and distorted earthly knowledge. In the end, the cloud declares itself a "daughter of Earth and Water" but a "nursling of the Sky": that is, the mind is fundamentally sublunar and limited but has been inspired by divine creative energy. When the cloud further says, "I change, but I cannot die," Shelley portrays through myth both the perpetuation of imaginative creativity and the persistent limitations of all sublunar manifestations of that divine energy.

The Witch of Atlas presents a somewhat more exalted parentage than the cloud: a daughter of the Sun and "one of the Atlantides," she was born in that idyllic age before "incestuous Change" had given birth to the "cruel Twins . . . Error and Truth," who destroyed all myths and fables. The pre-scientific, pre-literal age of her birth frees the Witch from being judged by rules of probability or by the manners of any historical age. She is purely mythopoeic, an experiment in a kind of poetry that, Shelley says in his "Defence of Poetry," is found only infrequently: "Few poets of the highest class have chosen to exhibit the beauty of their conceptions in its naked truth and splendour; and it is doubtful whether the alloy of costume, habit, &c., be not necessary to temper this planetary music for mortal ears."[20]

The Witch herself is a sublunar embodiment of the ideal. At her birth, the animals and nature deities come to worship her. "Universal Pan" himself "passed out of his everlasting lair / Where the quick heart of the great world doth pant" (117–18) to encounter the Witch, who seemed to be of similar power but more divine than this supreme spirit of nature. The lady was beautiful, and her beauty seemed to eclipse the beauties of the natural world—"everything beside / Seemed like the fleeting image of a shade" (138–39). When the lady knew her power, she wove a veil from mist, light, and starbeams that shaded "the splendour of her love" from earthly creatures. Her cavern was stored with sounds, visions, odors, and "liquors clear and sweet" (stanzas xiv–xvii)—in short, things appealing to each of the senses except touch, the most mundane—as well as with scrolls that taught how "men . . . might win that happy age / Too lightly lost, redeeming native vice" (188–89). She possessed the qualities and knowledge that could lift men out of their inert slavery to surrounding impressions by making them desire a better life and by showing them the means to attain it. The "wizard maid" refused to associate with the nature deities because they were subject to time and mutability, whereas she was immortal. Instead, she sat aloof, studying ancient writings and adding to them new poetic effects (249–56).

The Witch's one outlet from her self-contained existence was a boat (of uncertain origin but associated with Venus or her child, Love), which moved by means of its internal "living spirit." Into the boat she put a hermaphrodite that she had created by kneading "fire and snow." This self-contained creature embodied a reconciliation of opposites such as Coleridge in *Biographia Literaria* (1817) had said lay at the heart of poetry: it combined the ideals of male and female beauty (that of Hermes and Aphrodite) that appears in Aristophanes' myth of the androgyne (in Plato's *Symposium*), in Ovid's *Metamorphoses,* and frequently in sculptures of the Italian Renaissance. The hermaphrodite, in short, represents that perfected creation that lacks nothing and, therefore, has no need for love, no reason to seek the good or the beautiful outside itself.

By developing this myth, Shelley affirms once again his belief in the existence—or at least the possibility—of a Spirit of Intellectual Beauty. But in "The Witch of Atlas" he implies no sense of personal relationship with this spirit. Such a spirit *could* redeem human life, but the Witch of Atlas, for all her beauty, does far less: She plays pranks; she toys with both nature and man. This poem, in spite of the grace and lightness of its *ottava rima* stanzas, is (when set in the context of Shelley's thought and art) ironic in the root meaning of the word "irony." The poet and his readers, being human, can understand the full implications of the goddess's fun and games, but she cannot. As she floats down the Nile, she can mingle with the dreams of human souls, a power denied to man-created deities like Aurora, Venus, and Proserpine; but she "doth not know its value yet" (584).

Shelley's myth includes, however, an intimation of change in the attitude of the Witch: "'Tis said in after times her spirit free / Knew what love was, and felt itself alone—" (585–86). She could give the most beautiful souls—like the Youth in *Alastor* or Rousseau in "The Triumph of Life"—"strange panacea in a crystal bowl" which caused them to live "as if some control, / Mightier than life, were in them" so that they welcomed death. It was in her power to foil evil plans, causing soldiers, for example, to beat "their swords to ploughshares." But she did not end war or pursue any consistent plan of reform; having absolute power over evil, she was content to toy with it like a cat with a mouse or a child with a butterfly, catching it and letting it go as her mood changed.

The tone of "The Witch of Atlas" is, on the surface, playful throughout. In the dedicatory stanzas "To Mary," Shelley demands freedom for himself to vacation from his poetry of high seriousness and to play like a kitten or act the part of an ephemera ("silken-wingèd fly") instead of a swan. Stanza iii of the dedication alludes to *The Revolt of Islam,* which Shelley had dedicated to Mary in high seriousness only three years before, only to have it smothered beneath a wave of hostile criticism;

now, overcome by the sense of the untimely death of that "wingèd Vision," Shelley asks that he not be deluded by more false hopes: "O, let me not believe / That anything of mine is fit to live!" The final three stanzas of the dedication compare the Witch of Atlas to Wordsworth's Peter Bell, and Shelley declares that, though his Witch "is not so sweet a creature / As Ruth or Lucy" of Wordsworth's earlier poems, she surpasses Peter. For Peter, whom Wordsworth sets up as an ethical example, is the product of a narrow, dogmatic morality rather than a truly imaginative one. If the reader unveils Shelley's Witch, he will fall in love with her to the extent that love "becomes idolatry" (though whether this constitutes a sin or not, Shelley refuses to say). Shelley, then, sees the Witch—this infusion of the divine spirit into the sublunar realm of nature and mankind—as an ideal, completely beautiful to mortal eyes.

But he sees her at the same time as potentially dangerous because she is beyond human good and evil. She at once frees man from his narrow categories and betrays him into desires and expectations too great for fulfillment within the world he inhabits—desires and expectations which she, as an immortal, cannot feel and for which she takes no responsibility. Shelley in this poem stands back from his *beau idéal* to make clear that mortal eyes may not gaze upon the immortal with impunity. Yet he has not allowed his perspective as a limited human being to distort his appreciation of the *beau idéal* that his imagination conceives. In "To Autumn" Keats embodied his acceptance of man's nature and destiny as he conceived it—merely a natural creature among other creatures; Shelley in like manner in "The Witch of Atlas" demonstrates his acceptance of a quite different view of human life. Were man merely a child of nature, Shelley would not even recognize a problem; animals and flowers do not curse their destiny. Man's vision of the ideal is what makes his life difficult, and that vision itself rather than the natural cycle is, in a sense, the villain.

In "The Witch" Shelley accepts the ideal as a good *in itself* without dwelling on (though he alludes to) the implications that its relation to the world holds for men. "The Witch of Atlas" marks the maturity of Shelley's vision. From this serious holiday, he could return to the central human dilemma without self-pity and embody in art his answer to the problem facing limited men who can conceive illimitable ideals: This answer was that man can best fulfill himself through his experience of great art.

Chapter Seven
Built beyond the Grave

On October 20, 1820, Shelley accompanied Claire Clairmont to Florence, where it had been arranged that she should live in the home of Dr. Bojti, one of the physicians to the Grand Duke of Tuscany. Shelley returned to the Baths of San Giuliano (near Pisa) on October 22, but three days later heavy rains caused flooding there; the household, now including Shelley's cousin Thomas Medwin, evacuated by boat and returned to Pisa, where they rented a *palazzo* along the Arno. Medwin's account of Shelley's intellectual habits of 1820–22 gives valuable testimony, corroborated in the poet's letters, that Shelley studied the supremely great artists in each literature and thereby chose for himself the finest literary models of the Western world. Shelley gave Medwin a list of books that belong in a well-chosen library, naming the Bible, "the Greek plays," English Renaissance drama, and the works of Plato, Bacon, Shakespeare, Milton, Goethe, Schiller, Dante, Petrarch, Boccaccio, Machiavelli, Guicciardini, and Calderón.

I "A Defence of Poetry"

Shelley's view of the importance of creative artists in the history of civilization is set forth in his finest prose work, "A Defence of Poetry," which he wrote during February and March, 1821, as an answer to "The Four Ages of Poetry," Peacock's brilliant satirical essay that had appeared in the single issue of Ollier's *Literary Miscellany* (1820).[1] According to Peacock, poetry passes through four ages analogous to the ages of man: an age of iron, in which all is crude and untutored (the period of folk-ballads and romances, primitive and Medieval); an age of gold, in which the natural genius is full blown in the larger epic and tragic forms (fifth-century Athens and Renaissance Europe); a silver age, in which the luxuriant growth of the imagination is pruned and given rules (the times of Virgil and Lucretius, of Dryden and Pope); and an age of bronze, in which poetry returns to an artificial simplicity, a second childhood of senility (the declining Classical period and, in England, the current age of Wordsworth, Scott, Byron, *et al.*). Peacock declared that, as civilization and science increased, the role of poetry became smaller and smaller until literature became a waste of time for intelligent men, who could be devoting themselves to the natural or social sciences. This attack provoked Shelley to state his mature view of the role of poetry in the life of the individual and of society.

In the opening paragraph of the "Defence," Shelley distinguishes between reason, the analytic operation of the human mind, and imagination, the synthetic process; reason enumerates known quantities, while imagination combines and perceives the value of these quantities. Next, Shelley says that "poetry, *in a general sense,*" is "the expression of the imagination" (italics added). Because all aspects of human civilization derive from the operation of the imagination, "language, colour, form, and religious and civil habits of action . . . may be called poetry by that figure of speech which considers the effect as a synonyme of the cause. But *poetry in a more restricted sense* expresses those arrangements of language, and especially metrical language, which are created by [the imagination]. . . . And this springs from the nature itself of language, which is a more direct representation of the actions and passions of our internal being, and . . . is more plastic and obedient to the control of that faculty of which it is the creation" (Paragraph 5, italics added). In the other arts and in religious or civil institutions, the imagination encounters arbitrary obstacles that "interpose between conception and expression."

Shelley says clearly that the only art that can be called *poetry* consists of imaginative "arrangements of language, and especially metrical language." Even when he calls Plato and Bacon poets, he does so on the basis of the qualities in their language; and, to make this irreplaceable criterion clearer, he states: "All the authors of revolutions in opinion are not necessarily poets as they are inventors, nor even as their words unveil the permanent analogy of things by images . . . ; but *as their periods are harmonious and rhythmical, and contain in themselves the elements of verse . . .*" (Paragraph 8, italics added).

Peacock and Shelley agreed, then, that poetry and other products of the imagination (scientific thought, political theory) compete for the imaginative energy of the human mind. Shelley, however, wished to justify poetry as the highest and most useful expression of the imagination. He began to do so by saying that language, the arbitrary product of the imagination, can give expression to it more directly and faithfully than can materials produced by nature (the sculptor's stone, the scientist's chemicals, the economist's crops and people).

Having defined "poetry" in the first ten paragraphs, Shelley turns in paragraphs eleven to thirty-one to show, through a chronological study of the relations between literature and society, that "Poetry is ever found to coexist with whatever other arts contribute to the happiness and perfection of man" (Paragraph 14). There is an especially close relationship between drama ("poetry in its most perfect and universal form" [Paragraph 16]) and the morality of a society. Epic poetry, on the other hand, though not so accurate an index of the current moral health of a society as the drama, indicates the relation of a society's past to its future. The epics of Homer, Dante, and Milton "bore a defined and intelligible relation to the knowledge and sentiment and religion and political conditions of the age in which [each poet] lived, and of the ages which followed it" (Paragraph 28). Thus Homer paved the way for Greek greatness by embodying in his epics all the best elements of the heroic age; Dante linked the best of Medieval religion and the courtly love tradition with the Renaissance and Reformation; and Milton, knowingly or unconsciously, pioneered the Enlightenment by his questioning of old dogmas, while preserving the imaginative heritage of the Classical and Christian traditions.[2]

In paragraphs 32–42 Shelley argues against Peacock's standard of "utility." He agrees that *pleasure* is the measure of good, but declares (as John Stuart Mill was later to do) that there are two different kinds of pleasure, one based solely on the "wants of our animal nature" and the other, "durable, universal and permanent," that, though "difficult to define," is found "often wholly unalloyed" in such forms as "the delight of love and friendship, the ecstasy of the admiration of nature, the joy of the perception and still more of the creation of poetry . . ." (Paragraphs 32, 34). Poetry can give a man pleasure within his narrow sphere of time and place as "it creates anew the universe, after it has been annihilated in our minds by the recurrence of impressions blunted by reiteration" and it can also defeat "the curse which binds us to be subjected to the accident of surrounding impressions" (Paragraph 42).

Paragraphs 43–45 take up a subject that has been raised earlier— the nature of the poet. Here Shelley asserts that the best poets have been the best men, though they, too, have had weak moments. Whenever the involuntary creative inspiration fails, poets, who are more familiar with high points of pleasure than other men, frequently pursue pleasure in forms that prove to be illusory.

Shelley concludes with a promise to write a defense of the poetry of his own age. Since poetic inspiration is involuntary, even those poets (like Wordsworth) who may consciously support the side of reaction are allies in the struggle for liberty: "it is less their spirit than the spirit of the age" (Paragraph 48). In the context of the upsurge of liberty that he had discussed in "A Philosophical View of Reform," Shelley can repeat his assertion that "Poets are the unacknowledged legislators of the world." From the utterances of the poet who is closely attuned to his own inner creative universe, the world gets a picture of the new religious, political, and social order that is both the natural consequence of past history and the unuttered desire of the people.

"A Defence of Poetry" is the natural outgrowth of Shelley's thinking during the period of *Prometheus Unbound, The Cenci,* and the miscellaneous poems of 1819–20. Poetry by its beauty engenders human love (which is defined as "a going out of our own nature, and an identification of ourselves with the beautiful which exists in thought, action, or person, not our own" ["Defence," Paragraph 13]); and poetry is seen as the highest product of human endeavor, producing unalloyed, virtuous pleasure both in its creation and in its appreciation. Whereas Shelley earlier had set as his goal some specific amelioration in human history (improvement of conditions in Ireland, or reform of Parliament) or a relationship of mutual love and understanding with one or more fellow human beings (Hogg, Harriet Westbrook, Mary Godwin), he from this time forward had his mind clearly set on the distinction between the inalienable limitations of the phenomenal world and the potentialities for perfection in the realm of poetry, which "makes us the inhabitants of a world to which the familiar world is a chaos" ("Defence," Paragraph 42). We should keep this development in mind when reading *Epipsychidion,* one of Shelley's best but most misunderstood poems.

II *Epipsychidion*

On November 29, 1820, Claire and Mary were introduced to Teresa Viviani,[3] daughter of the Governor of Pisa; Teresa was confined in a girls' school at the Convent of St. Anna until her father could arrange for her marriage. Mary, Claire, and Shelley all visited and corresponded regularly with the nineteen-year-old girl from the time of this first introduction until her marriage ten months later; for Teresa's intelligence and the seeming neglect by her parents won their sympathy.

Teresa's plight stirred Shelley's imagination and inspired him to idealize her as "Emily" in *Epipsychidion*. Shelley composed the poem in late January and early February, 1821. On February 16 he sent it to Ollier, specifying that it was "to be published simply for the esoteric few . . . in the simplest form, and merely one hundred copies."[4] It appeared—anonymously as Shelley had requested—during the summer of 1821.

The ultimate subject of the poem is suggested by its title, *"epipsy-chidion"* being a Greek word of Shelley's coinage that means, "concerning the dear little soul." The poem explores the origin, nature, and function of the central core of meaning and value within the human *psyche*. In his essay "On Love" Shelley had described this *psychidion* clearly and exactly: "We dimly see within our intellectual nature a miniature as it were of our entire self, yet deprived of all that we condemn or despise, the ideal prototype of every thing excellent or lovely that we are capable of conceiving as belonging to the nature of man." This is the *beau idéal* whose origin Shelley had described in his Preface to *Alastor*. The imaginative individual creates from the external impressions of natural beauty and human civilization an ideal of perfection within himself and then seeks to find its embodiment in the external world; if he is sensitive and if his ideal is worthy of the name, its quality exceeds anything in the external phenomenal world and all his attempts at sustained relationship with it during human life are doomed.

Shelley's mythmaking poems like "To a Skylark" and "The Witch of Atlas" had, however, stimulated another train of thought: If the *beau idéal* was the internal manifestation of the human imagination, its ideal antitype in the external world must also be a product of that same imagination. Because the external objectification of this inner ideal was poetry itself, the most nearly direct expression of the imagination, poetry must be the most worthy object of human love.

Epipsychidion has three major movements, followed by the Poet's short address to his poem. The first (1–189), corresponding to the *protasis* of a drama, identifies the "characters" and defines the terms. This division, in turn, contains some sections addressed to "Emily" and some to a "Stranger," the reader of the poem. Emily is a woman idealized (as in *Song of Songs*) beyond her actual nature into a portrait of the antitype for which the *beau idéal* within the Poet is seeking. The first line invokes her as a "Spirit" that is "Sister" of the Poet's "orphan [spirit]." She becomes, successively, a "poor captive bird," "high, spirit-wingèd Heart," and "seraph of Heaven! too gentle to be human";

in these and other metaphors the Poet invokes her aid in bringing his poem to perfection: "I pray thee that thou blot from this sad song / All of its much mortality and wrong."

This purifying of the poem is to be achieved, curiously, through the *tears* ("those clear drops") of Emily, who will weep "till sorrow becomes ecstasy: / Then smile on [this sad song], so that it may not die" (35–40). Shelley seems to be saying in this forty-line invocation that Emily's sorrow is necessary to the perfection of his poem, as he has said earlier that the poem will be the fulfillment of her desire: "This song shall be thy rose: its petals pale / Are dead, indeed, my adored Nightingale! / But soft and fragrant is the faded blossom, / And it has no thorn left to wound thy bosom" (9–12). The "thorns of *life*" mentioned in "Ode to the West Wind" are absent from art, which, though "dead," has been purified of "all we condemn or despise." The "seraph of Heaven" does not appear before the Poet in her unearthly brightness, but rather, has veiled "beneath that radiant form of Woman" all that mortality is unable to bear, and even this "veiled Glory" (26) is further obscured by the Poet's "dim words," though they "flash, lightning-like, with unaccustomed glow" (33–34).

The intricate relationships here expressed between *life* and the *Ideal*, on the one hand, and *life* and *poetry*, on the other, are somewhat as follows: when the Ideal is projected into life, it is inevitably veiled and distorted; "becoming" thus turns the Ideal itself into a prisoner beating its "unfeeling bars with vain endeavour" and, hence, an occasion for sorrow and weeping. The poem preserves the beauty of life while removing the sorrows (the thorns), but it lacks the vitality that characterizes both the creative Ideal and its living human projection. Thus the human being and the poem possess (in limited measure) the complementary attributes of ideal perfection—life exhibits its vitality, art its formal order.

In the subsequent passage the Poet declares that he loves Emily because she embodies "youth's vision thus made perfect." He goes on to compare her, once again in a number of metaphors, to "a well," "a Star," "a Solitude, a Refuge, a Delight"; but he must finally admit the limits of human poetic powers: "I measure / The world of fancies, seeking one like thee, / And find—alas! mine own infirmity" (69–71). To recapitulate: Emily is a mortal embodiment of the immortal Ideal, but the very act of embodying implies a limitation which is paralleled by an equivalent limitation of poetic expression; neither the *person* nor the *poem* fully expresses the vision that inspires it.

The opening seventy-one lines were addressed to Emily's spirit, but the Poet addresses his next verse paragraph to his unknown reader ("She met me, *Stranger,* upon life's rough way"), telling how the ideal vision lured him toward Death as Day lures Night and Spring lures Winter; she who possessed "light, life, peace" attracted him, who lacked these things, inspiring in him *eros,* love for the good and beautiful absent from self or, as Shelley was later to characterize it,

> The desire of the moth for the star,
> Of the night for the morrow,
> The devotion to something afar
> From the sphere of our sorrow.
>   (OSA, p. 645)

Such love, which kills "the sense with passion" and is "too deep / For the brief fathom-line of thought or sense," is not lust but the pursuit of Beauty far more universal than fleshly beauty.

If his spirit had worshipped Emily's spirit either before birth or after death, says the Poet, people would not misinterpret the relationship (as they now do), but he determines not to remain silent but to "beacon the rocks on which high hearts are wrecked." Lines 147–59 argue for free love, but love as it has already been defined—a pursuit of the Ideal, something too deep for either "thought or sense." This "true Love" differs from materials like "gold and clay" because it can multiply itself and because to divide it among many is not to diminish anyone's share in it. Mind differs from "its object" (that which it contemplates), and good differs from evil in this respect: "If you divide pleasure and love and thought, / Each part exceeds the whole," and "this truth" is what gives hope to those who work to repair the ravaged garden of "this world of life" (174–89).

The second major movement of *Epipsychidion* (190–387) is the Poet's idealized autobiography. First (190–216) he discusses his early youth, when vague intimations of the Ideal were shaped by the records of past human achievements ("whatever checks that Storm / Which with the shattered present chokes the past" [211–12]) and by "that best philosophy" which makes "our life" ("this cold common hell") a fate "as glorious as a fiery martyrdom" (213–15). In plain language, the Poet says that the "best philosophy" is one that looks on human sufferings as meaningful rather than meaningless; that is, the "best philosophy" is the philosophy of Julian rather than Maddalo, hope rather than despair.

In the second—and most important—paragraph of the second movement (217–66), the Poet recounts (as he did in "Hymn to Intellectual Beauty" and in the Dedication to *The Revolt of Islam*) how his moral nature sprang suddenly into being. But here he makes clear that what occurred was not simply *moral* but *personal* as well; what sprang forth was not simply the Poet's ethical nature but his very *ego:* "Then, from the caverns of my dreamy youth / *I* sprang" (217–18, italics added). The vision of the Ideal was "the lodestar of my one desire" (219), a magnet that polarized the disparate elements of the *psyche* into a unified, integrated personality. When the Ideal, "She, whom prayers or tears then could not tame," first disappeared "into the dreary cone of our life's shade," the Poet wished to follow her even beyond the grave; but, when a voice said, "the phantom is beside thee whom thou seekest," he continued to pursue "this soul out of [his] soul" (238). The Poet's prayers and poems were unable to liberate the projection of his idealized self-conception from "the night which closed on her," but neither could the same prayers or verse "uncreate / That world within this Chaos, mine and me . . . / The world I say of thoughts that worshipped her" (241–45).

Here Shelley articulates an idea that had heretofore been implicit rather than explicit in his works—that there is a distinction within the human personality between "me," an organized universe of values, and "mine," the chaos of disparate, unorganized, and rebellious thoughts and passions. Later in the poem, in the opening lines of the third movement, the Poet makes this distinction again, reiterating that his love for "Emily" is the love of his internal *"psychidion"* (an imaginative universe within him that projects a pattern of purpose and value on the universe) for her central soul:

> To whatsoe'er of dull mortality
> Is *mine,* remain a vestal sister still;
> To the intense, the deep, the imperishable,
> Not *mine* but *me,* henceforth be thou united
> Even as a bride, delighting and delighted.
> (389–93; italics added)

Although Shelley did not conceive of the *libido, ego,* and *superego* in Freudian terms, he clearly distinguished between the central core of human personality and the peripheral, random energy and appetites of mind and body. "On Life" and "A Defence of Poetry" show his belief that the elements of the human "value-personality" sprang from the unconscious and, hopefully, derived ultimately from a great unknown spiritual force that underlay all creation. But, within the confused and distorted realm of phenomenal experience, these values could be promoted only insofar as the value-personality ruled consciously over all aspects of human life, examining, judging, and either approving or refusing to permit various ideas and emotions to be expressed in words or actions.

The Poet continues his autobiography (ll. 246 ff.) by telling how, soon after encountering his vision of the Ideal, he sought in "the wintry forest of our life," among other young people ("those untaught foresters"), one resembling that vision. He describes "One, whose voice was venomed melody," who "sate by a well," whose "touch was as electric poison," whose looks sent flame into his vitals, and whose "cheeks and bosom" sent "a killing air, which pierced like honey-dew / Into the core of my green heart" (256–64). Collation of this section of *Epipsychidion* with autobiographical references in other poems and with evidence from early letters and Medwin's biography (the only one by a person who knew him in his pre-Oxford days) suggests that Shelley here refers to his first romance with his cousin Harriet Grove. The phrases that some commentators have elaborated into confessions of an encounter with a prostitute and a bout with venereal disease say simply, when the metaphors are stripped away, that, while seeking the ideal vision among real people, Shelley encountered a girl who aroused him sexually (not a surprising event during adolescence). In the context of the distinction between "I" or "me" and "mine," such an arousing of sexual desires becomes a dangerous event because it distracts the Poet's *psychidion* from its quest for its antitype. During adolescence, then, Shelley confused his normal sexual desires with his idealistic goals and rationalized passions into principles. Lines 256–66 tell how his moral vision became confused with passions that he sees in retrospect to have been quite extraneous to it.

In the passage that follows Shelley tells how he "rashly sought" an embodiment of his ideal "in many mortal forms":[5] some, perhaps Harriet Westbrook and Cornelia Turner, were fair; some, probably Elizabeth Hitchener and Mrs. Boinville, were wise; "One was true—oh! why not true to me?"—either a reference to Harriet Westbrook Shelley and Shelley's suspicions about infidelity on her part, or perhaps an allusion to Harriet Grove. Adapting a Shakespearean simile, Shelley writes: "as a hunted deer . . . / I turned upon my thoughts, and stood at bay,"[6] until there came deliverance in the shape of the Moon—Mary Godwin. Under her beautiful but cold influence, he was like the passive sea. The next paragraph (308–20) alludes to Harriet's suicide by drowning ("when She, / The Planet of that hour, was quenched"), to the Chancery Court suit that deprived Shelley of his children ("what earthquakes made it gape and split") initiated by Eliza Westbrook (the "Tempest"), and to Mary's continuing loving care of him ("the white Moon smiling all the while"). "At length" Shelley encountered another woman, described as Dante described Matilda in *Purgatorio* xxviii. This creature, "soft as an Incarnation of the Sun," called to the Poet's spirit, "and the dreaming clay / Was lifted by the thing that dreamed below / As smoke by fire" (335–40). That is, the imaginative dreamer within the Poet elevated or oriented his entire being.

The Poet, now in the present tense (345–83), addresses the "twin Spheres of light" (Mary, the Moon, and Emily, the Sun) who rule him and asks a "Comet beautiful and fierce" (Claire Clairmont) to "float into our azure heaven again" and become "Love's folding-star" (Venus, as Hesperus, the Evening Star). Finally, to conclude the second movement, the Poet asks his lady to perfect his "flowers of thought" into fruit "as of the trees of Paradise."

The last third of the poem, envisioning an imaginary elopement of the Poet and Emily to an island paradise similar to the one described at the end of "Lines written among the Euganean Hills," derives from Dante's sonnet to Guido Cavalcante (Shelley's translation of which had appeared in the *Alastor* volume). But to the metaphor of an effortless flight by boat is added one of sexual union to express the sense of freedom and complete mutual understanding between the Poet and his *beau idéal*. Shelley had, of course, earlier used the metaphor of sexual union for similar purposes in *Alastor* and *The Revolt of Islam* (as Keats had in *Endymion*). But, whereas in those narratives another protagonist was involved, in *Epipsychidion* the Poet, speaking in the first person, has the boldness to use sexual intercourse as a metaphor for the marriage of true minds: "to whatsoe'er of dull mortality / Is mine [his body], remain a vestal sister still." This passage is replete with mythic geography, including allusions to the Saturnian Golden Age and to Milton's Garden of Paradise. Shelley, in fact, strains for figures of speech to convey the idea of the union between his own *psychidion* and that of Emily, its antitype. But, at the end, mere human expression is inadequate to the vision:

> Woe is me!
> The wingèd words on which my soul would pierce
> Into the height of Love's rare Universe,

Are chains of lead around its flight of fire—
I pant, I sink, I tremble, I expire!

This moment of failure is, however, not the end of the story; in the three main movements of *Epipsychidion* Shelley had identified "Emily" as the human incarnation of the Ideal, recounted the history of his search for that antitype to his own central being, and proposed that his *psychidion* and that of Emily be joined in a union uninhibited either by social conventions or by the very encumbrances of flesh and blood. In the *envoi*, however, the Poet makes clear—as he has hinted throughout the poem—that the real achievement of his inner being lies in its projection of itself, not in a pseudo-erotic union with a woman's soul, but in the creation of the poem. He writes: "Weak Verses, go, kneel at your Sovereign's [Emily's] feet, / And say:—'We [the verses] are the masters of thy slave [the poet].'" He then commands them to call their "sisters" (his other poems) "from Oblivion's cave"—all the verses singing: "'Love's very pain is sweet, / But [Love's] reward is in the world divine / Which, if not here, [Love] builds beyond the grave.' / So [in such a manner—singing, etc.] shall ye [verses] live when I am there [in the grave]."

Shelley says, therefore, that his love—the sacred rage for order that has oriented his life toward a vision of the Ideal—has enabled him to create, even through his pain, a divine world that will live when he is in the grave. Like Keats in "Ode on a Grecian Urn," Shelley says that, when old age shall this generation waste, his poems will remain, friends to man, to whom they will say, "Love's very pain is sweet"—and, though this immortality of art is all that man can know on earth, it is all that he really needs to know in order to participate in the timeless and immortal realm.

The closest literary analogue to *Epipsychidion* is, as Shelley hints in the Advertisement, *La vita nuova* of Dante. In that narrative Dante comes to the conclusion that, because it may be beyond his power to possess Beatrice or even to win from her recognition of his love, he will base his happiness on something that *is* within his power:

Then I said to them: "Ladies, the end and aim of my love formerly lay in the greeting of this lady. . . . But since it pleased her to deny it to me, my lord, Love, through his grace, has placed all my bliss in something that can not fail me." . . . And after these ladies had spoken among themselves awhile, that lady who had first addressed me spoke to me again, saying: "We beg you to tell us wherein this bliss of yours now lies." And I answered her by saying: "In those words that praise my lady."[7]

Shelley had come to realize that, whereas he was, perhaps, seeking in a mortal form something that must, ultimately, remain eternal, and whereas union with that Ideal was impossible, he could place all his happiness in something that could not fail him—in his poems, those words that praise the Ideal.

The mundane Teresa Viviani was not, as Shelley realized by the time he published his poem, a model of perfection. Several months after she married Luigi Biondi (September 8, 1821) and left Pisa, both Shelley and Mary apparently became disillusioned with "Emilia" because of her requests for money. On June 18, 1822, recommending *Epipsychidion* to John Gisborne as "an idealized history of my life and feelings," he confessed that he himself could not look at it: "the person whom it celebrates was a cloud instead of a Juno." According to Charles Ollier, Shelley asked that the edition be suppressed.

III *Adonais*

Late in July, 1820, Shelley had invited John Keats to visit him in Italy. He knew, through a letter from the Gisbornes, that Keats was ill with tuberculosis and that the climate of Italy was recommended in such cases; he also knew that Keats had not the means to support himself in a foreign land and he hoped, by guaranteeing the promising young poet a place to stay, to convince him to plan for the journey at the earliest possible moment so that he might reach Italy before the disease had made too much headway. Keats replied on August 16, saying conditionally, "If I do not take advantage of your invitation it will be prevented by a circumstance I have very much at heart to prophesy" (his death). After delays occasioned by difficulties in raising money for the voyage, Keats and Joseph Severn, a young painter, sailed in mid-September, 1820, for Naples, arriving there on October 21. Following quarantine and about a week in Naples, they proceeded to Rome; there, after a lingering illness, Keats died on February 23, 1821.

On April 11 Shelley learned of Keats's death and began *Adonais* soon afterward, for he had completed the poem before receiving "Colonel" Robert Finch's sentimentalized account of Keats's last days.[8] Shelley had heard that Keats had been severely hurt by the unfavorable notice of *Endymion* in *The Quarterly Review* (April, 1818, by John Wilson Croker), and he associated Keats's early death and its supposed cause with his own mistreatment at the hands of reviewers, particularly the brutal attack on *The Revolt of Islam* in *The Quarterly* (April, 1819, by John Taylor Coleridge). On June 8, 1821, he wrote to Ollier that he had finished the poem, "of about forty Spenser stanzas," and the entire fifty-five stanzas had been completed and printed (at Pisa) by July 13, when Shelley sent a copy to the Gisbornes.

In "A Defence" Shelley had described the role of *poetry* in society; in *Epipsychidion* he had shown the importance of the *poem* as a means of orienting phenomenal life toward the Ideal; in *Adonais* he portrays the *poet* as victorious over the limitations of phenomenal existence.

In the first seventeen stanzas the Poet urges the fatal Hour (in which Adonais died) and Urania to mourn the young man, as his Dreams, Desires, Adorations, Persuasions—"all he had loved, and moulded into thought" (his ideas and the poems in which they were expressed)— already mourn him. In the middle section (stanzas xviii–xxxviii), nature is reborn as Urania visits the grave of Adonais; there, unable to revive him as she revives nature, she grieves for him, and some other poets mourn their dead colleague. The movement concludes with a retort to the anonymous reviewer whose cowardly attack has killed Adonais. The third movement (like the first, seventeen stanzas long) asserts that Adonais has not really died, but rather that we, the living, exist in a realm of distorted vision and illusion from which Adonais has escaped to be reunited with the One, the spirit of beauty in both nature and human history (xxxix–xlvi), and that he is far better off than the living (xlvii–li). The Poet, realizing that little of value remains in his own life, is caught up by the spirit of beauty and drawn toward the higher realm from which "the soul of Adonais, like a star," shines as a beacon (lii–lv).

This, in barest outline, is the progression of the poem; but no summary or paraphrase of *Adonais* can more than suggest the artistry with which Shelley has interwoven Classical and Judeo-Christian myths, conventions of the pastoral elegy and scientific imagery, into his most nearly perfect work of art. In it, as in other late poems, we find significant echoes of Milton and Dante, Shelley's most important mentors, along with echoes of Bion's "Lament for Adonis" and Moschus' elegy on Bion.[9] The Spenserian stanza, with which Shelley had experimented in the Esdaile poems and had developed in *The Revolt of Islam*, had by this time become Shelley's own instrument, with a tone unlike that found in *The Faerie Queen,* "The Eve of St. Agnes," or *Childe Harold's Pilgrimage.*

Adonais is a drama or a tableau with a cast of characters whose functions and significance develop gradually. The name "Adonais" is a conflation of Adonis (the youth beloved by Aphrodite who was killed on a boar-hunt and whose death so distraught the goddess of fertility that she mourns for a long period each year and thereby creates the seasons) and the Hebrew word "Adonai" or "Lord" (thought by the historians of religion and myth in Shelley's day to derive from the same root as the Greek and near-Eastern Adonis).[10] Urania is, in Shelley's conception, both Aphrodite, the earth-mother of the Adonis myth, and the spiritual influence whom Milton addressed as the "heavenly muse" in *Paradise Lost;* she is both a goddess of nature and the muse of astronomy, potent within *and* beyond sublunar creation—"that Power . . . Which wields the world with never-wearied love, / Sustains it from beneath, and kindles it above" (375–78).

The persona of the Poet and the reader participate, at different levels, in the "progressive revelation" of the poem as together they move from sorrow at the death of Adonais to a realization that he is better off than they are; in the end, the Poet parts company from his reader by deciding to pursue death, while the reader remains behind in doubt and uncertainty. Only by understanding the different conclusions reached by the persona of the Poet, the imagined reader whom the Poet addresses, and the "pardlike Spirit beautiful and swift" (an objectified Shelley) can one avoid over-simplifying the poem into a pat generalization that death is better than life. In *Adonais* Shelley suggests the possibility that this may be so, but his emphasis is, in part, required because Keats died unfulfilled as a man and as a poet; Shelley could derive meaning from this death only by emphasizing the extreme idealistic monism that he explores in "On Life" (where, however, he does not suggest that death is preferable to life).

The poem opens with the Poet weeping for Adonais and urging the reader to join him, "though our tears / Thaw not the frost" (2–3). In stanzas i–vi, the Poet urges Urania, the "mighty Mother," to lament again as she did at the death of Milton, "who was the Sire of an immortal strain . . . the third among the sons of light" (along with Homer and Dante, the other two epic poets, according to "A Defence of Poetry"). Because Shelley thought that Keats's Miltonic epic fragment "Hyperion" was his best poem and the basis of his claim to recognition, he represents Adonais as being Milton's posthumous child, whose mother is Urania ("the nursling of thy widowhood"). The sixth stanza echoes Keats's "Isabella" in comparing the dead poet to "a pale flower by some sad maiden cherished"; as the poem develops, the flower becomes the representation of earthly beauty whose counterpart beyond the sublunar realm is the star.

When the Poet speaks in the seventh stanza of "the vault of blue Italian day" as a "charnel-roof" of Adonais, he introduces the image of the refraction of light into the colors of the rainbow by the moisture of Earth's atmosphere. In the following stanzas, before Corruption (female) begins to consume the corpse, the livng ("quick") Dreams of Adonais mourn him; allusions to "Ode on a Grecian Urn," "Ode on Melancholy," "To Autumn," "Ode to a Nightingale," and *Endymion* show that the "quick Dreams" are Keats's poems. The first seventeen stanzas thus explore the relation of a creative artist to his works and the relation of the artist to the creative power personified in Urania. At the end of this movement, Adonais' creations mourn him; but Urania remains indifferent, even oblivious to his death.

The second section begins with the theme of the late Latin poem *Pervigilium Veneris*—man's isolation during the spring, when nature is reborn under the influence of Venus as earth-mother. Ants, bees, birds, flowers, lizards, and snakes reappear, "a quickening life from the Earth's heart has burst / As it has ever done" (164–65); even the corpse of Adonais "exhales itself in flowers . . . / Like incarnations of the stars" (172–74). Yet this rebirth brings no comfort to the Poet; for, although matter is conserved and nature is renewed, the individual human mind seems to disappear forever. In despair, the Poet cries: "Nought we know, dies. Shall that alone which knows [human self-consciousness] /Be as a sword consumed before the sheath . . .?" (177–79). He concludes (Stanza xxi) that there is no hope for the preservation of humane values so long as the mutability of the natural cycle persists—"as long as skies are blue, and fields are green, / Evening must usher night, night urge the morrow, / Month follow month with woe, and year wake year to sorrow"; in all this, death merely "lends what life must borrow" (185–89).

But, when the Poet despairs (as had Prometheus, tormented by doubts and fears), he is answered by Urania, a creative force related to those "spirits" that had restored hope in the Titan. On the journey "out of her secret Paradise," Urania passes "camps and cities" that are "rough with stone, and steel, / And human hearts," which wound her; but the very wounds resulting from the obduracy of man and man's creations are turned to beauty by the goddess, whose blood paves "with eternal flowers that undeserving way."

In the tomb Urania confronts Death; but, though he is at first awed by "that living Might," he soon realizes that she is powerless to restore Adonais to life. The goddess promises the dead youth that, if he can but speak or kiss her once again, the memory of that word or kiss shall survive all other thoughts. But she also admits her own limited condition: "I would give / All that I am to be as thou now art! / But I am chained to Time, and cannot thence depart!" (232–34).

In the three central stanzas of the poem (xxvii–xxix), Urania regrets that Adonais did not wait until he was better armed (more mature as a poet) before he dared "the unpastured dragon" (the critics). And she compares Keats's reaction to hostile criticism to Byron's response; "the Pythian of the age" sped "one arrow" (*English Bards and Scotch Reviewers*) and put to flight the critics, who now "fawn on the proud feet that spurn them lying low" (250–52). Then Urania develops a simile that relates the natural world to "the world of living men": The sun or godlike mind appears, and many ephemeral creatures bask in its light; when it sinks, "the swarms that dimmed or shared its light" disappear, and "the immortal stars" that were obscured by its brightness "awake again."

In human history, a supreme imagination like Byron dominates his era, and lesser writers (like Thomas Moore) who imitate him attain a derivative popularity while he is in vogue. When the influence of the single "godlike mind" wanes, the works of the ephemeral poets disappear from view, and there emerge the "kindred lamps" of excellent but unappreciated writers whose light had been obscured by the popular luminary. The simile of Stanza xxix unifies the poem's two major themes: first, the meaning of the life of Keats, who died while still a gifted but unappreciated poet; and, second, the relation between the phenomenal world and underlying ontological reality. On the one hand, Stanza xxix recalls stanzas iv–v, with their account of the fates of Milton (another "godlike mind") and other lesser poets; on the other, it looks forward to Stanza lii, in which will culminate the imagery of light and the theme of its distortion by the moist atmosphere.

Following Urania's speech, Adonais' brother writers, also described as shepherds, come to mourn him. Here Shelley's genius shows itself most precise, for those to whom he alludes—Byron ("the Pilgrim of Eternity"), Tom Moore ("the sweetest lyrist" of Ireland's "saddest wrong"), and Shelley himself ("a pardlike Spirit beautiful and

swift")—exemplify the types of poets Urania has described. The figure
representing Shelley is given more attention because, as he "in another's fate now wept his own," so he is a living surrogate for the dead
poet; his role *as poet honoring the good qualities and achievements of other
imaginative spirits* gives meaning to the life of young John Keats and to
all others who contribute to human civilization without themselves
becoming supremely influential. Leigh Hunt, the "gentlest of the
wise," is introduced not as a poet but as one who "taught, soothed,
loved, honoured" Adonais; he is a humanitarian and a critic who rec-
ognizes and defends poets of worth. The "silence of that heart's ac-
cepted sacrifice" thus contrasts with the cruelty of the anonymous critic
whose venom has killed Adonais.

Shelley again (Stanza xxxvi) effectively coalesces Greek and Hebrew
myth, for the "deaf and viperous murderer" is described in terms that
suggest both the destroyers of Orpheus and the serpent of Eden. The
reviewer's punishment (like Satan's in *Paradise Lost*) is simply to be
himself and to be conscious of his own evil nature. The "cold embers"
of the unimaginative reviewer will return to dust, but the "pure spirit"
of Adonais will "flow / Back to the burning fountain" that is the
source of all creative energy and will "glow / Through time and change,
unquenchably the same." Shelley does not argue for personal immortality, but neither does he deny its possibility: Adonais "wakes or sleeps
with the enduring dead" (336); in whatever state the great spirits of
the past are imagined, Adonais is among them, and that in itself makes
him blessed by comparison with the reviewer, a "noteless blot on a
remembered name."

In "Lines written among the Euganean Hills" the Poet had argued
that, if during life one can take no comfort from love or friendship,
"then 'twill wreak him little woe" whether there be immortality or
not; in the second movement of *Adonais* the Poet argues that the creative influence of young Adonais will perpetuate itself through the
ever-changing creative force personified in Urania and that such a fate
(even supposing that there is no personal immortality) is far better than
an eternity in the condition of the anonymous reviewer, who, blind
and deaf to all beauty, poisons both his own happiness and that of
others.

The poem's third part (xxxix–lv) elaborates these two sources of comfort, but it also exploits the third factor in the earlier discussion—the
Poet's doubt as to what constitutes reality. If ordinary human cognitive
faculties are untrustworthy, perhaps earthly existence is illusory, and

moments of imaginative inspiration are glimpses into a reality in which the Good, the True, and the Beautiful exist in perfection. As the reviewer comes to epitomize the "living" and Adonais to represent the "dead," the Poet asserts in a dramatic reversal of categories that the reviewer's existence cannot be called "life" at all; only the creativity embodied in Adonais will persist and prevail, and therefore Adonais "is not dead, he doth not sleep— / He hath awakened from the dream of life—" (343–44). Adonais lives because, even if he as an individual were to be forgotten, the influence of his life and words would help recreate natural beauty for unknowing men in the way characteristic of all poetry.[11] He will be one of "the splendours of the firmament of time" who "may be eclipsed, but are extinguished not"; for "the dead live" whenever "lofty thought" encourages a "young heart" to rise above its merely mortal nature.

Shelley had earlier shown young idealists (the Youth in *Alastor,* Laon, and Lionel) drawing their ideals from the writings and art of the great imaginative spirits of the past; now he asserts the significance not only of such notable "inheritors of unfulfilled renown" as Chatterton, Sidney, and Lucan, but also "many more, whose names on Earth are dark, / But whose transmitted effluence cannot die / So long as fire outlives the parent spark" (406–8). Whatever may be the fate of Adonais' self-conscious identity, he is one of "the kings of thought / Who waged contention with their time's decay, / And of the past are all that cannot pass away" (430–32).

Stanza xlix ("like an infant's smile . . .") and Stanza li allude to Shelley's son William, buried at Rome where Keats lies, and there may be other personal allusions in Stanza liii ("A light is passed from the revolving year, / And man, and woman; and what still is dear / Attracts to crush, repels to make thee wither"). The Poet realizes that his hopes may lie beyond the grave; but, as the previous stanza had made clear, this loss of light is a subjective phenomenon, not necessarily pertinent to the reader: "Life, like a dome of many-coloured glass, / Stains the white radiance of Eternity, / Until Death tramples it to fragments" (462–64). Each man's mind, like "the vault of blue Italian day" (59), distorts the one reality into colors of the phenomenal world. "From the contagion of the world's slow stain / [Adonais] is secure" (356–57); and, freed from the limitations of his subjective existence, "the soul of Adonais, like a star / Beacons from the abode where the Eternal are" (494–95).

The Poet is caught up (as was the persona of the Poet in *Epipsychi-*

dion) by the power that inspires him, as "the fire for which all thirst" kindles during the process of composing the poem. Thus he celebrates the power of his own creative act in writing *Adonais,* even as the poem celebrates the imaginative power that Keats-Adonais had displayed. The "pardlike Spirit" had in another's fate wept his own neglect by the reading public, but in the concluding stanzas the persona of the Poet rejoices that his own creativity has translated Adonais from the merely mortal realm of cause and effect, time and place, into an immutable product of the imagination. The soul of Adonais, no longer tied to the tubercular body of John Keats, participates in the eternity of art.

There is space to suggest only a few of the subtle verbal and symbolic patterns in *Adonais.* Urania, initially described as a vegetation goddess, is seen in the end as a spirit that infuses both nature and human creativity—in which human imagination participates and to which it contributes. The flowers of the early parts of the poem become stars in the final movement. The word "splendours" that at first referred to the lost creations of Adonais' imagination (100, 111) refers in the end to stars in the firmament of time (388). In other words, Keats's poems, which seemed at first meaningless after the death of their creator, are seen ultimately as undying embodiments of his soul.

In the act of declaring that the works of a dead poet will live to inspire others, Shelley created a poem that illustrates and proves this very point. Among all the monuments of stone or words erected to honor the memory of John Keats, there has never been another that approached in importance this poem, which asserted that Keats's influence would persist when some of the dead poet's closest friends thought it possible that his "name was writ in water."

Chapter Eight
Eyeless Charioteer

During most of their sojourn in Italy the Shelleys had been restless itinerants in the manner of many Englishmen who visited the Continent after the Napoleonic wars. By 1820 they had visited most of the ordinary sights; having lost two children to the vagaries of Italian climate and not intending to return immediately to England, they questioned whether to settle in a congenial part of Italy or turn to other, unseen lands—Spain, Greece, the Middle East, or even India.[1] That they remained in the proximity of Pisa until Shelley's death was, as Mary Shelley later wrote, due more to chance than to plan or inclination (see "Note on the Poems of 1820," OSA, p. 636).

At Pisa the Shelleys had, besides their friendship with Mr. and Mrs. Mason,[2] made some connections both with Italians and with a colony of Greek aristocrats, especially Prince Alexander Mavrocordato. Eventually, a number of congenial exiles gathered there, forming what has been called the "Pisan Circle." Shelley's cousin Tom Medwin joined them, as we have seen, in October, 1820. January, 1821, saw the arrival of Medwin's friend Edward Williams, a former lieutenant in the British army (like Medwin, retired on half pay), and Jane Cleveland Johnson—who, separated but not divorced from her unsavory first husband, lived with Williams as his wife.

In the meantime, the Shelleys had met John Taaffe, Jr., an Irishman of good family and literary pretensions (rather than talent) who had lived at Pisa for several years. When Shelley visited Ravenna in August, 1821, and found Byron on the verge of moving out of the Papal States from which Count Ruggero Gamba and Pietro Gamba (father and brother of Byron's mistress Teresa Gamba Guiccioli) had recently been expelled for revolutionary activities, Shelley urged Byron to settle at Pisa, promising that Claire would remain a safe distance away at Florence. Byron agreed and reached Pisa on November 1, 1821.

I *Hellas*

Between Shelley's visit to Ravenna and Byron's arrival in Pisa, Shelley wrote a drama on the war for Greek independence dedicated to Mavrocordato (a leader of the Greek nationalists) begun in October 1821 and entitled *Hellas*. Wishing to publish quickly that he might help arouse British sympathy for the Greek cause, Shelley expended less pains on revising *Hellas* than he had on *Adonais*; in the Preface he calls it "a mere improvise" and apologizes for his dependence on "common fame" and "newspaper erudition." Yet the poem shows Shelley's maturity both in thought and execution, and to say that it falls short of *Epipsychidion* and *Adonais,* or that the two major fragments that follow ("Charles the First" and "The Triumph of Life") offer greater promise, is to say only that Shelley's poetic powers had arrived at such a high level as to make anything short of greatness disappointing.

Surviving fragments of a Prologue strongly resembling the "Prologue in Heaven" of Goethe's *Faust*[3] suggest that Shelley at one point thought of developing a cosmic drama on the pattern of the Book of Job, but he abandoned this plan to maintain the human perspective in which men speak about the "unknown God," rather than one from which gods judge men. The "lyrical drama," as belatedly published by Ollier in 1822,[4] is modeled, as Shelley tells in the Preface, on *The Persians* of Æschylus: As in *The Persians,* the action of *Hellas* is viewed from the palace of the antagonist—in this case, the Turkish Sultan Mahmud II: Mahmud imagines that he speaks to the spirit of a great progenitor, Mahomet II (conqueror of Constantinople in 1453), as Atossa the Persian queen received counsel from the shade of Darius, her dead husband; the Chorus of captive Greek women naturally sympathizes with the Greek cause as Æschylus' Chorus of Elders favored dead Darius over the proud, young Xerxes. The blank-verse accounts of the battles between the Turks and Greeks have the ring of Æschylus' messengers from the Battle of Salamis.

Hellas consists of seven parts, three major sections of blank-verse dialogue flanked by four passages of choral lyrics. The opening group of lyrics (1–113) culminates in the first great chorus, beginning "In the great morning of the world." Here the theme is that of "Ode to Liberty," for the introductory semichoruses proclaim that life, hope, truth, and love are all ineffectual or misdirected without liberty, the keystone of all other virtues. In the first major section of blank verse (114–96), Mahmud, arising from nightmares, arranges to meet with

Ahasuerus, "a Jew, whose spirit is a chronicle / Of strange and secret and forgotten things" (132–33).

There follows a second major chorus, "Worlds on worlds are rolling ever" (197–238), which states the second theme of the drama. This relates to the first theme because the flux of all created things and especially the continual upheavals in human history make imperative the liberty of individual thought and conscience as a safeguard against the otherwise inevitable stagnation and decay of any ideal. In the second stanza Jesus is pictured as a "Promethean conqueror" from "the unknown God," and the Greek women of the Chorus aver that "the moon of Mahomet / Arose, and it shall set," while "the cross leads generations on." This assurance of the relative longevity of Christianity does not, however, affect the statements on mutability of the first stanza, and "generations" itself is a limiting, temporal word.

The third stanza (echoing Milton's "On the Morning of Christ's Nativity") speaks of the flight of the Classical gods, "the Powers of earth and air," at the birth of Christ; yet the Greek women do not portray this victory as being entirely desirable, for "our hills and seas and streams, / Dispeopled of their dreams / Their waters turned to blood, their dew to tears, / Wailed for the golden years" (235–38). The imagery and themes of this chorus are to be taken up once again, with new emphasis, in the final chorus, "The world's great age begins anew."

In the meantime, the Chorus's prediction of Greek "Christian" victory over the Islamic Turks seems to be vindicated in the following section (239–647), in which Mahmud, having been forced to buy the loyalty of his own Janizary palace guard with "the treasures of victorious Solyman" (252), listens as Hassan describes the insurgents' courage at the Battle of Bucharest and a Greek naval victory and then as four messengers give successive accounts of new reverses for the Turks—first, the precipitous departure of the Russian ambassador; second, the Greek conquest of several cities and the massacre of their Turkish inhabitants (together with the neutralizing of such Turkish war-lords as Ali Pacha); third, unrest or uprisings by dissident groups in such other parts of the Turkish empire as the Levant, Arabia, Ethiopia, Mesopotamia, Crete, and Cyprus; finally, news of a naval battle between Greek and Turkish forces, the outcome of which yet seems doubtful when Mahmud impatiently silences the messenger and leaves to keep his appointment with Ahasuerus.

That the following choral lyrics (648–737) are, except for one brief passage, recited antiphonally by the two semichoruses (which interrupt each other in their haste) is symptomatic of the eager expectancy of the captive Greek women at this crisis point of the drama. But their words warn against interpreting the reports of Ottoman reverses as Greek victories: as in "Ode to the West Wind," the cloud, rain, lightning, and wind are unfettered, while men have been corrupted by "Slavery! thou frost of the world's prime" (676). In reasserting their freedom, men should understand clearly that their true glory consists, not in "temples and towers, / Citadels and marts" which "have been ours, / And may be thine, and must decay."[5] What is real, eternally vital, and worth fighting to preserve is not the mutable material glory that was Greece, but the underlying ideals of the highest Greek civilization that persist in the best aspects of Western humanism:

> . . . Greece and her foundations are
> Built below the tide of war,
> Based on the crystàlline sea
> Of thought and its eternity;
> Her citizens, imperial spirits,
>   Rule the present from the past,
> On all this world of men inherits
>   Their seal is set.
>   (696–703)

Semichorus II sees that "The world's eyeless charioteer, / Destiny, is hurrying by"—preceded by the "shadow," "ruin." But his career does not correct anything unless in its track follows a "splendour" named "renovation" and unless the shouts of "kill! kill! kill!" give way to "a small still voice" saying: "Revenge and Wrong bring forth their kind, / The foul cubs like their parents are" (729–30). The ideal, the god-image of man, must be not a war-god of racial or sectarian vengeance, but a spirit of a religion pure and undefiled:

> In sacred Athens, near the fane
> Of Wisdom, Pity's altar stood:
> Serve not the unknown God in vain,
> But pay that broken shrine again,
>   Love for hate and tears for blood.
>   (733–37)

In the third and final section of dramatic blank verse (738–939), Ahasuerus echoes Prospero's outburst in *The Tempest* when he responds to Mahmud's desire to know the future:

> . . . this Whole
> Of suns, and worlds, and men, and beasts, and flowers,
> . . . .
> Is but a vision;—all that it inherits
> Are motes of a sick eye, bubbles and dreams;
> Thought is its cradle and its grave . . . .
> Nought is but that which feels itself to be.
>
> (776–85)

To clarify this speech, Ahasuerus gives another equally paradoxical "Thought" and its living elements, "Will, Passion, / Reason, Imagination, cannot die";[6] for these vital aspects or functions of thought are, in fact, what their objects ("that which they regard") appear to be— the material out of which the process of change forms all that mutability controls—"worlds, worms, / Empires, and superstitions" (795–801). Shelley, through this mature conception of the Wandering Jew who had haunted his youthful writings, seems, at first glance, to have set forth a clear and unequivocal statement of an extreme monistic Idealism—that all reality consists of one stuff and that this reality is of the nature of Mind or Idea rather than body or matter.

Yet he has really said both more and less: On the one hand, Thought and "its quick elements" make up everything that exists within the "dominion" of mutability, and only that exists which has self-consciousness of its existence ("Nought is but that which feels itself to be"). But here, as in *Prometheus Unbound* and "On Life," Shelley reaches out beyond "existence" as human beings experience it to imply that, though we can know nothing of it, there is prior to thought or self-consciousness a Power—call it "the unknown God"—that contains even that of which men have no knowledge.

For the purposes of this drama—historical and ethical rather than ontological in perspective—Ahasuerus has said enough when he concludes, "The coming age is shadowed on the Past / As on a glass" (805–6); having convinced Mahmud of the power of mind over time, he evokes by subtle suggestion the mental image of the Sultan's ancestor Mahomet the Second, conqueror of Constantinople. Mahmud, without additional suggestion from Ahasuerus (who exits at line 861), projects a conversation between himself and the "Phantom" of his progenitor, who articulates what Mahmud already senses—that, as Mahomet's conquest of Byzantium marked the end of the Roman Empire and the summertime of the Ottoman rule, now "a later Empire nods in its decay: / The autumn of a greener faith is come" (870–71). Having seen human life *sub specie aeternitatis*, Mahmud cannot be duped by the hollow cries of "Victory! Victory!" which promise only another turn to the meaningless cycle of wronged and avenger, destroyer and destroyed— "those that suffer and inflict"—and, as he exits for the last time, he has been reduced to total nihilism.

Such is not, of course, the burden of the drama as a whole: Although Mahmud, whose hopes were tied to material glory, has sunk into cynical nihilism and greets the news of victory with despair, the Chorus draws hope even from the abysm of defeat. At the end of *The Revolt of Islam* the physical destruction of the reformers was accompanied by their spiritual apotheosis; in *Hellas,* where the emphasis is on a rebirth of ideals rather than renovation of institutions, the news—the idea— of physical defeat elicits from the Chorus an affirmation of the persistence of Hellas as an eternal ideal. So far as political rejuvenation is concerned, the United States, "young Atlantis," shall be the reincarnation of Roman power (992–95). Greece, however, is of a different order of excellence; her greatest moments rest in such exploits as the retreat of "the ten thousand from the limits of the morn," refugees from a lost military cause but, through their unconquerable ideals, survivors of "many an hostile Anarchy."[7]

The action of *Hellas* takes place in twenty-four hours: The time at the beginning of the drama is "Sunset" and at the beginning of the final semichoruses, "darkness has dawned in the East / . . . The weak day is dead, / But the night is not born" (1023, 1034–35). This closing of the presumably unsuccessful day's struggle of the Greeks for their political independence is likened to "the sunset of hope" presided over by Hesperus that will, in time and through mutability, yield a new morning when "Greece, which is dead, is arisen!"

The final chorus—one of the supreme achievements of Shelley's art—parallels the earlier chorus, "Worlds on worlds" (197–238), which is also forty-two lines long. The earlier chorus had ended with "hills and seas and streams" wailing "for the golden years," but in this vision (modeled, as Shelley tells, on Isaiah's prophecy and Virgil's Fourth Eclogue) "the golden years return," the snake of necessity renews its vitality by casting off its old outer skin, and "faiths and empires" dissolve under the smile of Heaven.

In this rejuvenation, a new Hellas of great natural beauty comes into view, one worthy of the veneration of imaginative men (1066–71); and a series of new myths evolve–from the quest-motif of the Argonauts to the myth of Orpheus the Poet to that of Ulysses, who left behind the sensuality of Calypso for the love of home, wife, and duty. But in the new, more perfect mythology, the Chorus hopes, there will be no renewed stories of pride, war, murder, and vengeance like those of the Trojan and Theban cycles. Rather, the ideal Athens will be revived and—"if nought so bright may live"—will in its sunset bequeath to posterity "all earth can take or Heaven can give." The religious ideals of the new era will be those of love and reason: "Not gold, not blood, their altar dowers, / But votive tears and symbol flowers" (1094–95).

As in *Prometheus Unbound,* Shelley is too much the realist to believe that, even should the long-awaited "world's great age" dawn, it could remain forever. Because everything in existence is subject to the mutability of thought and its quick elements, the Chorus foresees once more the return of "hate and death." Yet in their disappointment at the present defeat of the Greek cause, the captive women do not have the courage to gaze upon the entire turn of the wheel; they draw back from what they know lies at the bottom of the urn of prophecy, crying out, "The world is weary of the past, / Oh, might it die or rest at last!" A common mistake attributes to Shelley the straw-grasping optimism of this dramatic chorus of captive women. But Shelley himself foresaw the ultimate destruction of the reforms to which he had devoted his life; he simply knew that hope was necessary for most men, if they were to continue to struggle against chaos and nothingness.

II Late Lyrics and Minor Fragments

Hellas and the intricate poem that was also published in the same volume, "Written on Hearing the News of the Death of Napoleon" (which underscores the ineffectualness of men who merely ride the wheel of historical necessity to make any permanent impression on the realm of sublunar mutability), are the last poems that Shelley is known to have completed for publication. But they by no means mark the end of his poetic productivity, and, indeed, several of the lyrics for which he was best known during the Victorian period and two unfinished

longer works that are highly regarded today belong (solely or chiefly)
to the few months between the completion of *Hellas* and Shelley's death
in July, 1822.

Until recently readers of these late poems have been handicapped by
the lack of accurate texts, and they have been unaware how tentative
and incorrect the printed texts were. In 1846 Walter Savage Landor
wrote of Shelley: "I would rather have written his 'Music, when soft
voices die,' than all that Beaumont and Fletcher ever wrote, together
with all their contemporaries, excepting Shakespeare."[8] In the twentieth century, during the reaction against Shelley's poetry, there were
many attacks on this lyric, which had been first published by Mary
Shelley in *Posthumous Poems of Percy Bysshe Shelley* (1824); critics con-
tended that the sequence of images was illogical and the thought in-
coherent for a love poem. In 1960, however, Irving Massey examined
Shelley's notebook from which Mary Shelley presumably took the text
of the poem, and he found that Mrs. Shelley had added the title ("To
———") and had reversed the order of the two quatrains. When the lines
are read in the proposed order, the poem proves to be a much more
coherent one, and the subject is not love but immortality.[9]

Or, to take another example, in 1862 Richard Garnett published in
his *Relics of Shelley* "Lines written in the Bay of Lerici," a poem of fifty-
two lines, and later in the volume among "Miscellaneous Fragments"
he included five and a half lines beginning "Bright wanderer, fair co-
quette of heaven," that, as later editors rightly noted, were addressed
to the moon. In 1961 G. M. Matthews published a complete text of
"Lines written in the Bay of Lerici," including the opening lines to the
moon and the connecting lines that had baffled Garnett.

Because it is impossible to discuss definitively poems that Shelley
himself did not prepare for the press until they have been reedited from
the manuscripts, we can write only in a general way about the fragments of Shelley's drama "Charles the First." His interest in choosing
such a subject for dramatic presentation shows the increasing objectiv-
ity and distance that he was putting into his writings, for his feelings
were mixed on the issues involved in the struggle between the cultured
humanistic aristocrats and churchmen supporting the king's tyranny
and the narrower and often-bigoted dissenters and supporters of
Parliament.

The discrepancy between appearance and reality governs the beginning of "Charles the First": in the opening scene, the Second Citizen
sees the masque as a false covering for a corrupt and ungodly society;

but the Youth, his son, is content to enjoy the beauty of the surface rather than plumb beneath. In the second scene, Archy the court fool can, like the Fool in *King Lear,* see beyond the king's power and the archbishop's religiosity to the essential weakness of a regime built on oppression of popular sentiments, one that futilely attempts "to strike dead the Spirit of the Time" and to "keep the fierce spirit of the hour at bay" (ii.115, 165).

Shelley, in short, read the struggle not in terms of the simple categories of the oppressors and the oppressed that had governed *The Cenci,* but rather as a drama of the irony of historical necessity in which Charles is to be crushed by the Jacobin-like violence of the Second Citizen, whose bloodthirstiness matches that of Archbishop Laud. When Laud asks permission to punish Archy, the king replies prophetically, "Prithee / For this once do not as Prynne would, were he / Primate of England" (ii.95–97). Clearly, Laud is to be the villain of the play, while Charles, the queen, and Strafford on the one side and probably Hampden, Pym, Cromwell, and young Sir Harry Vane on the other are to represent two groups of limited human beings whose glory or infamy rests not so much on the virtues or vices of their personal characters as on whether they advanced or attempted to check the revolutionary spirit of their age.

Another uncompleted work belonging to the winter of 1821–22, known simply as "Fragments of an Unfinished Drama," is written in quite a different vein. This play was "undertaken," Mary Shelley said, "for the amusement of the individuals who composed our intimate society"; and it centers around the adventures of a pirate "of savage but noble nature" who is involved with a Calypsoesque enchantress "in one of the islands of the Indian Archipelago." This projected amusement was, no doubt, sketched after the arrival at Pisa on January 14, 1822, of Williams' friend Edward John Trelawny, the Cornishman who boasted that he had once been a pirate in the East Indies, who was to sail with Byron on his last voyage to Greece, and who was later to write untrustworthy but eminently readable narratives of his own youth in *Adventures of a Younger Son* (1831) and of his first encounter with poets in *Recollections of the Last Days of Shelley and Byron* (1858), revised as *Records of Shelley, Byron, and the Author* (1878).

Shelley needed no special reason to abandon the artificial entertainment that has as its literary ancestors the Renaissance masques and particularly Milton's *Comus;* what was initiated by whim could end as easily. But the failure to complete "Charles the First" goes far deeper.

Shelley had long before begun to feel the lack of a reading public, and his awareness of his inability to strike a responsive chord in British readers was always greatest when he contrasted himself directly with Byron. Recently he had come to feel neglected by Charles Ollier, his publisher. By the beginning of 1822, Shelley's patience had reached the breaking point. In a letter to Ollier in which frustrated rage is covered lightly by the good breeding of an English gentleman, Shelley concluded: "Should you pay the same attention to my present letter as its late predecessors have received from you, you will scarcely think it extraordinary that this should be the last time I intend to trouble you" (January 11 [1822]; *Letters,* II, 372).

On March 2, after Leigh Hunt had written that he could raise no money by selling the copyright of the unwritten drama, Shelley confides: "Indeed I have written nothing for this last two months; a slight circumstance gave a new train to my ideas & shattered the fragile edifice when half built.—" (*Letters,* II, 394). Perhaps the "slight circumstance" was Shelley's attempt to write the "Fragments of an Unfinished Drama," or perhaps by March he was upset by his domestic problems. Certainly, Mary Shelley was becoming increasingly difficult to live with.

Some of Shelley's more-than-momentary feelings about his marriage are to be seen in the sad lyric called "To Edward Williams" ("The serpent is shut out from Paradise"), sent to his friend on January 26, 1822, in which Shelley contrasts the happiness of Edward and Jane with his own "cold home" (OSA, pp. 644–45). Again, in the lyric entitled by Mary Shelley simply "To ———," beginning "When passion's trance is overpast," Shelley contrasts the transitory revival of "tenderness and truth" during brief moments of "passion's trance" with their absence in the relationship at other times. He would be willing to suppress his sexual desires, he says, "couldst thou but be as thou hast been" (OSA, pp. 645–46).

Amid these clear indications of growing estrangement between Shelley and Mary, we find Shelley during the early months of 1822 addressing Jane Williams in such beautiful poems as "To Jane: The Invitation" and "To Jane: The Recollection" (commemorating a January outing in the pine forest of the Cascine near Pisa that Jane, Mary, and Shelley took together on February 2, 1822) and "With a Guitar, to Jane" (accompanying Shelley's gift of the instrument), and, very late, "To Jane: 'The keen stars were twinkling'" (recounting the beauty of Jane's playing and singing). But neither these poems nor such others as "The Magnetic Lady to Her Patient" and the expanded "Lines written in the Bay of Lerici" evince the same kind of passionate idealization of Jane that *Epipsychidion* does of Teresa Viviani; and, when all the evidence is scrutinized, no clear conclusion emerges as to what—if anything—beyond congenial friendship passed between Shelley and Jane.

Tensions were increased during the spring of 1822 by Claire's continual agitating to remove Allegra from the convent near Ravenna where Byron had left her to be educated and, second, by the financial ruin of Godwin in a lawsuit. The Pisan circle, though it stimulated Shelley, also irritated him. The better he knew Byron, the more clearly he saw his personal and intellectual limitations—and he resented Byron's overwhelming fame. Even before Hunt had finally embarked from England with his large family, hoping to mend his fortune in partnership with Byron and Shelley in a new periodical, Shelley wrote that "particular dispositions in Lord B's character render the close & exclusive intimacy with him in which I find myself, intolerable to me. . . ."

The Pisan group dispersed following an incident on March 24. When Taaffe was jostled by a Tuscan dragoon as the party returned from a ride, he incited his companions to pursue the soldier. After a scuffle, one of Byron's servants gravely wounded Sergeant-Major Masi. The Tuscan authorities could not determine the guilt in the case; and, when Masi recovered, they released the two (innocent) servants they had arrested, but ordered the Gambas out of Tuscany. Byron followed his mistress and her family to the duchy of Lucca.[10]

III "The Triumph of Life"

The Shelleys and the Williamses determined to spend the summer living and boating on the Bay of Spezia. Although they could find only one house, Casa Magni at San Terenzo, they managed not only to settle their two families there but even to take Claire with them for a few days early in May so that she would not be near Byron when they told her that Allegra had died of typhus on April 20 (at the age of five years and three months).

Shelley's health improved markedly during the months of May and June. His companions noticed chiefly his delight in the *Don Juan*, the sailboat built for him at Genoa by Trelawny's friend Captain Daniel Roberts. But in his letters, particularly in one to John Gisborne on June 18, Shelley confided his inability to communicate freely with Mary and his deep disappointment at his literary isolation: "It is impossible to compose except under the strong excitement of an assurance of finding sympathy in what you write. Imagine Demosthenes reciting a Philippic to the waves of Atlantic! . . . I do not go on with 'Charles the First.' I feel too little certainty of the future, and too little satisfaction with regard to the past, to undertake any subject seriously and deeply" (June 18, 1822; *Letters,* II, 435–36).

But—and there can never be, it seems, an unqualified statement about this complex man—Shelley may have been at the very time he wrote that letter to Gisborne engaged in "The Triumph of Life," perhaps his first poem since *Prometheus Unbound* not inspired or initiated by a specific occasion or by a pragmatic purpose but by Shelley's desire to render poetically his total mature vision of the nature and destiny of man. Unfinished at his death, this fragmentary work has nevertheless been pronounced by T. S. Eliot and other modern critics to be the apex of Shelley's poetry, even though until recently some of its finest effects have been muted by a very imperfect text.[11]

"The Triumph of Life" is Shelley's last important exploration of the problem of evil, and the lines of the poem that most succinctly state the *problem* are 224–34; after the shade of Rousseau has pointed out Napoleon among the important captives who are chained to the chariot of the malevolent shape, the Poet feels a despair comparable to that experienced by Prometheus. He says,

> And much I grieved to think how power & will
> In opposition rule our mortal day—
>
> And why God made irreconcilable
> Good & the means of good . . . .
>
> (228–31)

Rousseau, his mentor, will not permit him to remain in despair, but turns him back to the pageant of historical figures to see that there are, in fact, distinctions to be made among the victims of Life. Some have been conquered and have left nothing to redeem themselves, but others like Plato and Rousseau himself have inspired the efforts of other generations to overcome the world, even though they personally fell victim to it. A great part of the poem's message is that the Poet-idealist's first disillusionment is dangerous, merely playing into the hands of the mundane conqueror; for the consequent withdrawal of the relatively virtuous from the stage of history leaves an open field for the activities of evil men.

In the introductory lines of the poem (1–40), the sun rises on a joyful world in which all the elements of natural creation "rise as the Sun their father rose" to share the burden of natural existence; the Poet, out of tune with nature and free from the rule of natural necessity, has remained awake with the stars and now at dawn prepares to sleep. But the "thoughts which must remain untold" that have kept him awake project themselves on his consciousness in a trance-like vision such as Ahasuerus elicited from Mahmud's inner thoughts.

In the first major section of the vision (41–175), the Poet becomes progressively more deeply involved in the plight of those in the pageant. At first he sees only a barren highway and "a great stream / Of people" blindly rushing along, tormenting themselves or one another, and ignoring the "fountains," "grassy paths," and "violet banks" while "they / Pursued their serious folly as of old" (41–73). This initial view of human life as random motion is modified immediately when there appears, in "a cold glare, intenser than the noon / But icy cold," a moon-like chariot in which there sits a "Shape," described in terms deriving from Milton's portrayal of Death in *Paradise Lost*. While the death-like Shape crouches, a four-faced "Shadow" of destiny acts as charioteer, guiding a "wonder-winged team."

The details of the chariot, its motive power, and its guiding charioteer derive from a description found in Ezekiel's vision of the manifest power of God, Dante's car of the church, and Milton's "Chariot of Paternal Deitie"; but Shelley—as so often in his use of myths and symbols[12]—has changed the moral implications of the description. For Ezekiel, Dante, and Milton, the God of Power that rules nature and shapes the external destinies of men was a beneficent force assuring the ultimate triumph of virtue. But for Shelley, moral coercion is in itself evil; there can be no good fruit from an evil tree. The influence of this triumphant chariot is thus pernicious, destroying the human freedom that is the basis of all morality and virtue. Because necessity is blind, "ill was the car guided," no matter what its speed or power.

At this point the Poet "arose aghast," no longer indifferent to his vision, and he saw "the million" celebrating the triumphant progress of this amoral chariot. If the ignorant, aimless wanderings of the first group seemed folly, the active worship of amoral power, like the old triumphs of Roman emperors, seems a positive evil. Bound to this chariot are the leading figures of all ages, both the oppressors and the oppressed—all "who had grown old in power / Or misery"—except two groups: first, a "sacred few" who had died young and "fled back like eagles to their native noon" before they had been corrupted by the

world's slow stain, and, second, a group "who put aside the diadem /
Of earthly thrones or gems"—those men "of Athens & Jerusalem," the
best of the Hellenic and Hebraic traditions, who had either fled the
world before their disillusionment or else resisted (as Jesus and Socrates
did) the temptation to turn their personal power—whether physical,
political, intellectual, or spiritual—into any kind of tyranny over their
fellow men.

The chariot, besides being followed by chained men of notable
power or suffering, is preceded by a hoard of nameless "maidens &
youths" driven by lusts that lead them to destroy themselves and one
another; and it is also followed by a second crowd of anonymous older
men and women who, arid and impotent, go through the motions of
lust though their natures lead them to a cold death in dust rather than
a passionate destruction of lightning and foam: "And frost in these
performs what fire in those" (175).

By this time the Poet, "struck to the heart" by what he has seen,
cries out to know the meaning of the vision. He is answered by the
decayed ruin of Rousseau's spirit. This "grim Feature"—yet another
projection of the Poet's mind (as the shade of Mahomet was of Mahmud's)—explains part of the meaning of the pageant and identifies
Napoleon among "the Wise, / The great, the unforgotten." The Poet
is shocked to despair by the destructive power of mundane life over
both Rousseau, inspired with an inner fire but corrupted (like Beatrice
Cenci) by unpropitious external circumstances, and Napoleon, unable
to "repress the mutiny within" even though given every external
advantage.

But, when the Poet tries to turn away from the pageant, Rousseau
will not let him rest in the self-gratification of easy despair. He
commands him to "behold . . . those spoilers spoiled"—Voltaire,
Frederick the Great, Kant, Catherine of Russia, and Leopold of Austria—and distinguishes between their slavery to external influences and
his own destruction by his unfulfilled desires: "I was overcome / By my
own heart alone" (240–41). Although the Poet has no wish to see any
more of those who, in spite of great talents and opportunities, have
left the world "not so much more glorious than it was," Rousseau
reminds him that every generation casts its influence for good or ill on
human history and points to the "mighty phantoms of an elder day"—
those of Greek civilization including Plato, who, like Rousseau himself, was corrupted by excessive love for an improper object,[13] and
Aristotle and Alexander (260–68), who, like Voltaire and Frederick,
were intellectual and military conquerors.

Rousseau points out also "the great bards of old," who were able to quell "the passions which they sung," whereas he himself "suffered what I wrote, or viler pain!" But, when he says, "my words were seeds of misery— / Even as the deeds of others," the Poet remonstrates with him, insisting that Rousseau's writings produced no such evil as the deeds of Roman emperors ("the heirs / Of Caesar's crime"), the "Anarchs old" who founded the feudal states out of which European nations grew, or the popes, "who rose like shadows between Man & god." After Rousseau acknowledges that "their power was given / But to destroy," the Poet asks him to tell his story, which he does in a symbolic narrative in the manner of *Alastor* and *Epipsychidion*.

Awakening in the spring, Rousseau found himself in a beautiful valley beside a "gentle rivulet" that emerged from the shadowy mountain that separates the realm of birth from whatever preceded it.

> "Whether my life had been before that sleep
> The Heaven which I imagine, or a Hell
>
> "Like this harsh world in which I wake to weep,
> I know not."
>
> (332–35)

For a brief interval he senses a "trace / Of light diviner than the common Sun / Sheds on the common Earth," but this light is quickly swallowed up by a melange of sounds and the bright glare of the morning sun. The sunlight flows through the gorge in the mountain (from which the stream of life issued) and shines on a pool. Amid the pool's reflection of the sun there appears "a shape all light." This beautiful female form proves to be a vision of the Ideal as it is distorted both by the limitations of the human condition and by those of the individual mind. The "shape," associated with mist, foam, "leaves & winds & waves & birds & bees," and especially with the rainbow, tramples out the sparks of Rousseau's mind as "Day" (not the sun itself but the distorted diffusion of sunlight) "treads out the lamps of night." In other words, the vision of the partial ideal destroys Rousseau's initial appreciation of individual people and particular things of beauty.

When Rousseau asks his self-projected ideal for the answers to life's ultimate questions, she bids him drink from the crystal glass in her hand; but, when he does, he (like Eve and Adam, who sought similar knowledge) is confronted first by a vision of wolfish evil and then by the cold bright chariot, which eclipses the vision of the "shape all light." By absolutizing the relative and by seeking within the limited world of mutability the vision of what was eternal and unconditional, Rousseau has blinded himself to the virtue and beauty of sublunar things without having found anything with which to replace them. Confronted by the triumphal progress of random experience, the disillusioned idealist plunges "among / The thickest billows of the living storm," giving himself up to despair and sensuality (465–68). But the memory of his partial ideal lingers, and he continues to glimpse that vision and to hope that his day's path may end as he began it, in the smile of Venus, both morning star of love and evening star of hope (412–33).

The fragment concludes with a lengthy section in which Rousseau tells how, as he approached middle age, he beheld "a wonder worthy of the rhyme" of Dante. In this vision, he describes by means of animal similes a series of "phantoms"—"dim forms" that were "sent forth incessantly" from aging human beings. These forms prove to be masks created by the artificial roles people play—from the delegated power of kings to those of "lawyer, statesman, priest & theorist" (495–510). Potentially autonomous moral agents are distorted into formalized, unfeeling automatons fulfilling preconceived functions without making personal ethical choices. As these masks "fell from the countenance / And form of all," those who gave them off lost all joy and spontaneity and some, like Rousseau himself, "grew weary of the ghastly dance / And fell . . . by the way side" (535–43). The Poet at this point interrupts his guide:

> "Then, what is Life?" I said . . . the cripple cast
>   His eye upon the car which now had rolled
>   Onward, as if that look must be the last,
>
> And answered . . . . "Happy those for whom the fold
>   Of
>
>   (544–48)

These were not the last words Shelley ever wrote; we cannot even be certain that they were his last lines of poetry. But there is reason to think that he wrote them shortly before he, Edward Williams, and Captain Daniel Roberts sailed the *Don Juan* down the coast from the Bay of Spezia to Leghorn on July 1, 1822, to welcome Leigh Hunt to Italy. On Monday, July 8, Shelley and Williams (along with a sailor boy named Charles Vivian) left Leghorn to return to San Terenzo. From the shore Roberts and Trelawny separately watched the small sailing craft until, about ten miles out to sea, it disappeared into the dark cloud of a sudden squall.

At Casa Magni, Mary and Jane waited with some uneasiness until Friday, July 12, when a letter arrived from Hunt to Shelley saying, "pray write to tell us how you got home, for they say that you had bad weather after you sailed on monday [*sic*], & we are anxious."[14] After an intensive search of the coastline between Leghorn and Lerici, the bodies of Shelley and Williams were found washed up about three miles apart on the shore near Viareggio, Shelley's within the duchy of Lucca and Williams' in Tuscany. Trelawny took charge of carrying out the widows' wishes to bury Shelley in Rome near William Shelley and to send Edward Williams' remains to England for final burial. Because of strict quarantine laws, the decomposing bodies could not be transported across national boundaries. Trelawny, therefore (with the help of the English minister at Florence), asked and received permission to cremate the bodies near their respective places of temporary burial on the beach.

There is no need here to go into the aftermath of Shelley's sudden death. One unfortunate result was that his absence permitted the whole enterprise of Hunt's journal—named *The Liberal* at Byron's suggestion—to founder.[15] Jane Williams soon returned to England, where she eventually married Thomas Jefferson Hogg. Mary and her young son returned in 1823; she edited a volume of Shelley's *Posthumous Poems* (1824) and, later, his *Poetical Works* (4 vols., 1839) and *Essays, Letters from Abroad, Translations and Fragments* (2 vols., 1840), all containing notes of biographical interest that partly compensated for her inability (because of the financial threats of Sir Timothy Shelley) to publish a full biography of her husband. At Sir Timothy's death in 1844, Percy Florence Shelley succeeded his grandfather in the baronetcy, and was able to ease the last years of Mary Shelley (d. 1851). In 1848 Sir Percy Florence married Jane St. John, a fervent admirer of both Shelley and Mary, who undertook a role as caretaker of their reputations that has had repercussions that still echo in studies of Shelley.[16]

IV Epilogue

Although Shelley probably faced death with equanimity, this is not to say that he sought it. We do not have the feeling that Shelley's death was a tragedy for him (though it was for his family and several friends), because his life and thought were mature before the end—not simply turning from bud to bloom, as in the case of John Keats. "If I die tomorrow," Shelley is reported to have said the day before his death, "I have lived to be older than my father."[17]

Shelley could face death and life with equal strength and courage because he had learned, after many trials and not a few errors, wherein his happiness lay: It was neither to be found in political panaceas, such as reform bills (though he would have welcomed the progressive democratization of England during the later nineteenth century), nor in an ideal antitype of his psyche embodied in another man or woman (though he highly valued true friendship); rather, his happiness lay in *words that praised* the social and personal ideals he had cherished so intensely during all his adult years.

In the life of the imagination, especially as that experience could be communicated to others through creative actions and gestures, through the plastic and performing arts, and most effectually through written words, Shelley saw the seeds of the values that could continually regenerate individual men and, at fortunate moments in human history, renovate entire societies. *Prometheus Unbound,* "A Defence of Poetry," *Epipsychidion, Adonais, Hellas,* and "The Triumph of Life" all say with one voice that the virtues of any living individual man are inspired, nurtured, and brought to fruition (or limited) by the imaginative ideals he holds—his personal vision of what a man ought to be. The *telos,* the goal of human life, thus lies within the best of the imaginative ideals available to men; and the greatest service one man can perform for his fellows is to augment and enhance those ideals.

If we were asked to evaluate Shelley's life and work, we could point to the practical effectiveness of his poetry and prose in the history of British political and social reform movements[18] or to his pervading influence among great literary figures of the later nineteenth and the twentieth centuries—Tennyson, Browning, Rossetti, Swinburne, Meredith, Hardy, Shaw, Yeats, and (in spite of his early criticisms) T. S. Eliot. But a truer test, and one that Shelley himself would have approved, is the degree to which his imaginative mythic formulations have been diffused into the general cultural imagination. The figures of Prometheus, Queen Mab, Count Cenci and Beatrice, and such natural phenomena as Mont Blanc, the west wind, a cloud, or a skylark evoke in literate English-speaking people conceptions that are as vividly informed by Shelley's imagination as the characters of Falstaff,

Richard III, Romeo and Juliet are by Shakespeare's, those of Comus, Adam and Eve, and Satan by Milton's, and the whole panoply of Canterbury pilgrimages by Chaucer's. The public understanding of each of these representations has grown and changed over the years and will continue to do so, for the imaginative conception remains alive to reinterpretation as the matter-of-fact discourse does not. The measure of Shelley's success will remain, however, in the number of elements of public thought and discourse upon which he has placed the ineradicable stamp of his imagination.

Notes and References

Preface to the Updated Edition

1. Among the many analyses of the fall of Shelley's reputation from the 1920s through the 1950s, see: 1) Frederick A. Pottle, "The Case of Shelley," *PMLA* 67 (1952): 589–608, reprinted in *English Romantic Poets: Modern Essays in Criticism,* ed. M. H. Abrams (New York: Oxford University Press, 1960); 2) Carl Woodring, "Dip of the Skylark," *Keats-Shelley Journal* 9 (Winter 1960):10–13; and 3) Sylva Norman, "Twentieth-Century Theories on Shelley," *Texas Studies in Literature and Language* 9 (1967): 223–37.

2. The best general account of Shelley's reputation in the nineteenth century is still Sylva Norman's *The Flight of the Skylark: The Development of Shelley's Reputation* (Norman: University of Oklahoma Press, 1954).

3. Robert Pattison's *The Triumph of Vulgarity: Rock Music in the Mirror of Romanticism* (New York: Oxford University Press, 1987) names some twentieth-century "artists" who think that they are following in the steps of the Romantics. (I strongly disagree with Pattison's contention that they are actually doing so.)

4. *The Journals of Claire Clairmont,* ed. Marion Kingston Stocking, with the assistance of David Mackenzie Stocking (Cambridge, Mass.: Harvard University Press, 1968); *The Letters of Mary Wollstonecraft Shelley,* ed. Betty T. Bennett, 3 vols. (Baltimore: Johns Hopkins University Press, 1980–88). Recently joining these much praised editions as a basic source is *The Journals of Mary Shelley, 1814–1844,* ed. Paula R. Feldman and Diana Scott-Kilvert, 2 vols. (Oxford: Clarendon Press, 1987).

5. *Shelley and his Circle,* ed. Kenneth Neill Cameron and Donald H. Reiman, 8 vols. to date (Cambridge, Mass.: Harvard University Press, 1961—). For an account of the history and policies of the edition to 1971, see Donald H. Reiman, "Editing Shelley," in *Editing Texts of the Romantic Period,* ed. John D. Baird (Toronto: A. M. Hakkert, 1972). The essay has been slightly revised and reprinted in Reiman's *Romantic Texts and Contexts* (Columbia: University of Missouri Press, 1987).

6. These two series, published by Garland Publishing, Inc., of New York, at present involve twenty scholars from the United States, Canada, the United Kingdom, and Japan and list twenty-nine volumes either issued, scheduled, or announced for early publication; fifteen of these volumes are devoted to Shelley's manuscripts.

7. See Curran's essay "Percy Bysshe Shelley" in *The English Romantic Poets: A Review of Research and Criticism,* ed. Frank Jordan (New York: Modern

Language Association of America, 1985), where the quotation appears on page 598.

8. Shelley's relations with such older women as Madame de Boinville, Maria Gisborne, and Lady Mount Cashell ("Mrs. Mason") seem to have been more successful than his relations with male mentors, against whom he reenacted his rebellion against his father.

9. For the textual history of this poem and an extended analysis of its place in Shelley's development, see *Shelley and his Circle,* VII (1986), 110–60.

10. See "Sad Reality and Self-Knowledge: *The Cenci,*" in Earl R. Wasserman, *Shelley: A Critical Reading* (Baltimore: Johns Hopkins Press, 1971), 84–128.

11. For the text of this review, see *The Romantics Reviewed: Contemporary Reviews of Romantic Poetry,* ed. Donald H. Reiman (New York: Garland, 1972), part C, II, 770–76. For Shelley's initial reaction to the review, see *Shelley and his Circle,* VI (1973), 931–34.

12. The so-called Whig Connexion was a group of great landowning titled families, including prominently, among others of note, the families Howard (e.g., Shelley's father's patron, the Duke of Norfolk, and Byron's cousin, the Earl of Carlisle), Russell (e.g., the Duke of Bedford and Thomas Moore's friend Lord John Russell), Fox (e.g., Lord Holland and his uncle Charles James Fox), Petty (Marquis of Lansdowne), Ponsonby (Earl of Besborough), and Grey (Earl Grey). Through intermarriages and family alliances, they controlled a great deal of the best arable land in England.

13. Godwin's influence on Shelley has been much talked about but frequently misunderstood. In November 1811, when that influence was at its height, Shelley wrote Elizabeth Hitchener his views of Godwin's various works, suggesting that she read, first, *The Enquirer,* next *St. Leon,* then "his political justice" (which Shelley described as "long, sceptical good"), and, finally, *Caleb Williams.* See Shelley, *Letters,* ed. F. L. Jones (Oxford: Clarendon Press, 1964), I, 195.

14. On the influence on Cobbett, Carlyle, and others of medieval ideals of community, see Alice Chandler, *A Dream of Order: the Medieval Ideal in 19th-Century English Literature* (Lincoln: University of Nebraska Press, 1970).

15. For details on the economic situation in Great Britain about the time of the first census (1801), see the first three chapters of A. D. Harvey's *Britain in the Early Nineteenth Century* (New York: St. Martin's Press, 1978), 1–63.

16. The phrases "wake to weep" and "wake and weep" appear no less than nine times in F. S. Ellis's *A Lexical Concordance to the Poetical Works of Percy Bysshe Shelley* (London: Bernard Quaritch, 1892), 766.

17. See "Wordsworth, Shelley, and the Romantic Inheritance," in Reiman, *Romantic Texts and Contexts,* 359.

18. Sperry, *Shelley's Major Verse: The Narrative and Dramatic Poetry* (Cambridge, Mass.: Harvard University Press, 1988).

19. For one aspect of his moral and political influence that extends even beyond the Western world, see Art Young, *Shelley and Nonviolence* (The Hague: Mouton, 1975).

Chapter One: A World to Reform

1. General authorities for Shelley's family background and early life are: Newman I. White, *Shelley* (New York: Knopf, 1940), the standard biography; Kenneth Neill Cameron, *The Young Shelley* (New York: Macmillan, 1950); Roger Ingpen, *Shelley in England* (London: Kegan Paul, Trench, Trubner, 1917); *Letters of Percy Bysshe Shelley*. New information can be found in *Shelley and his Circle*, volumes I and II.

2. Cameron, *Young Shelley*, 40.

3. Humbert Wolfe, ed., *The Life of Percy Bysshe Shelley* (London: Dent, 1933), II, 326–27. This clergyman, hitherto unidentified, was Evan Edwards (1751–1839). His nickname was "Taffy," and some measure of his influence on Shelley is suggested by Shelley's mention of him in his letter to Elizabeth Hitchener, ?December 10, 1811 (*Letters*, I, 200).

4. Wolfe, ed., *Life of PBS*, I, 30.

5. *Letters*, I, 2–4. The correct date of the first letter is probably, as Cameron suggested in *Young Shelley* (295, note 46), January 10, 1809, not 1808.

6. The novel is dated 1811, but see *Letters*, I, 26.

7. On the authorship, dating, and publication of these two works, see Cameron, *Young Shelley*, 304–6, 307–13.

8. See Cameron, *Shelley and his Circle*, I, 35–38.

9. See *Shelley and his Circle*, II, 475–540.

10. *Letters*, I, 219[n]. See also Southey to Charles Danvers, January 13, 1812, *New Letters of Robert Southey*, ed. Kenneth Curry (New York and London: Columbia University Press, 1965), II, 19–22.

11. See Kenneth Neill Cameron, "Shelley vs. Southey: New Light on an Old Quarrel," *Publications of the Modern Language Association* 57 (June 1942): 489–512.

12. Denis Florence MacCarthy, *Shelley's Early Life* (London: John Camden Hotten, 1872), 240–43.

13. Later in the century, however, the *Letter to Lord Ellenborough* gained some currency among radicals and was at least twice reprinted upon similar infringements of freedom of the press (Cameron, *Young Shelley*, 186).

14. *Letters*, I, 336. See also *Letters*, I, 331[n], and White, *Shelley*, I, 238–42, 262–65, 645–46.

15. Cameron, *Young Shelley*, 187–91.

16. *Letters*, I, 355[n]–56[n].

17. Cameron, *Young Shelley*, 205–14; H. M. Dowling, *Keats-Shelley Memorial Bulletin* 12 (1961): 28–36, and White, *Shelley*, I, 281–85.

18. The best discussions of this important but little-known work are: Cameron, *Young Shelley*, 274–87, and C. E. Pulos, *The Deep Truth: A Study of Shelley's Scepticism* (Lincoln: University of Nebraska, 1954), 91–97.

19. See, for example, *Letters*, I, 315–16 (to Godwin, July 29, 1812).

20. Harry Buxton Forman, *The Shelley Library* (London: Reeves and Turner, 1886), 35–58.

21. *The Esdaile Notebook: A Volume of Early Poems by Percy Bysshe Shelley* (New York: Knopf, 1964).

22. Of the poems in the notebook, six are sonnets, two are in Spenserian stanzas; and there appear sixteen other rhymed stanzaic patterns of from six to twelve lines (besides unrhymed and irregularly rhymed poems and poems in quatrains).

Chapter Two: Student to Poets

1. For an interpretation by an acknowledged partisan of Harriet, see Louise Schutz Boas, *Harriet Shelley: Five Long Years* (London and New York: Oxford, 1962).

2. See *Letters*, I, 423[n] and, especially, F. L. Jones's essay in *Shelley and his Circle*, III, 423–34.

3. Louise Schutz Boas, "'Erasmus Perkins' and Shelley," *Modern Language Notes* 70 (June 1955): 408–13.

4. Edward Dowden, *The Life of Percy Bysshe Shelley* (London, 1886), I, 525–30; Wolfe, ed., *Life of PBS*, II, 340–41.

5. Harold Bloom, *The Visionary Company* (Garden City, N.Y.: Doubleday, 1961), 280.

6. "Love," for Shelley, is *eros*, a desire to possess good qualities that do not belong to the self. In "A Defence of Poetry" Shelley defines "Love" as "a going out of our own nature, and an identification of ourselves with the beautiful which exists in thought, action, or person, not our own." See also, "The Sensitive Plant," lines 74–77.

7. "Youth" refers to the young poet who is the protagonist; "Poet" refers to the persona of Shelley who speaks the two invocations and the concluding lines of *Alastor*.

8. See Joseph Raben, "Shelley's *Prometheus Unbound*: Why the Indian Caucasus?" *Keats-Shelley Journal* 12 (1963): 95–106. Raben, while explaining Shelley's use of the Hindu Kush (Indian Caucasus) in *Prometheus*, doubts that the same mountains were the goal of the Youth in *Alastor*; but the geography of *Alastor* indicates that the Indian, not the European range, is intended. For a correlation of the Youth's journey with modern geography, see *Shelley's Poetry and Prose*, ed. Donald H. Reiman and Sharon B. Powers (New York: W. W. Norton, 1977), 76, note 8.

9. Irene H. Chayes, "Plato's *Statesman* Myth in Shelley and Blake," *Comparative Literature* 13 (Fall 1961): 358–69.

10. Again the analogue is the myth in Plato's *Statesman*; the progress of the boat can be seen, geographically, as an ascent of the Oxus River from the Aral Sea to its source in the Hindu Kush range (the Indian Caucasus).

11. Pine trees also symbolize this struggle in "Mont Blanc" (20–24, 109–11) and other poems.

12. Leslie Marchand, *Byron: A Biography* (New York: Knopf, 1957), II, 603–8.

Chapter Three: A Hermit at Marlow

1. See Fanny's letters in *Shelley and Mary*, I, 93–95, 104–13, 140–42, 143–46. For other interpretations of this tragedy, see White, *Shelley*, I, 470–71, and Burton R. Pollin, "Fanny Godwin's Suicide Re-examined," *Etudes Anglaises* 18 (Fall 1965): 258–68.

2. White, *Shelley*, I, 480–85; cf. Cameron, "The Last Days of Harriet Shelley," *Shelley and his Circle*, IV, 769–802.

3. Boas, *Harriet Shelley*, 197–98.

4. C. Kegan Paul, *William Godwin: His Friends and Contemporaries* (Boston: Roberts Brothers, 1876), II, 246.

5. For the facts and problems relating to the publication of this pamphlet, see White, *Shelley*, I, 544–46, 744 (note 70).

6. Shelley alludes to the theory of poetic diction that Wordsworth enunciated in his Preface to *Lyrical Ballads* (1800; amended 1802 and supplemented 1815) and to which Coleridge replied in *Biographia Literaria* (1817).

7. In the notebook in which he began composing his poem, Shelley wrote: "Is this an imitation of Ld. Byron's poem? It is certainly written in the same metre. Coleridge and Wordsworth to be considered" (*Verse and Prose from the Manuscripts of Percy Bysshe Shelley*, ed. John C. E. Shelley-Rolls and Roger Ingpen [London: privately printed, 1934], 12). There are also verbal echoes of "The Rime of the Ancient Mariner" and "The Prisoner of Chillon" in Canto III of *The Revolt*, and the poem uses ideas and techniques drawn both from Wordsworth's early poems and from *The White Doe of Rylstone* (1815). The standard discussion is now Donald H. Reiman's "The Composition and Publication of *The Revolt of Islam*" and related commentaries in *Shelley and his Circle*, V (1973), 141–89.

8. The woman probably alludes here to the Youth of *Alastor*, thus making *The Revolt of Islam*, in a sense, a sequel to the earlier poem.

9. See Kenneth Neill Cameron, "A Major Source of *The Revolt of Islam*," *Publications of the Modern Language Association* 56 (March 1941): 175–206, for the influence of Volney's *Ruins of Empire* on this and many other passages of the poem.

10. *The Poetical Works of Percy Bysshe Shelley*, ed. H. Buxton Forman (London: Reeves and Turner, 1876), I, 97.

11. See Titus I.15. That Shelley was, in part, reacting to charges that

he, Byron, Mary, and Claire had formed a "league of incest" at Lake Geneva seems clear from his disclaimer in a footnote to the Preface: "The sentiments connected with and characteristic of this circumstance have no personal reference to the Writer" (*Poetical Works,* ed. Forman, I, 98). Certainly Shelley was foolhardy, in view of the personal slanders centering on this very question, to fly into the face of public opinion; as it was, the Tory *Quarterly Review* obtained a copy of *Laon and Cythna* in its unexpurgated form and in reviewing it made capital of Shelley's defense of incest.

12. Book X; Loeb Classical Library Edition (Cambridge, Mass.: Harvard University Press, 1961), III, 303–5.

13. For an account of Shelley's recurring use of earthquakes, volcanoes, and other terrestrial disturbances as symbols of the uprising of the human spirit against tyranny, see G. M. Matthews, "A Volcano's Voice in Shelley," *ELH: A Journal of English Literary History* 24 (1957): 191–228.

14. This apocalyptic horse is at once a symbol of destiny and of uncorrupted nature. Shelley's handling of its relationship to the theme owes much to Wordsworth's *White Doe of Rylstone* (1815).

15. Thomas Medwin, *The Life of Percy Bysshe Shelley,* ed. H. Buxton Forman (London, 1913), 178–79.

16. Julian, VI, 227–52. For a facsimile of the manuscript, with full transcription and the latest informed discussion of the date of this essay and related prose fragments, see P. M. S. Dawson's edition of *Bodleian MS. Shelley e. 4,* Volume III in *The Bodleian Shelley Manuscripts* (New York and London: Garland Publishing, 1987).

Chapter Four: Green Isles

1. See Mary's note on the poem (OSA, 188–89) and *Letters,* II, 29, 31 and note.

2. The holograph draft of "On Love" comes just before that of the "Discourse on the manners of the Antient Greeks relative to the subject of Love" in Bodleian MS Shelley adds. e. 11: "On Love," 1–9; "Discourse," 17–41. For two recent views of the essay, see Nathaniel Brown, *Sexuality and Feminism in Shelley* (Cambridge, Mass.: Harvard University Press, 1979), and Donald H. Reiman, *Shelley and his Circle,* VI (1973), 633–47.

3. *Letters,* II, 32–38; White, *Shelley,* II, 29.

4. Published with *Rosalind and Helen* (1819). See Donald H. Reiman, "Structure, Symbol, and Theme in 'Lines written among the Euganean Hills,'" *Publications of the Modern Language Association* 77 (September 1962): 404–13; reprinted in *Shelley's Poetry and Prose,* ed. Reiman and Powers.

5. See "Boat on the Serchio," 26–27, the only other use of the word "rooks" in Shelley's poetry.

6. *Shelley,* II, 42–50.

7. Dowden, *Life of Percy Bysshe Shelley*, II, 238; Baker, *Shelley's Major Poetry*, 124–38; G. M. Matthews, "'Julian and Maddalo': The Draft and the Meaning," *Studia Neophilologica* 35 (1963): 57–84; for the date and circumstances of composition, see Reiman, *Shelley and his Circle*, VI (1973), 857–65.

8. For adverse comments on Byron, see Shelley to Peacock, December 17 or 18, 1818 (*Letters*, II, 57–58).

Chapter Five: Roman Scenes

1. The only account mentioning the Shelleys' stay in Naples (except their own letters and laconic journal entries) is that by Charles MacFarlane (1799–1858), *Reminiscences of a Literary Life*, intro. John F. Tattersall (New York: Charles Scribner's Sons, 1917), 1–12.

2. White, *Shelley*, II, 546–50 (Appendix VII).

3. *Letters*, II, 211 (July ?7, 1820).

4. See Marcel Kessel, "The Mark of X in Claire Clairmont's Journals," *Publications of the Modern Language Association* 66 (December 1951: 1180–83; Ivan Roe, *Shelley: The Last Phase* (New York: Roy Publishers, 1953), 161–81; Ursula Orange, "Elise, Nursemaid to the Shelleys," *Keats-Shelley Memorial Bulletin* 6 (1955): 24–34; White, *Shelley*, II, 71–83; Kenneth Neill Cameron, *Shelley: The Golden Years* (Cambridge, Mass.: Harvard University Press, 1974), 66–73 and 581–83 (notes).

5. See Joseph Raben, "A Computer-Aided Study of Literary Influence: Milton to Shelley," *Literary Data Processing Conference Proceedings*, September 9, 10, 11, 1964 (New York: MLA Materials Center), 230–74. For another interpretation of this scene, emphasizing its relations with Virgil's sixth Eclogue, see Earl R. Wasserman, *Shelley's "Prometheus Unbound": A Critical Reading* (Baltimore: Johns Hopkins University Press, 1965), 118–27. For commentaries on *Prometheus* before ca. 1950, see Lawrence John Zillman, *Shelley's "Prometheus Unbound": A Variorum Edition* (Seattle: University of Washington Press, 1959).

6. The most significant gloss to Shelley's conception of Demogorgon is Peacock's long note on "Dæmogorgon" in *Rhododaphne; or, The Thessalian Spell* (London: T. Hookham; Baldwin, Cradock, and Joy, 1818).

7. See E. M. W. Tillyard, "Shelley's *Prometheus Unbound* and Plato's *Statesman*," [London] *Times Literary Supplement* 31 (September 29, 1932): 691. See also Irene H. Chayes, "Plato's *Statesman* Myth in Shelley and Blake," *Comparative Literature* 13 (1961): 358–69.

8. Wasserman describes the union of Jupiter and Thetis as "a sterile rape" (90). A rape it certainly is, but its sterility is problematical; for the rape brings forth its own appropriate fruit—the overthrow of Jupiter through the agency of necessity.

9. See Wasserman, 145–46.

10. See Donald H. Reiman, "Roman Scenes in *Prometheus Unbound* III.iv," *Philological Quarterly* 46 (January 1967): 69–78; reprinted in Reiman, *Romantic Texts and Contexts,* 275–88.

11. From "Shelley, Dryden, and Mr. Eliot," in C. S. Lewis, *Rehabilitations and Other Essays* (London: Oxford University Press, 1939); reprinted in M. H. Abrams, ed., *English Romantic Poets: Modern Essays in Criticism,* 266.

12. Reprinted in the Shelley Society edition of *The Cenci* (London, 1886), 93–107. The manuscript of Mary W. Shelley's translation will be reproduced and edited in Volume X of *The Bodleian Shelley Manuscripts, Bodleian MS Shelley adds. d. 2 and adds. e. 13,* ed. Betty T. Bennett and Charles E. Robinson (New York: Garland Publishing, 1990).

Chapter Six: The Chameleon

1. See A. Stanley Walker, "Peterloo, Shelley and Reform," *Publications of the Modern Language Association* 40 (1925): 128–64. For the history of the composition and publication of Shelley's poem, as well as facsimiles of the primary textual authorities, see Donald H. Reiman, ed., *The Mask of Anarchy: Facsimiles . . . , The Manuscripts of the Younger Romantics: Shelley,* Volume II (New York and London: Garland Publishing, 1985).

2. Literary precedents for Shelley's use of "Anarch" are to be found in Milton's *Paradise Lost* (II.988) and Pope's *Dunciad* (IV.655).

3. White first called attention to the publication in *The Military Register and Weekly Gazette* (*Shelley,* II, 4); Charles E. Robinson first noted the earlier printing in the *Morning Chronicle* for September 26, 1820, in *Keats-Shelley Memorial Bulletin* 32 (1981), 57.

4. "Rhetoric as Drama: An Approach to the Romantic Ode," *Publications of the Modern Language Association* 79 (March 1964): 67–79, especially 71–74.

5. On the "fading coal" image, see D. J. Hughes, "Coherence and Collapse in Shelley . . . ," *Journal of English Literary History* 28 (September 1961): 260–83; "Potentiality in *Prometheus Unbound,*" *Studies in Romanticism* 2 (Winter 1963): 107–26; "Kindling and Dwindling: The Poetic Process in Shelley," *Keats-Shelley Journal* 13 (1964): 13–28.

6. Donald H. Reiman's authoritative transcription and annotation of "A Philosophical View of Reform" and discussion of its composition and significance appear in *Shelley and his Circle,* VI, 945–1066; the most reliable edited text remains that in the Julian Edition, VII, 1–55.

7. The identity of "Dr. J. Bell" has not hitherto been noted in Shelley studies. For the main facts of his career, see the *Dictionary of National Biography.*

8. For facsimiles of the drafts and press-copy manuscripts of *Peter Bell the Third,* together with analysis of the manuscript evidence on its composition

and meaning, see Volumes I (1986) and VII (1989) of *The Bodleian Shelley Manuscripts*, edited by Donald H. Reiman.

9. Peacock based the characters of Moley Mystic in *Melincourt* (1817) and Flosky in *Nightmare Abbey* (1818) on Coleridge. In the latter novel, Scythrop, a caricature of young Shelley, is an admirer of Flosky.

10. The immediate source of this phrase is Chapter XXI of *Melincourt*, where Peacock identifies his source as "Forsyth's *Principles of Moral Science*."

11. For a discussion of the surviving manuscript evidence on "Letter to Maria Gisborne," see Reiman's edition of *Hellas: A Lyrical Drama, A Facsimile* . . . [with other Shelley manuscripts] in the Henry E. Huntington Library, *The Manuscripts of the Younger Romantics: Shelley*, III (1985), 91–111; for detailed notes on the poem's allusions and thematic development, see *Shelley's Poetry and Prose*, ed. Reiman and Powers, 313–21.

12. Wasserman, *The Subtler Language* (1959), 251–84; also Wasserman, *Shelley: A Critical Reading*, 154–79.

13. James A. Notopoulos, *The Platonism of Shelley* (Durham, N.C.: Duke University Press, 1949), 440.

14. Carlos Baker, *Shelley's Major Poetry: The Fabric of a Vision* (Princeton: Princeton University Press, 1948), 174–81.

15. Forman, *The Shelley Library*, 98–99. See also Cameron, *Shelley: The Golden Years*, 357 and 628–29, note 38.

16. Compare "The Mask of Anarchy," lines 14–17.

17. These identifications come directly from Newman I. White, "Shelley's *Swellfoot the Tyrant* in Relation to Contemporary Political Satire," *Publications of the Modern Language Association* 36 (1921): 332–46, and Baker, *Shelley's Major Poetry*, 179–80.

18. See John E. Jordan, "Wordsworth and 'The Witch of Atlas,'" *Journal of English Literary History* 9 (1942): 320–25.

19. See Desmond King-Hele, *Shelley: His Thought and Work* (London: Macmillan, 1960), 220–27.

20. See Harold Bloom, *Shelley's Mythmaking* (New Haven: Yale University Press, 1959), 172–73.

Chapter Seven: Built Beyond the Grave

1. Shelley sent "A Defence of Poetry" to Ollier for insertion in a later *Literary Miscellany*, promising to send two more parts, which were apparently never written (Shelley to Ollier; *Letters*, II, 275). After Ollier's periodical failed, the essay was prepared for publication in *The Liberal* by John Hunt, but *The Liberal* also ceased publication before it was used. The "Defence" was first published in 1840 by Mrs. Shelley in her edition of Shelley's *Essays, Letters from Abroad* . . . without its original references to "The Four Ages of Poetry" (Julian, VII, 350–51).

2. Brian Wilkie elucidates Shelley's comprehension of the epic in *Romantic Poets and Epic Tradition* (Madison and Milwaukee: University of Wisconsin Press, 1965): 114–22; Reiman extends his argument with reference to Shelley's view of Byron in *"Don Juan* in Epic Context," *Studies in Romanticism* 16 (1977): 587–94; reprinted in his *Romantic Texts and Contexts,* 334–43.

3. Teresa Viviani's biographer argues that Shelley referred to her as "Emilia" (not one of her given names) because she occupied a position between two suitors similar to that of Emilia, the heroine of Boccaccio's *Teseida* (the model for Chaucer's *Knight's Tale*). See Enrica Viviani della Robbia, "Shelley e il Boccaccio," *Italica* 36 (September 1959): 181–97, and her *Vita di una donna: l'Emily di Shelley* (Firenze: G. C. Sansoni, 1936).

4. *Letters,* II, 262–63. Ollier ordered a larger printing, for after Shelley's death 160 copies of *Epipsychidion* remained unsold (Ollier to MWS, November 17, 1823; see Sylva Norman, *The Flight of the Skylark* [Norman, Oklahoma: University of Oklahoma Press, 1954], 46–47.

5. The discussion that follows is indebted to Kenneth Neill Cameron, "The Planet-Tempest Passage in *Epipsychidion,"* *Publications of the Modern Language Association* 63 (September 1948): 950–72.

6. Compare *Twelfth Night,* I.i.21–23.

7. *La vita nuova,* translated by Mark Musa (Bloomington: University of Indiana Press, 1962), 30.

8. Mary Shelley had not heard of it when she wrote to Maria Gisborne on April 5, 1821 (*MWS Letters,* I, 137–38). On April 11 Horace Smith's letter dated March 28 arrived (*MWS Journal,* 152); this mentioned Keats's death, as well as a temporary stoppage of Shelley's income (printed in *Shelley Memorials,* ed. Lady Shelley, 3rd edition [London: Smith, Elder & Co., 1875], 166–68). See also Shelley to John Gisborne, June 16, 1821 (*Letters,* II, 299–300). On Finch, see Elizabeth Nitchie, *The Reverend Colonel Finch* (New York: Columbia University Press, 1940).

9. For these and other literary influences, see Anthony D. Knerr, *Shelley's Adonais: A Critical Edition* (New York: Columbia University Press, 1984).

10. See Wasserman, *Shelley: A Critical Reading,* 464–65.

11. See "A Defence of Poetry," paragraphs 40–42.

Chapter Eight: Eyeless Charioteer

1. See *Letters,* II, 237, 242, 361[n].

2. On the "Masons"—George Tighe and Margaret, Countess of Mount Cashell—see Edward C. McAleer, *The Sensitive Plant: A Life of Lady Mount Cashell* (Chapel Hill: University of North Carolina Press, 1958).

3. Bodleian MS Shelley adds. e. 7, 13–38. Partially transcribed by Richard Garnett in *Relics of Shelley* (London: Edward Moxon, 1862), 4–13.

4. On Shelley's impatience with the delay in publication, see *Letters,* II, 356, 365, 372, 375, 382, 377[n]–78[n], 396, and 404.

5. Compare Shakespeare's *Othello*, III.iii.157–61.

6. Compare *Prometheus*, II.iv.10–12.

7. The reference is to *Anabasis* of Xenophon.

8. "Southey and Landor: Second Conversation," *Imaginary Conversations*, ed. Charles G. Crump (London: J. M. Dent, 1891), IV, 253.

9. Massey, "Shelley's 'Music, When Soft Voices Die': Text and Meaning," *Journal of English and Germanic Philology* 59 (1960): 430–38; see also E. D. Hirsch, Jr., *Journal of English and Germanic Philology* 60 (1961): 296–98.

10. The fullest account of the so-called Masi affair and its aftermath is to be found in chapters 6 and 7 of C. L. Cline, *Byron, Shelley and Their Pisan Circle* (London: John Murray, 1952).

11. The standard study of the poem is Donald H. Reiman, *Shelley's "The Triumph of Life"* (Urbana: University of Illinois Press, 1965); a revised edition of the text appeared in the Reiman and Powers edition of *Shelley's Poetry and Prose*, and Shelley's holograph manuscript was reproduced and further analyzed by Reiman in Volume I of *The Bodleian Shelley Manuscripts*.

12. The fullest and best discussion of Shelley's use of myth is now found in Chapter 9 of Wasserman's *Shelley: A Critical Reading*, 255–305.

13. Lines 256–59 refer to the legend of Plato's love for Aster, a boy whose name in Greek means "star" and is also the name of a flower (therefore, "flower of Heaven").

14. Mary Shelley to Maria Gisborne, August 15, 1822; *Letters of Mary Wollstonecraft Shelley*, ed. Betty T. Bennett, I, 247.

15. See William H. Marshall, *Byron, Shelley, Hunt and "The Liberal"* (Philadelphia: University of Pennsylvania Press, 1960).

16. For accounts of Shelley's posthumous reputation see White, *Shelley*, II, 389–418, and Sylva Norman, *Flight of the Skylark*.

17. See Mary Shelley to Maria Gisborne, ca. August 27, 1822; *Letters of MWS*, ed. Bennett, I, 255.

18. On Shelley's influence among active reformers and radical writers see Newman Ivey White, "Literature and the Law of Libel: Shelley and the Radicals of 1840–1842," *Studies in Philology* 22 (1925): 34–47, and "Shelley and the Active Radicals of the Early Nineteenth Century," *South Atlantic Quarterly* 29 (1930): 248–61; Kenneth Muir, "Shelley's Heirs," *Penguin New Writing*, ed. John Lehmann (Harmondsworth, Middlesex: Penguin, 1945), 117–32; N. Stephen Bauer, "Romantic Poets and Radical Journalists," *Neophilologische Mitteilungen* 79 (1978): 266–75; and Bouthaina Shaaban, "Shelley in the Chartist Press," *Keats-Shelley Memorial Bulletin* 34 (1983): 41–60.

Selected Bibliography

PRIMARY SOURCES

Items in each category are arranged chronologically.

Facsimiles of Manuscripts

Miscellaneous

A Proposal for Putting Reform to the Vote throughout the Kingdom. by The Hermit of Marlow [Percy Bysshe Shelley]. Fac-simile of the Holograph Manuscript with an Introduction by H. Buxton Forman. London: Published for the Shelley Society by Reeves and Turner, 1887.

The Mask of Anarchy[,] written on the Occasion of The Massacre at Manchester. by Percy Bysshe Shelley. Fac-simile of the Holograph Manuscript with an Introduction by H. Buxton Forman. London: Published for the Shelley Society by Reeves and Turner, 1887.

The Shelley Notebook in the Harvard College Library. Reproduced with Notes and a Postscript by George Edward Woodberry. Cambridge, Mass.: John Barnard Associates, 1929. Woodberry's notes, taken from a publication he did when he was an undergraduate in 1889, contain errors. A new facsimile edition of all the Harvard Shelley manuscripts will appear in *The Manuscripts of the Younger Romantics.*

Percy Bysshe Shelley: Epipsychidion, 1821, together with Shelley's Manuscript Draft. Menston, Yorkshire: Scolar Press, 1970. Photofacsimiles of the first edition and some fragments of the draft from Bodleian MS. Shelley d. 1, ff. 102 verso-92 verso.

The Manuscripts of the Younger Romantics: Percy Bysshe Shelley

Volume I. *The Esdaile Notebook: A Facsimile of the Intermediate Fair-Copy Manuscript in The Carl H. Pforzheimer Library.* Edited by Donald H. Reiman. New York and London: Garland Publishing, 1985.

Volume II. *The Mask of Anarchy: Facsimiles of the Intermediate Fair-Copy Holograph . . . ; The Press-Copy Transcription by Mary W. Shelley . . . ; Proofs of the First Edition, 1832 . . . .* Edited by Donald H. Reiman. New York and London: Garland Publishing, 1985.

Volume III. *Hellas: A Lyrical Drama: A Facsimile of the Press-Copy Transcript and Fair-Copy Transcripts of "Written on Hearing the News of the Death of Napoleon" and "Letter to Maria Gisborne," as well as . . . "Line written among*

the Euganean Hills": *All in the Henry E. Huntington Library.* Edited by
Donald H. Reiman. New York and London: Garland Publishing, 1985.
Volume IV. *Huntington Shelley Notebook, MS. 2177: A Facsimile Edition with a
Full Transcription.* Edited by Mary A. Quinn. New York and London:
Garland Publishing, 1989.

The Bodleian Shelley Manuscripts

Volume I. *Peter Bell the Third: A Facsimile of the Press-Copy Transcript . . .
(Bodleian MS. Shelley adds. c. 5, folios 50–69); and The Triumph of Life: A
Facsimile of Shelley's Holograph Draft (Bodleian MS. Shelley adds. c. 4, folios
18–58) . . . .* Edited by Donald H. Reiman. New York and London:
Garland Publishing, 1986.
Volume II. *Bodleian MS. Shelley adds. d. 7: A Facsimile Edition with Full Transcription and Textual Notes.* Edited by Irving Massey. New York and London: Garland Publishing, 1987.
Volume III. *Bodleian MS. Shelley adds. e. 4: A Facsimile Edition with Full Transcription and Textual Notes.* Edited by P[aul] M. S. Dawson. New York
and London: Garland Publishing, 1987.
Volume IV. *Bodleian MS. Shelley d. 1: A Facsimile Edition with Full Transcription
and Textual Notes.* Edited by E. B. Murray. New York and London: Garland Publishing, 1988.
Volume VII. *Bodleian MSS. Shelley adds. e. 15 and adds. e. 20, and Shelley adds.
c. 4, folios 212–246: A Facsimile Edition with Full Transcriptions and Notes.*
Edited by Donald H. Reiman. New York and London: Garland Publish-
ing, 1989.
Volume VIII. *Bodleian MS. Shelley d. 3: A Facsimile Edition with Full Transcrip-
tion and Textual Notes.* Edited by Tatsuo Tokoo. New York and London:
Garland Publishing, 1988.
Volume IX. *Bodleian MS. Shelley e. 1, e. 2, and e. 3: Intermediate Fair Copies of
Prometheus Unbound . . . : A Facsimile Edition with Full Transcriptions and
Notes.* Edited by Neil Fraistat. New York and London: Garland Publish-
ing, 1989.

First Editions of Shelley's Works

Zastrozzi, a Romance. London: G. Wilkie and J. Robinson, 1810.
Original Poetry; by Victor and Cazire. London: J. J. Stockdale, 1810.
*Posthumous Fragments of Margaret Nicholson; Being Poems Found Amongst the Papers
of that Noted Female Who Attempted the Life of the King in 1786.* Oxford: J.
Munday, 1810.
St. Irvyne; or, The Rosicrucian. London: J. J. Stockdale, 1811.
The Necessity of Atheism. Worthing: Printed by C. & W. Phillips, 1811.
An Address, to the Irish People. Dublin: [no publisher], 1812.

Proposals for an Association of those Philanthropists, Who Convinced of the Inadequacy of the Moral and Political State of Ireland to Produce Benefits which Are Nevertheless Attainable Are Willing to Unite to Accomplish its Regeneration. Dublin: Printed by I. Eton, 1812.

Declaration of Rights. [A broadside; Dublin: no publisher, 1812].

The Devil's Walk, a Ballad. [A broadside; circumstances of printing unknown, 1812].

A Letter to Lord Ellenborough, Occasioned by the Sentence which He Passed on Mr. D. I. Eaton, as Publisher of the Third Part of Paine's Age of Reason. [Barnstable: Printed by Syle, 1812].

Queen Mab; a Philosophical Poem: with Notes. London: [no publisher], 1813.

A Vindication of Natural Diet. Being One in a Series of Notes to Queen Mab, a Philosophical Poem. London: J. Callow, 1813.

A Refutation of Deism: in a Dialogue. London: Printed by Schulze and Dean, 1814.

Alastor; or, The Spirit of Solitude: and Other Poems. London: Baldwin, Cradock, and Joy; and Carpenter and Son, 1816.

A Proposal for Putting Reform to the Vote Throughout the Kingdom. London: C. and J. Ollier, 1817.

An Address to the People on the Death of the Princess Charlotte. [1817]. [No extant copy of the first edition.]

History of a Six Weeks' Tour through a Part of France, Switzerland, Germany, and Holland: with Letters Descriptive of a Sail Round the Lake of Geneva, and of the Glaciers of Chamouni. London: T. Hookham, Jr., and C. and J. Ollier, 1817.

Laon and Cythna; or, The Revolution of the Golden City: A Vision of the Nineteenth Century. London: Sherwood, Neely, & Jones; and C. and J. Ollier, 1818.

The Revolt of Islam; A Poem, in Twelve Cantos. London: C. and J. Ollier, 1818.

Rosalind and Helen, A Modern Eclogue; with Other Poems. London: C. and J. Ollier, 1819.

The Cenci: A Tragedy, in Five Acts. Italy: C. and J. Ollier, London, 1819.

Prometheus Unbound: A Lyrical Drama in Four Acts, with Other Poems. London: C. and J. Ollier, 1820.

Œdipus Tyrannus; or, Swellfoot the Tyrant. A Tragedy in Two Acts. London: The Author, 1820.

Epipsychidion: Verses Addressed to the Noble and Unfortunate Lady Emilia V——— Now Imprisoned in the Convent of ———. London: C. and J. Ollier, 1821.

Adonais: An Elegy on the Death of John Keats, Author of Endymion, Hyperion etc. Pisa, 1821.

Hellas: A Lyrical Drama. London: Charles and James Ollier, 1822.

Posthumous Poems of Percy Bysshe Shelley [ed. Mary Shelley]. London: John and Henry L. Hunt, 1824.

The Masque of Anarchy. A Poem. Ed. Leigh Hunt. London: Edward Moxon, 1832.

The Poetical Works of Percy Bysshe Shelley. Ed. Mrs. Shelley. 4 vols. London: Edward Moxon, 1839.

Essays, Letters from Abroad, Translations and Fragments. Ed. Mrs. Shelley. 2 vols. London: Edward Moxon, 1840.

Shelley Memorials, from Authentic Sources. Ed. Lady Shelley. London: Smith, Edler & Co., 1859.

Relics of Shelley. Ed. Richard Garnett. London: Edward Moxon, 1862.

The Wandering Jew. A Poem. Ed. Bertram Dobell. London: Shelley Society, 1887.

A Philosophical View of Reform, Now Printed for the First Time. Ed. T. W. Rolleston. London: Oxford University Press, 1920.

Verse and Prose from the Manuscripts of Percy Bysshe Shelley. Ed. Sir John C. E. Shelley-Rolls and Roger Ingpen. London: Privately printed, 1934.

The Esdaile Notebook: A Volume of Early Poems. Ed. Kenneth Neill Cameron, New York: Alfred A. Knopf, 1964. First full text of these poems, with extensive notes and commentary.

Critical Editions and Textual Criticism

Rossetti, William Michael, ed. *The Poetical Works of Percy Bysshe Shelley.* 2 vols. London: Moxon, 1870; revised in 3 vols., 1878. Rossetti's strength was his poetic sensitivity, but he sometimes emended Shelley's text to correspond with his own taste and he rushed his editing to earn his living.

Forman, Harry Buxton, ed. *The Poetical Works of Percy Bysshe Shelley.* 4 vols. London: Reeves and Turner, 1876; with *Prose Works,* 4 vols., 1880, an eight-vol. collected edition. Forman revised *Poetical Works* in condensed edition for Reeves and Turner, 1882 (2 vols.), and the "Aldine Edition" for George Bell, 1892 (5 vols.). All are accurate, outdated only where new evidence has since appeared.

Locock, C[harles] D. *An Examination of the Shelley Manuscripts in the Bodleian Library.* Oxford: Clarendon Press, 1903. Rough collation of some of Shelley's poetic manuscripts with final printed texts of his poems; these manuscripts (now being reproduced in *The Bodleian Shelley Manuscripts*) lack final authority for most of the poetry.

Hutchinson, Thomas, ed. *The Complete Poetical Works of Shelley.* Oxford: Clarendon Press, 1904. Reset as *The Poetical Works of Percy Bysshe Shelley.* Oxford Edition. London: Henry Frowde, 1905, et seq.; reset in 1943 for Oxford Standard Authors; corrected by G. M. Matthews, 1970. A conservative text, based chiefly on Forman; still the best one-volume, nearly complete edition.

Koszul, A[ndre] H., ed. *Shelley's Prose in the Bodleian Manuscripts, Edited with Corrections, Additions, Notes, and Unpublished Fragments.* London: Henry Frowde, 1910. Companion to Locock's 1903 study of the poetry, but done in a more scholarly way.

Locock, C. D., ed. *The Poems of Percy Bysshe Shelley.* 2 vols. London: Methuen, 1911. Useful for its notes, but introduces unauthorized readings from Shelley's drafts into the final texts.

Forman, H. Buxton, ed. *Note Books of Percy Bysshe Shelley: From the Originals in the Library of W. K. Bixby.* 3 vols. Boston: Bibliophile Society, 1911. Sporadic transcription and elaborate commentary on the contents of Shelley's three draft notebooks now in the Huntington Library.

Ingpen, Roger, and Walter E. Peck, eds. *The Complete Works of Percy Bysshe Shelley.* 10 vols. London: Ernest Benn; New York: Charles Scribners' Sons, 1926–30. The latest attempt at a complete edition, still useful for its text of Shelley's prose and collations of the poems.

Notopoulos, James A. *The Platonism of Shelley: A Study of Platonism and the Poetic Mind.* Durham, N.C.: Duke University Press, 1949. Most valuable for its texts of Shelley's translations from Plato, supplemented by Notopoulos in "New Texts from Plato," *Keats-Shelley Journal* 15 (Winter 1966): 99–115; see also Webb, *The Violet in the Crucible.*

Clark, David Lee, ed. *Shelley's Prose; or, The Trumpet of a Prophecy.* Albuquerque: University of New Mexico Press, 1954. The only accessible edition of Shelley's prose, but misleadingly inaccurate in both text and notes; the Oxford edition, long in preparation, is badly needed.

Taylor, Charles H., Jr. *The Early Collected Editions of Shelley's Poems: A Study in the History and Transmission of the Printed Text.* New Haven: Yale University Press, 1958. Important bibliographical analysis of Mary Shelley's editions of Shelley's poems.

Zillman, Lawrence John, ed. *Shelley's Prometheus Unbound: A Variorum Edition.* Seattle: University of Washington Press, 1959. Useful for summarizing earlier commentary and collating the early printed texts with the intermediate fair-copy manuscripts and with other editions.

Cameron, Kenneth Neill, and Donald H. Reiman, eds. *Shelley and his Circle, 1773–1822.* Cambridge, Mass.: Harvard University Press; Cameron, vols. I–II (1961) and III–IV (1971); Reiman, vols. V–VI (1973) and VII–VIII (1986); to be completed in 12 vols. A catalog edition, with extensive commentaries, of the manuscripts of the Shelleys, Byron, Godwin, Wollstonecraft, Hunt, Peacock, et al. in the Pforzheimer Shelley and His Circle Collection, New York Public Library.

Matthews, G[eoffrey] M., ed. *Shelley: Selected Poems and Prose.* London: Oxford University, 1964. Annotated student text, its small selection of Shelley's works and parts of works edited from primary authorities.

Reiman, Donald H. *Shelley's "The Triumph of Life": A Critical Study, Based on a text Newly Edited from the Bodleian Manuscript.* Urbana: University of Illinois Press, 1965. Comprehensive materials for studying Shelley's last poem.

Zillman, Lawrence John, ed. *Shelley's Prometheus Unbound: The Text and the Drafts, Toward a Modern Definitive Edition.* New Haven: Yale University

Press, 1968. An attempted critical edition done on false principles; useful for its transcriptions of the drafts.

Reiman, Donald H., and Sharon B. Powers, eds. *Shelley's Poetry and Prose.* Norton Critical Edition. New York & London: W. W. Norton, 1977 [et seq.]. For now, the standard text of Shelley's major poems and three of his essays, with notes, student helps, and fifteen scholarly essays.

Webb, Timothy, ed. *Percy Bysshe Shelley: Selected Poems.* London: J. M. Dent; Totowa, N.J.: Rowman and Littlefield, 1977. Selection for students, critically edited from primary sources and annotated.

Knerr, Anthony D. *Shelley's Adonais: A Critical Edition.* New York: Columbia University Press, 1984. Provides a critical edition of the poem, a textual and contextual study, and an interpretive essay that weaves together variorum commentary on the poem.

Primary Biographical Sources

Clairmont, Mary Jane Clara. *The Journals of Claire Clairmont,* ed. Marion Kingston Stocking. Cambridge, Mass.: Harvard University Press, 1968.

Gisborne, Maria, and Edward E. Williams. *Maria Gisborne & Edward E. Williams, Shelley's Friends: Their Journals and Letters,* ed. Frederick L. Jones. Norman: University of Oklahoma Press, 1951. For corrections to the Gisborne journal, see George H. Ford's review, *Modern Philology* 50 (1952): 69–72; for corrections to Williams' journal, see *Journals of Mary Shelley,* I, 417–418n.

Hunt, Leigh. *Lord Byron and Some of His Contemporaries; with Recollections of the Author's Life, and of His Visit to Italy.* London: Henry Colburn, 1828. Hunt's comments on Shelley also appear (with revisions) in his *Autobiography* (1850).

Medwin, Thomas. *The Life of Percy Bysshe Shelley: A New Edition . . . Amended and Extended by the Author . . . ,* ed. H. Buxton Forman. London: Humphrey Milford / Oxford University, 1913.

Shelley, Mary W. *The Journals of Mary Shelley, 1814–1844,* ed. Paula R. Feldman and Diana Scott-Kilvert. 2 vols. Oxford: Clarendon Press, 1987.

———. *The Letters of Mary Wollstonecraft Shelley,* ed. Betty T. Bennett. 3 vols. Baltimore: Johns Hopkins University Press, 1980–88.

Shelley, Percy Bysshe. *The Letters of Percy Bysshe Shelley,* ed. Frederick L. Jones. 2 vols. Oxford: Clarendon Press, 1964. Additional letters appear in *Shelley and his Circle, Keats-Shelley Memorial Bulletin,* and *Keats-Shelley Journal.*

Shelley and Mary. 3 vols., occasionally bound as 4 vols. "For private circulation only" [1882]. Sponsored by Sir Percy Florence Shelley and Jane, Lady Shelley, these volumes contain (sometimes censored) versions of letters, journals, and other documents relating to the lives of both Shelleys.

Wolfe, Humbert, ed. *The Life of Percy Bysshe Shelley, as Comprised in The Life of Percy Bysshe Shelley by Thomas Jefferson Hogg, The Recollections of Shelley &*

Byron by Edward John Trelawny, Memoirs of Shelley by Thomas Love Peacock.
2 vols. London: Dent, 1933. A convenient collection of three basic primary biographical records; for correction of the tampered texts of Shelley's
early letters to Hogg, see *Shelley and his Circle,* II–IV.

SECONDARY SOURCES

Bibliographies and Reference Works

Curran, Stuart. "Percy Bysshe Shelley," in *The English Romantic Poets: A Review
of Research and Criticism,* 4th ed., edited by Frank Jordan. New York:
Modern Language Association of America, 1985. The most up-to-date
critical survey of scholarship and opinion on Shelley.
Dunbar, Clement. *A Bibliography of Shelley Studies: 1823–1950.* New York:
Garland Publishing, 1976; 2nd ed., 1988. Detailed entries on publica-
tions in English discussing Shelley from 1825 till the *Keats-Shelley Journal
(K-SJ)* began its bibliography.
Ellis, F. S. *A Lexical Concordance to the Poetical Works of Percy Bysshe Shelley.*
London: Quaritch, 1892.
Forman, Harry Buxton. *The Shelley Library: An Essay in Bibliography.* London:
Reeves and Turner, 1886.
Green, David Bonnell, and Edwin Graves Wilson, eds. *Keats, Shelley, Byron,
Hunt, and Their Circles. A Bibliography: July 1, 1950–June 30, 1962.* Lin-
coln: University of Nebraska Press, 1964. Collects the first twelve annual
bibliographies from *K-SJ.*
Hartley, Robert A. *Keats, Shelley, Byron, Hunt, and Their Circles. A Bibliog-
raphy: July 1, 1962–December 31, 1974.* Lincoln: University of Nebraska
Press, 1978. Collects more bibliographies from *K-SJ.*
Keats-Shelley Journal. "Current Bibliography" (1951 to date). Besides its annual bibliography, *K-SJ*—like *Keats-Shelley Memorial Bulletin (KSMB),*
since 1986 *Keats-Shelley Review (K-SR)*—publishes articles, notes, and reviews on Keats, Byron, Shelley, and their circles.
Reiman, Donald H. *English Romantic Poetry, 1800–1835: A Guide to Information Sources.* Detroit: Gale Research, 1979. Selective, annotated bibliography on each major poet (except Blake) and on the background poets
and history of the period.
Reiman, Donald H., ed. *The Romantics Reviewed: Contemporary Reviews of British Romantic Writers. Part C: Shelley, Keats, and London Radical Writers.* 2
vols. New York: Garland Publishing, 1972. Contains facsimiles of the

original periodical texts of most of the known reviews of Shelley, as well as relevant ancillary materials.

White, Newman Ivey. *The Unextinguished Hearth: Shelley and His Contemporary Critics.* Durham, N.C.: Duke University Press, 1938. Reprints reviews and other contemporary references to Shelley through 1824.

Wise, Thomas James. *A Shelley Library.* London: privately printed, 1924; reprinted as part of Wise's catalogue *The Ashley Library* (11 vols., 1922–36). With Forman's earlier catalogue, the fullest description of first editions and other rare items relating to the Shelleys; Wise's Ashley collection is now in the British Library.

Biographies and Biographical Studies

Cameron, Kenneth Neill. *The Young Shelley: Genesis of a Radical.* New York: Macmillan, 1950. Supplements White's *Shelley* with scholarly Marxist account of Shelley's early life and works.

———. *Shelley: The Golden Years.* Cambridge, Mass.: Harvard University Press, 1974. Takes up chronology from *The Young Shelley,* with less emphasis on life, more on Shelley's major writings.

Crook, Nora, and Derek Guiton. *Shelley's Venomed Melody.* Cambridge: Cambridge University Press, 1986. Explores Shelley's possible health problems (including his possible encounters with venereal disease) and evidence from his writings of his reactions.

Dowden, Edward. *The Life of Percy Bysshe Shelley.* 2 vols. London: Kegan Paul, Trench, 1886. The "official" life, authorized by Shelley's son; though reticent on some matters, a notably accurate work of scholarship.

Holmes, Richard. *Shelley: The Pursuit.* London: Weidenfeld & Nicholson, 1974; New York: E. P. Dutton, 1975. Imaginative and lively life, marred by factual errors, by a journalist-scholar with limited sympathy for Shelley's poetry.

Ingpen, Roger. *Shelley in England: New Facts and Letters from the Shelley-Whitton Papers.* London: Kegan Paul, Trench, Trubner, 1917 (sometimes bound as 2 vols.). Important information on Shelley's finances, legal problems, and relations with his father.

Peck, Walter Edwin. *Shelley: His Life and Work.* 2 vols. Boston and New York: Houghton Mifflin, 1927. Flawed by Peck's idiosyncratic views, but filled with detailed information drawn from primary sources. The appendixes in vol. II are especially valuable.

White, Newman Ivey. *Shelley.* 2 vols. New York: Alfred A. Knopf, 1940 (one volume condensed revision, *Portrait of Shelley,* 1945). Still the best biography, a monument to a lifetime of devoted study, though it has been corrected and supplemented in *Shelley and his Circle* and other subsequent studies.

Studies of Shelley's Thought and Art

Studies of Shelley's writings now number in the hundreds, but the list of individual topics discussed is more manageable. The following books and essays retain their value in relation to other studies by virtue of comprehensive treatment of their chosen topics, accurate and thorough scholarship, and/or a unique perspective or persuasive exposition of a viable viewpoint.

Allsup, James O. *The Magic Circle: A Study of Shelley's Concept of Love.* Port Washington, N.Y., and London: Kennikat, 1976. An eloquent meditation on the interactions of *eros* and *agape* in Shelley's poetry. See also Nathaniel Brown's study.

Baker, Carlos. *Shelley's Major Poetry: The Fabric of a Vision.* Princeton: Princeton University, 1948. Excellent interpretive essays emphasizing Shelley's use of earlier literature.

Barnard, Ellsworth. *Shelley's Religion.* Minneapolis: University of Minnesota Press, 1937. Still the best account of its topic.

Bloom, Harold. *Shelley's Mythmaking.* New Haven: Yale University Press, 1959. Speculative and stimulating, though factually unreliable.

Brown, Nathaniel. *Sexuality and Feminism in Shelley.* Cambridge, Mass.: Harvard University Press, 1979. A full study of Shelley's thinking on sexuality and gender, illuminated from the thought of his own age, what he read from earlier times, and modern studies of human sexuality and gender differentiation.

Butter, P[eter] H. *Shelley's Idols of the Cave.* Edinburgh: Edinburgh University Press, 1954. Following Yeats, Butter explores characteristic symbols and modes of thought in Shelley's writings.

Chernaik, Judith. *The Lyrics of Shelley.* Cleveland: Case Western Reserve University Press, 1972. Detailed readings of Shelley's major lyrics from new texts (some now superseded by the Norton edition).

Cronin, Richard. *Shelley's Poetic Thoughts.* New York: St. Martin's, 1981.

Curran, Stuart. *Shelley's Annus Mirabilis: The Maturing of an Epic Vision.* San Marino, Calif.: Huntington Library, 1975. A rich study of Shelley's poems of 1819–20.

————. *Shelley's Cenci: Scorpions Ringed with Fire.* Princeton: Princeton University Press, 1970. The standard study of *The Cenci* both as a drama and as a poem.

Dawson, P[aul] M. S. *The Unacknowledged Legislator: Shelley and Politics.* Oxford: Clarendon Press, 1980. An important study of Shelley's political perspective, set against the ideas current in his family and those of his own mentors.

Duffy, Edward. *Rousseau in England: The Context for Shelley's Critique of the Enlightenment.* Berkeley: University of California Press, 1979.

Everest, Kelvin, ed. *Shelley Revalued: Essays from the Gregynog Conference.* Leicester: Leicester University Press, 1983. Ten significant essays by British and American Shelleyans.

Fraistat, Neil. *The Poem and the Book: Interpreting Collections of Romantic Poetry.* Chapel Hill and London: University of North Carolina Press, 1985. Illustrates the "contexture" of the arrangement of poems within volumes by reading *Lyrical Ballads* (1798), Keats's *Lamia* volume, and Shelley's *Prometheus Unbound; with Other Poems.*

Grabo, Carl. *The Magic Plant: The Growth of Shelley's Thought.* Chapel Hill: University of North Carolina Press, 1935. The culminating 1930s study of Shelley's thought, with special attention to scientific and Neoplatonic influences on his ideas.

Hall, Jean. *The Transforming Image: A Study of Shelley's Major Poetry.* Urbana: University of Illinois Press, 1980.

Hogle, Jerrold E. *Shelley's Process: Radical Transference and the Development of His Major Works.* New York and Oxford: Oxford University Press, 1988.

Hughes, D[aniel] J. Hughes has no book on Shelley, but has made his mark as a major Shelleyan through essays and reviews dating from the early 1960s to the present; see under his name in the indexes to the annual bibliographies in *K-SJ*—and as collected by D. B. Green and E. G. Wilson (1964) and by R. A. Hartley (1978).

Keach, William. *Shelley's Style.* New York and London: Methuen, 1984. The best book on Shelley's interest in language, the relations between his linguistic ideas and those of his contemporaries, and on several specific stylistic topics.

Matthews, G[eoffrey] M. Though Matthews, like Hughes, wrote mainly essays and reviews on Shelley, he was recognized as England's major Shelleyan for nearly two decades; see the bibliographies listed above.

Pulos, C. E. *The Deep Truth: A Study of Shelley's Scepticism.* Lincoln: University of Nebraska Press, 1954. Seminal for later studies relating Shelley's thought to Academic Skepticism.

Reiman, Donald H. *Intervals of Inspiration: The Skeptical Tradition and the Psychology of Romanticism.* Greenwood, Fla.: Penkevill, 1988. Surveys the Skeptical tradition from the Hellenistic schools and Cicero, through Ockham, Montaigne, and Hume and the use of this tradition by the English Romantics; Chapter 5: "Shelley: The Mythology of Aspiration."

———. *Romantic Texts and Contexts.* Columbia: University of Missouri Press, 1987. Six of its nineteen essays center on Shelley or the editing of his writings.

Robinson, Charles E. *Shelley and Byron: The Snake and Eagle Wreathed in Flight.* Baltimore: Johns Hopkins University Press, 1976. Carefully researched analysis of interactions between Shelley and Byron in life and poetry.

Sperry, Stuart M. *Shelley's Major Verse: The Narrative and Dramatic Poetry.* Cambridge, Mass.: Harvard University Press, 1988. A major study and defense of Shelley as a moral idealist.

Scrivener, Michael. *Radical Shelley: The Philosophical Anarchism and Utopian Thought of Percy Bysshe Shelley.* Princeton: Princeton University Press, 1982. The fullest chronological account of Shelley's political radicalism and his search for an audience.

Wasserman, Earl R. *Shelley: A Critical Reading.* Baltimore: Johns Hopkins University Press, 1971. A comprehensive reading incorporating Wasserman's earlier influential studies of particular works by Shelley. Still the most influential critical book on Shelley.

Weaver, Bennett. *Toward the Understanding of Shelley.* Ann Arbor: University of Michigan Press, 1932. Explores the impact of the Bible and the Hebraic prophetic tradition on Shelley.

Webb, Timothy. *Shelley: A Voice Not Understood.* Atlantic Highlands, N.J.: Humanities Press, 1977. A mature introduction to Shelley, arranged topically to refute old myths about Shelley and his poetry.

————. *The Violet in the Crucible: Shelley and Translation.* Oxford: Clarendon Press, 1976. The standard study of Shelley as a translator, with much information on his reading in other languages.

Wilson, Milton. *Shelley's Later Poetry: A Study of His Prophetic Imagination.* New York: Columbia University Press, 1959. A solid study that retains much of its original value.

Woodman, Ross Greig. *The Apocalyptic Vision in the Poetry of Shelley.* Toronto: University of Toronto, 1964. A good dissertation-book that Woodman is now supplementing with a series of essays on Shelley's poetry and ideas.

Woodring, Carl. *Politics in English Romantic Poetry.* Cambridge, Mass.: Harvard University Press, 1970. Shelley receives an important chapter in this fine study of the interrelations of the Romantics' poetry with the political events and ideas of their time.

Young, Art. *Shelley and Nonviolence.* The Hague: Mouton, 1975. Explores Shelley's philosophy of active but nonviolent action in relation to the ideas and practice of Gandhi, King, and others.

Index

This Index covers the new Preface, the text, and the notes, but not the Preface (1969), the Chronology, or the Selected Bibliography.

161